The Red Gate Guide to SQL Server Team-based Development

By Phil Factor, Grant Fritchey, Alex Kuznetsov, and Mladen Prajdić

First published by Simple Talk Publishing 2010

Editor: Tony Davis
Technical Reviewer: Peter Larsson
Additional Material: Roger Hart and Allen White
Cover Image: Paul Vlaar
Copy Edit: Gower Associates
Typeset & Designed: Matthew Tye & Gower Associates

Table of Contents

Chapter 6: Reusing T-SQL Code 171

The paid versions of this book contain two additional chapters: Chapter 10, Automating CRUD, by Phil Factor, and Chapter 11, Refactoring SQL Code, by Mladen Prajdić.

About the Authors

Phil Factor

Phil Factor (real name withheld to protect the guilty), aka Database Mole, has 25 years of experience with database-intensive applications. Despite having once been shouted at by a furious Bill Gates at an exhibition in the early 1980s, he has remained resolutely anonymous throughout his career.

Phil contributed Chapters 1, 2, 8, 9 and 10.

Grant Fritchey

Grant Fritchey, Microsoft SQL Server MVP 2009–2010, works for an industry-leading engineering and insurance company as a principal DBA. Grant has performed development of large-scale applications in languages such as Visual Basic, C#, and Java, and has worked with SQL Server since version 6.0. Grant spends a lot of time involved in the SQL Server community, including speaking and blogging, and he is an active participant in the SQLServerCentral.Com forums. He is the author of several books including *SQL Server Execution Plans* (Simple Talk Publishing, 2008) and *SQL Server Query Performance Tuning Distilled* (Apress, 2008).

Grant contributed Chapters 3, 4, and 7.

Alex Kuznetsov

Alex Kuznetsov has been working with object-oriented languages and databases for more than a decade. He has worked with Sybase, SQL Server, Oracle and DB2. He currently works with DRW Trading Group in Chicago, where he leads a team of developers, practicing agile development, defensive programming, and database unit testing every day.

Alex contributes regularly to the SQL Server community. He blogs regularly on sqlblog. com and has written numerous articles on simple-talk.com and devx.com. He wrote the book *Defensive Database Programming with SQL Server*, contributed a chapter to the *MVP Deep Dives* book, and speaks at various community events, such as SQL Saturday.

In his leisure time, Alex prepares for, and runs, ultra-marathons.

Alex contributed Chapter 6.

Mladen Prajdić

Mladen Prajdić is a SQL Server MVP from Slovenia. He started programming in 1999 in Visual C++. Since 2002 he's been actively developing different types of applications in .Net (C#) and SQL Server, ranging from standard line of business to image processing applications.

He graduated at the college of Electrical Engineering at the University of Ljubljana, majoring in Medical Cybernetics. He's a regular speaker at various conferences and user-group meetings. He blogs at HTTP://WEBLOGS.SQLTEAM.COM/MLADENP and has authored various articles about SQL Server. He really likes to optimize slow SQL Statements, analyze performance, and find unconventional solutions to difficult SQL Server problems. In his free time, among other things, he also develops a very popular free add-in for SQL Server Management Studio called SSMS Tools Pack.

Mladen contributed Chapters 5 and 11.

Peter Larsson (Technical reviewer)

Peter Larsson has been working with development and administration of Microsoft SQL Server since 1997. He has been developing high-performance SQL Server BI-solutions since 1998, and also specializes in algorithms, optimizations, and performance tuning. He has been a Microsoft SQL Server MVP since 2009. He recharges his batteries by watching movies, and spending time with his friends and his amazing, intelligent and beautiful wife Jennie, and his daughters, Filippa and Isabelle, and his son, Samuel.

Roger Hart (additional material)

Roger is a technical author and content strategist at Red Gate Software. He creates user assistance for Red Gate's flagship SQL Tools products. He worries that a brief secondment to Marketing might have damaged him somehow, but the result seems to be an enthusiasm for bringing the skills and values of Tech Comms to the organization's wider approach to the Web. Roger blogs for Simple-Talk (WWW.SIMPLE-TALK.COM/COMMUNITY/BLOGS/ROGER/DEFAULT.ASPX), about technical communications, content strategy, and things that generally get his goat.

Roger contributed the Continuous Integration section to Chapter 4.

Allen White (additional material)

Allen is a Consultant/Mentor who has been in IT for over 35 years, and working with SQL Server for 18 years. He's a SQL Server MVP who discovered PowerShell while trying to teach SMO to database administrators. He blogs at HTTP://SQLBLOG.COM/BLOGS/ALLEN_WHITE/DEFAULT.ASPX.

Allen contributed the Powershell material to Chapter 3.

Introduction

Only small projects, relevant to very few people, are built by the sweat and toil of a lone developer. Larger projects, affecting whole organizations, will invariably require a team of people to design and develop the application and its storage layer, or database.

In some cases, this will mean some developers and one or two DBAs, but larger organizations can afford a higher degree of specialization, so there will be developers who work exclusively within the data access layer of an application, database developers who specialize in writing T-SQL, architects who design databases from scratch based on business requirements, and so on. Stepping up the scale even further, some projects require multiple development teams, each working on a different aspect of the application and database, and each team performing of a collection of these specialized tasks. All these people will have to work together, mixing and matching their bits and pieces of work, to arrive at a unified delivery: an application and its database.

While performing this feat of legerdemain, they'll also have to deal with the fact that the different teams may be at different points in the development life cycle, and that each team may have dependencies on another. These various differences and dependencies will lead to conflict as the teams attempt to work on a single shared system.

Before you throw up your hands and declare this a lost cause, understand that you're not alone. Fortunately, these problems are not unique. There are a number of tools and techniques that can help you write clear, well-documented, reusable database code, then manage that code so that multiple versions of it can be deployed cleanly and reliably to any number of systems.

This book shows how to use of mixture of home-grown scripts, native SQL Server tools, and tools from the Red Gate SQL toolbelt (such as SQL Compare, SQL Source Control, SQL Prompt, and so on), to successfully develop database applications in a team environment, and make database development as similar as possible to "normal" development.

It shows how to solve many of the problems that the team will face when writing, documenting, and testing database code in a team environment, including all the areas below.

- **Writing readable code** – a fundamental requirement when developing and maintaining an application and its database, in a team environment, is that the whole team adopts a single standard for naming objects and, ideally, for laying out their SQL code in a logical and readable manner.

- **Documenting code** – all members of a team must be able to quickly find out exactly what a piece of code is supposed to do, and how it is intended to be used. The only effective way to document a database is to keep that documentation with the code, then extract it into whatever format is required for distribution among the team.

- **Source control and change management** – during the course of a team development cycle it is vital to protect the integrity of the database design throughout the development process, to identify what changes have been made, when, and by whom and, where necessary, to undo individual modifications. Tools such as Red Gate's SQL Source Control fully integrate the normal database development environment (SSMS) with the source control system, and so help to make source control a fundamental part of the database development process.

- **Deploying code between environments** – a huge pain point for many teams is the lack of a consistent and reliable mechanism by which to deploy a given version of the application and database to each environment, or to synchronize a database in two different environments.

- **Unit testing** – despite advances in test-driven development testing methodologies for applications, testing databases is a somewhat neglected skill, and yet an effective testing regime during development will save many hours of painful debugging further down the line.

- **Reusing code** – huge maintenance problems arise when a team is prone to cutting and pasting code around their code base, so that essentially the same routine, subtle modified, pops up in about fifteen different places. Common logic should be refactored into a single reusable code unit, in the form of a constraint, stored procedure, trigger, user-defined function (UDF), or index. Furthermore the team needs access tools that will allow them to easily share and implement standard routines (error handling, and so on).

- **Searching and refactoring your code base** – although developers would like to spend most of their time developing cool new applications and databases, the sad fact is that much time is spent trying to refactor the existing code base to improve performance, security, and so on. It's vital that the team has effective techniques for searching quickly through your database schema and build scripts, and understands the basic techniques that will lead to fast, efficient, set-based, SQL code.

Code examples

Throughout this book are code examples, demonstrating the use of the various tools and techniques for team-based development.

In order to work through the examples, you'll need access to any edition of SQL Server 2005 or later (except Compact Edition). A 2008 copy of SQL Server Express Edition, plus associated tools, can be downloaded for free from: HTTP://WWW.MICROSOFT.COM/SQLSERVER/2008/EN/US/EXPRESS.ASPX.

You'll also need access to several Red Gate SQL tools, all of which can be downloaded for a free 14-day trial from: WWW.RED-GATE.COM/PRODUCTS/INDEX.HTM.

To download all the code samples presented in this book, visit the following URL:

HTTP://WWW.SIMPLE-TALK.COM/REDGATEBOOKS/SQLSERVERTEAMDEVELOPMENT/SQL-CODE.ZIP.

Chapter 1: Writing Readable SQL

It is important to ensure that SQL code is laid out in the way that makes it easiest for the team to use and maintain it. Before you work out how to enforce a standard, you have to work out what that standard should be, and this is where the trouble often starts. SQL, unlike a language such as Python, doesn't require code to follow any formatting or layout rules in order to compile and run and, as William Brewer (see the summary at the end of this chapter) has noted, it's hard to find two database developers who agree in detail on how it should be done.

In large corporations, there is often a software architect who decides on an organization-wide standard, and expects all developers to adopt the naming and layout conventions it prescribes. In smaller companies, the standard is often worked out between developers and maintenance teams at the application level. In either case, if there is no existing standard, one must be devised before coding starts. By laying SQL out carefully and choosing sensible object names you greatly assist your team members, as well as anyone who inherits your code.

Why Adopt a Standard?

It has often been said that every language marks its practitioners for keeps. Developers approach SQL as a second language and, as such, almost always write and format SQL in a way that is strongly inflected by their native language.

In fact, it is often possible to detect what language a database developer first cut his teeth on from looking at the way they format SQL. Fortran programmers tend to write thin columns of abbreviated code; Java programmers often like their SQL code to be in lower case; BASIC programmers never seem to get used to multi-line strings.

There is no single correct way of laying out SQL or naming your database objects, and the multiple influences on the way we write SQL code mean that even consensus agreement is hard to reach. When a developer spends forty hours a week staring at SQL code, he or she gets to like it laid out to a particular style; other people's code looks all wrong. This only causes difficulties when team members find no way of agreeing on a format, and much time is wasted lining things up or changing the case of object names before starting to work on existing code.

There was a time when unlearning old habits, in order to comply with existing layout standards in the workplace, was painful. However, the emergence of code formatting tools that work within the IDEs, such as SSMS, has given us a new freedom. We configure multiple layout templates, one to conform to our preferred, personal layout style, and another that conforms to the agreed standard, and to which the code layout can be converted as part of the Source-Control process. In development work, one can, and should, do all sorts of wild formatting of SQL, but once it is tested, and "put to bed," it should be tidied up to make it easier for others to understand.

Using good naming conventions for your database objects is still a chore, and allowances have to be made for a team to get familiar with the standard, and learn how to review the work of colleagues. If you can, produce a style guide before any code is cut, so that nothing need be saved in Source Control that doesn't conform. Any style guide should, I think, cover object naming conventions and code layout. I would keep the topic of structured code-headers, and code-portability, separate. Although ISO/IEC 11179 will help a great deal in defining a common language for talking about metadata, it is, inevitably, less prescriptive when discussing the practicalities of a style guide for a project. I have not found any adopted standard at all for layout, so I hope I can help with some suggestions in this chapter.

Object Naming Conventions

Object naming is really a different subject altogether from layout. There are tools now available to implement your code layout standard in the blink of an eye, but there is no equivalent tool to refactor the naming of all your SQL objects, to conform to a given standard (though SQL Refactor will help you with renaming tables).

Naming has to be done right, from the start. Because object naming is so bound up with our culture, it causes many arguments in development teams. There are standards for doing this (ISO/IEC 11179-5 – Naming and Identification Principles for Data Elements), but everyone likes to bring their own familiar rituals to the process. Here are a few points that cause arguments.

Tibbling

The habit most resistant to eradication is "Tibbling," the use of reverse Hungarian notation, a habit endemic among those who started out with Microsoft Access. A tibbler will prefix the name of a table with "tbl," thereby making it difficult to pronounce. So, for example, a tibbler will take a table that should be called `Node`, and call it `tblNode`. Stored procedures will be called something like `spCreateCustomer` and table-valued functions will be called `tvfSubscription`.

All this tibbling makes talking about your data difficult, but the habit is now, unfortunately, rather entrenched at Microsoft, in a mutated version that gives a `PK_`, `FK_`, `IX_`, `SP_` or `DF_` prefix to object names (but not mercifully to tables yet), so I doubt that it will ever be eradicated amongst SQL Server programmers.

Such object-class naming conventions have never been part of any national or international standard for naming data objects. However, there are well-established prefixes in DataWarehousing practice to make it possible to differentiate the different types of table (`dim`, `fact`, and so on).

Pluralizing

A pluralizer will always name a table after a quantity of entities rather than an entity. The `Customer` table will be called `Customers`, and `Invoice` will be `Invoices`. Ideally, the use of a collective name for the entities within a table is best, but failing that, the singular noun is considered better than the plural.

Abbreviating (or abrvtng)

An abbreviator will try to make all names as short as possible, in the mistaken belief that the code will run faster, take less space, or be, in some mystical sense, more efficient.

Heaving out the vowels (the "vowel movement") is a start, so that `Subscription` becomes `Sbscrptn`, but the urge towards the mad extreme will lead to `Sn`. I've heard this being called "Custing," after the habit of using the term Cust instead of Customer. To them, I dedicate Listing 1-1.

```
CREATE TABLE ## ( # INT )
DECLARE @ INT
SET @ = 8
INSERT  INTO ##
        ( # )
        SELECT  @ % 2
SELECT  *
FROM    ##
```

Listing 1-1: Abrvtng mdnss.

This habit came from the old Fortran days when you could only use six characters at the most. SQL 92 allows 18 characters, but SQL Server has no practical limit, though you must keep it under 128 characters.

[Escaping]

Spaces are not allowed in object names, unless the name is escaped, so SQL names need some way of separating words. One could write customerAccounts, CustomerAccounts, customer_Accounts or Customer_Accounts. Yes, you need to make up your mind.

Desktop databases, such as Access, are more liberal about the character set you can use for object names, and so came the idea came of "escaping," "quoting," or delimiting such names so that they could be copied, without modification, into a full relational database.

Those of us who take the trouble to write legal SQL object names find the rash of square brackets that are generated by SSMS acutely irritating. Listing 1-2 shows some code that runs perfectly happily in SQL Server, purely because of the use of escaping with square brackets.

```
/* we see if we can execute a verse of Macauley's famous poem "Horatius." */
--create a table with a slightly unusual name
CREATE TABLE [many a stately market-place;
    From many a fruitful plain;
    From many a lonely hamlet,]
  (
    [The horsemen and the footmen
    Are pouring in amain] INT ,
    [, hid by beech and pine,] VARCHAR(100)
  )
--put a value into this table
INSERT INTO [many a stately market-place;
    From many a fruitful plain;
    From many a lonely hamlet,]
        ( [The horsemen and the footmen
    Are pouring in amain] ,
        [, hid by beech and pine,]
        )
        SELECT  1 ,
                'an eagle's nest, hangs on the crest
    Of purple Apennine;'
```

```
/* now, with that preparation work done, we can execute the third verse */
SELECT  [The horsemen and the footmen
    Are pouring in amain]
FROM    [many a stately market-place;
    From many a fruitful plain;
    From many a lonely hamlet,]
WHERE    [, hid by beech and pine,]
    LIKE 'an eagle's nest, hangs on the crest
        Of purple Apennine;'
```

Listing 1-2: Horatius and the square bracket.

It is true that "delimited" names used to be handy for non-Latin languages, such as Chinese, but nowadays you can use Unicode characters for names, so Listing 1-3 runs perfectly happily.

```
CREATE TABLE 中國數據庫表
    (
    我的主鍵 CHAR(2) NOT NULL
                PRIMARY KEY ,
    我的數據列 INTEGER NOT NULL
                CHECK ( 我的數據列 > 0 )
    ) ;
```

Listing 1-3: Chinese tables.

Herein lies another horrifying possibility: SQL Server will allow you to use "shapes," as demonstrated in Listing 1-4.

```
CREATE TABLE "⌐⌐" ( "⌐⌐" NVARCHAR(10) )
DECLARE @ NVARCHAR(10)
SET @ = '='
INSERT  INTO "⌐⌐"
        ( "⌐⌐" )
        SELECT  replicate(@, 5)
SELECT  *
FROM    "⌐⌐"
```

Listing 1-4: Shape tables.

The ISO ODBC standard allows quotation marks to delimit identifiers and literal strings. Identifiers that are delimited by double quotation marks can either be Transact-SQL reserved keywords or they can contain characters not generally allowed by the Transact-SQL syntax rules for identifiers. This behavior can, mercifully, be turned off by simply by issuing: SET QUOTED_IDENTIFIER OFF.

Restricting

A habit that has crept into SQL from ex-Cobol programmers, I believe, is the use of a very restricted vocabulary of terms. This is rather like the development of cool street-argot with a highly restricted set of 400 words, rather than the 40,000 that are within the grasp of the normal adult. With SQL, this typically involves using words like GET, PUT or SAVE, in a variety of combinations.

SQL is perfectly happy to oblige, even though the results are difficult to understand. Taking this to extremes, the code in Listing 1-5 is perfectly acceptable to SQL Server.

```
--first create a GetDate schema
CREATE SCHEMA GetDate
--and a GetDate table to go in it.
CREATE TABLE GetDate.GetDate
(
GetDate DATETIME,
[GetDate GetDate] DATETIME
)
GO
--and a function called GetDate
CREATE FUNCTION GetDate ( )
RETURNS TABLE
AS RETURN
  ( SELECT  getdate() AS [GetDate]
  )
GO
- - Now we can write some startlingly silly code
INSERT  INTO GetDate.GetDate
```

```
             ( GetDate.GetDate.GetDate.GetDate ,
               [GetDate GetDate]
             )
       SELECT   getdate() AS GetDate ,
                GetDate
       FROM     getdate()
- - but we can do far far siller stuff if we wanted
- - purely because there is no restriction on what
- - goes between angle-brackets.
CREATE FUNCTION [GetDate.GetDate.GetDate.GetDate
GetDate.GetDate.GetDate.GetDate
GetDate.GetDate.GetDate.GetDate] ( )
RETURNS TABLE
AS RETURN
  ( SELECT   getdate() AS [GetDate]
  )
GO
INSERT   INTO GetDate.GetDate
             ( GetDate.GetDate.GetDate.GetDate ,
               [GetDate GetDate]
             )
       SELECT   getdate() AS GetDate ,
                GetDate
       FROM     [GetDate.GetDate.GetDate.GetDate
GetDate.GetDate.GetDate.GetDate
GetDate.GetDate.GetDate.GetDate]()
```

Listing 1-5:   The dangers of restricting your SQL vocabulary.

A guide to sensible object names

The existing standards for naming objects are more concerned with the way of discussing how you name database objects, and the sort of ways you might document your decisions. We can't discuss here the complications of creating data definitions, which are important where organizations or countries have to share data and be certain that it can be compared or aggregated. However, the developer who is creating a database application will need to be familiar with the standard naming conventions for database entities, objects, constraints, routines, and relationships.

Hopefully, the developer will already have been provided with the standard data definitions for the attributes of the data elements, data element concepts, value domains, conceptual domains, and classification schemes that impinge on the scope of the application. Even so, there is still the task of naming things within the application context. For this, there are international standards for naming conventions, which are mostly taken from ISO 11179-5:

- procedures should be a phrase, consisting of singular nouns and a verb in the present tense, to describe what they do (e.g. `removeMultipleSpaces or splitStringToTable`)

- be consistent with the way you denote word boundaries, the use of the underline character, the use of a capital letter or hyphen

- tables, sets, views, and other collections should use a collective name, a name for a group of entities, such as "flock," "ledger," "team," "staff"

- scalar names should be in the singular (e.g. "cost," "date," "zip")

- any object name should use only commonly understood abbreviations, such as ZIP for "Zone Improvement Plan"

- use standard and consistent postfixes (e.g. `_ID, _name, _date, _quantity`)

- where there is no established business term in the organization, use commonly understood words for relationship tables (e.g. `meeting, booking, marriage, purchase`)

- use capitalization consistently, as in written language, particularly where it is used for acronyms and other abbreviations, such as ID.

- names should consist of one or more of the following components:

  - **object class**: the name can include just one "object class," which is the terminology used within the community of users of the application.
    Examples: Words like "Cost," "Member" or "Purchase" in data element names like `EmployeeLastName, CostBudgetPeriod, TotalAmount, TreeHeight-Measure` or `MemberLastName`

- **property term**: these represent the category of the data.
  Examples: `Total_Amount`, `Date`, `Sequence`, `LastName`, `TotalAmount`, `Period`, `Size`, `Height`

- **qualifiers**: these can be used, if necessary, to describe the data element and make it unique within a specified context; they need appear in no particular order, but they must precede the term being qualified; qualifier terms are optional
  Examples: **Budget_**Period, **Financial**Year, **Last**Name

- **the representation term**: this describes the representation of the valid value set of the data element. It will be a word like "Text," "Number," "Amount," "Name," "Measure" or "Quantity." There should be only one, as the final part of the name, and it should add precision to the preceding terms.
  Examples: ProductClass**Identifier**, CountryIdentifier**Code**, ShoeSize**Metric**.

The type of separator used between words should be consistent, but will depend on the language being used. For example, the CamelCase convention is much easier for speakers of Germanic or Dutch languages, whereas hyphens fit better with English.

It isn't always easy to come up with a word to attach to a table.

> *Not all ideas are simply expressed in a natural language, either. For example, "women between the ages of 15 and 45 who have had at least one live birth in the last 12 months" is a valid object class not easily named in English.*
> *ISO/IEC 11179-1:2004(E): Page 19.*

You can see from these simple rules that naming conventions have to cover semantics (the meaning to be conveyed), the syntax (ordering items in a consistent order), lexical issues (word form and vocabulary), and uniqueness. A naming convention will have a scope (per application? company-wide? national? international?) and an authority (who supervises and enforces the conventions?).

Code Layout

The layout of SQL is important because SQL was always intended to be close to a real, declarative human sentence, with phrases for the various parts of the command. It was written in the days when it was considered that a computer language should be easy to understand.

In this section, we will deal purely with the way that code is laid out on the page to help with its maintenance and legibility.

Line-breaks

SQL code doesn't have to be broken into short lines like a Haiku poem. Since SQL is designed to be as intelligible as an English sentence, it can be written as an English sentence. It can, of course, be written as a poem, but not as a thin smear down the left-hand side of the query window. Line-breaking (and indenting) is done purely to emphasize the structure of SQL, and aid readability.

The urge to insert large numbers of line-breaks comes from procedural coders where a vertical style is traditional, dating back to the days of Fortran and Basic. An advantage of the vertical style is that, when an error just reports a line-number, it takes less time to work out the problem. However, it means an over-familiarity with the scroll-bar, if the routine runs to any length.

Line breaks have to be inserted at certain points (I rather like to have a line-break at around the 80th character), and they shouldn't be mid-phrase. However, to specify that there must always be a line-break between each phrase (before the FROM, ON, and WHERE clauses, for example) can introduce an unnecessary amount of white space into code. Such indenting should never become mere ritual activity to make things look neat, like obsessively painting the rocks in front of your house with white paint.

Indenting

Code without indenting is very difficult to follow. Indentation follows a very similar practice to a structured document, where the left margin is indented according to the nesting of the section heading. There should be a fixed number of spaces for each level of nesting.

Generally, the use of tabs for indenting has resulted in indenting that is way too wide. Of course, written text can have wide indents, but it isn't done to around eight levels, skidding the text hard against the right-hand side of the page. Usually, two or three spaces is fine.

It is at the point where we need to decide what comprises a change in the nesting level that things get difficult. We can be sure that, in a `SELECT` statement, all clauses are subordinate to the `SELECT`. Most of us choose to indent the `FROM` or the `WHERE` clause at the same level, but one usually sees the lists of columns indented. On the other hand, it is quite usual to see `AND`, `ON`, `ORDER BY`, `OR`, and so on, indented to the next level.

What rules lie behind the current best practice? Many of us like to have one set of rules for DDL code, such as `CREATE TABLE` statements, and another for DML such as `INSERT`, `UPDATE` or `SELECT` statements. A `CREATE TABLE` statement, for example, will have a list of columns with quite a lot of information in them, and they are never nested, so indenting is likely to be less important than readability. You'd probably also want to insist on a new line after each column definition. The use of curly brackets in DDL also makes it likely that indenting will be used less.

Formatting lists

Lists occur all over the place in code. As in printed text, you can handle them in a number of different ways. If, for example, you are just listing entities, then you'd do it like this. I like many French cheeses, including Abbaye de Belloc, Baguette Laonnaise, Brie de

Melun, Calenzana, Crayeux de Roncq, Esbareich, Frinault, Mixte, Pavé du Berry, Port-Salut, Quercy Petit, Regal de la Dombes, Sainte Maure, Sourire Lozerien, Truffe and Vignotte. Now, no typesetter would agree to arrange this in a vertical list, because the page would contain too much white space...

I like many French cheeses, including:

- *Abbaye de Belloc*

- *Baguette Laonnaise*

- *Brie de Melun*

- *Calenzana*

- *Crayeux de Roncq*

- *Esbareich*

- *etc.*

...and they'd be most unlikely to want to put commas at the beginning of list elements. However, if the list elements consisted of longer strings, then it would be perfectly acceptable. In the same way, the rules for formatting SQL have to take into account the type of SQL statement being formatted, and the average length of each list element.

Punctuation

Commas, used as list separators, are often put at the beginning of lines. I realize that it makes the "commenting out" of list members easier during development, but it makes it difficult for those of us who are used to reading English text in books. Commas come at the end of phrases, with no space before them, but if they are followed by a word or phrase on the same line, then there is a space after the comma.

Semicolons are a rather more unfamiliar punctuation mark but their use has been a part of the SQL Standard since ANSI SQL-92 and, as statement terminators, they are being seen increasingly often in SQL.

Generally speaking, their use in T-SQL is recommended but optional, with a few exceptions. They must be used to precede CTEs and Service Broker statements when they are not the first statement in the batch, and a trailing semicolon is required after a `MERGE` statement.

Capitalization

Before we start, I'd like to define what I mean by the various terms.

- This_Is_Capitalized
- this_is_lowercase (or *minuscule*)
- this_Is_CamelCase
- THIS_IS_UPPERCASE – (or *majuscule*).

Schema objects are, I believe, better capitalized. I would strongly advise against using a binary or case-sensitive collation for the database itself, since this will cause all sorts of unintended errors. A quirk of all European languages is that words mean the same thing, whether capital or lowercase letters are used. Uppercase, or *majuscule*, lettering was used exclusively by the Roman Empire, and lowercase, or *minuscule*, was developed later on, purely as a cursive script. The idea that the case of letters changed the meaning of words is a very recent novelty, of the Information Technology Age. The idea that the use uppercase is equivalent to shouting, may one day be adopted as a convention, probably at around the time that "smileys" are finally accepted as part of legitimate literary punctuation.

Of course, one would not expect SQL programmers to be so perverse as to do this sort of thing, but I've seen C# code that approaches the scale of awfulness demonstrated in Listing 1-6.

```
CREATE DATABASE casesensitive
ALTER DATABASE casesensitive COLLATE SQL_Latin1_General_CP1_CS_AS
USE casesensitive
CREATE TABLE thing
  (
    Thing INT IDENTITY(1, 1) ,
    tHing VARCHAR(20) ,
    thIng INT NOT NULL ,
    thiNg FLOAT NOT NULL ,
    thinG DATETIME NOT NULL
  )
INSERT   INTO thing
        ( tHing ,
          thIng ,
          thiNg ,
          thinG
        )
        SELECT  'thing' ,
                1 ,
                34.659 ,
                '1 Oct 2009'
SELECT   *
FROM     thing
DROP TABLE thing
```

Listing 1-6:   A capital idea.

Getting off the fence...

I wouldn't want to impose my views on anyone else. However, if you are looking for recommendations, here's what I usually suggest. I'd stick to the conventions below.

- Keep your database case-insensitive, even if your data has to be case-sensitive, unless you are developing in a language for which this is inappropriate.

- Capitalize all the Scalars and Schema object names (e.g. `Invoice`, `Basket`, `Customer`, `CustomerBase`, `Ledger`).

- Uppercase all reserved words (such as `SELECT`, `WITH`, `PIVOT`, `FROM`, `WHERE`), including functions and data types.

- Put a line-break between list items only when each list item averages more than thirty or so characters.

- Put block delimiters (such as `BEGIN` and `END`) on a new line by themselves, correctly indented.

- Put line breaks within SQL statements before the clause (`FROM`, `ON`, `WHERE`, `HAVING`, `GROUP BY`) only where it aids clarity in long statements, but not in every case.

- Use the semicolon to aid the reading of code, even where SQL syntax states that it is only optional.

- Use an increased indent for subordinate clauses if the `ON`, `INTO`, and `HAVING` statement is at the start of the line.

For sheer practicality, I'd opt for a layout that can be achieved automatically by your favorite code-layout tool (I use SQL Refactor and SQL Prompt, but there are several others). There is nothing more irritating than to find that someone has trashed a beautifully laid-out procedure by mangling it with a badly set up layout tool.

I tend to write my SQL fast and sloppily, to get some initial results quickly, and then refine and rewrite the code until it is fast and efficient. At that point, it is usually a mess, and it is very satisfying to run it through a layout tool to smarten it up. In fact, some time ago, before layout tools existed for SQL, I created a stored procedure that tidied up SQL code. It gradually ended up as the SQL Prettifier (www.simple-talk.com/prettifier), repurposed to render SQL in HTML, and with the formatting part taken out once SQL Refactor appeared. A tool like this can save a lot of inevitable arguments amongst developers as to the "correct" way to format SQL code.

Listing 1-7 shows the table-valued function from AdventureWorks, reformatted according to my preferences but, I suspect, perfectly horrible to anyone with strong feelings on the subject. The routine should, of course, have a structured header with a summary of what it does, and examples of its use, but that is a story for another chapter (Chapter 2, in fact).

```sql
CREATE FUNCTION dbo.ufnGetContactInformation (@ContactID INT)
RETURNS @retContactInformation TABLE (
  -- Columns returned by the function
  ContactID INT PRIMARY KEY NOT NULL,
  FirstName NVARCHAR(50) NULL,
  LastName NVARCHAR(50) NULL,
  JobTitle NVARCHAR(50) NULL,
  ContactType NVARCHAR(50) NULL)
AS /* Returns the first name, last name, job title and contact
type for the specified contact.*/
BEGIN
  DECLARE @FirstName NVARCHAR(50),
    @LastName NVARCHAR(50),
    @JobTitle NVARCHAR(50),
    @ContactType NVARCHAR(50);
  -- Get common contact information
  SELECT @ContactID = ContactID, @FirstName = FirstName,
        @LastName = LastName
  FROM Person.Contact WHERE ContactID = @ContactID;
  /* now find out what the contact's job title is, checking the
  individual tables.*/
  SET @JobTitle
    = CASE
      WHEN EXISTS -- Check for employee
        ( SELECT * FROM HumanResources.Employee e
          WHERE e.ContactID = @ContactID )
        THEN
          (SELECT Title FROM HumanResources.Employee
            WHERE ContactID = @ContactID)
      WHEN EXISTS -- Check for vendor
        ( SELECT * FROM Purchasing.VendorContact vc
```

```sql
                    INNER JOIN Person.ContactType ct
                        ON vc.ContactTypeID = ct.ContactTypeID
                  WHERE vc.ContactID = @ContactID )
              THEN
                 (SELECT ct.Name FROM
                                Purchasing.VendorContact vc
                    INNER JOIN Person.ContactType ct
                       ON vc.ContactTypeID =
                                        ct.ContactTypeID
                  WHERE vc.ContactID = @ContactID)
           WHEN EXISTS - - Check for store
             ( SELECT * FROM Sales.StoreContact sc
                  INNER JOIN Person.ContactType ct
                      ON sc.ContactTypeID = ct.ContactTypeID
                  WHERE sc.ContactID = @ContactID )
              THEN
                 (SELECT ct.Name FROM Sales.StoreContact sc
                     INNER JOIN Person.ContactType ct
                        ON sc.ContactTypeID =
                                        ct.ContactTypeID
                  WHERE ContactID = @ContactID)
          ELSE NULL
        END ;
SET @ContactType
   = CASE- - Check for employee
      WHEN EXISTS
        ( SELECT * FROM HumanResources.Employee e
             WHERE e.ContactID = @ContactID )
      THEN 'Employee'
      WHEN EXISTS - - Check for vendor
        ( SELECT * FROM Purchasing.VendorContact vc
             INNER JOIN Person.ContactType ct
                ON vc.ContactTypeID = ct.ContactTypeID
          WHERE vc.ContactID = @ContactID )
      THEN 'Vendor Contact'
      WHEN EXISTS - - Check for store
        ( SELECT * FROM Sales.StoreContact sc
             INNER JOIN Person.ContactType ct
                ON sc.ContactTypeID = ct.ContactTypeID
          WHERE sc.ContactID = @ContactID )
      THEN 'Store Contact'
      WHEN EXISTS - - Check for individual consumer
        ( SELECT * FROM Sales.Individual i
             WHERE i.ContactID = @ContactID )
```

```
            THEN 'Consumer'
        END ;
 -- -- Return the information to the caller
   IF @ContactID IS NOT NULL
     BEGIN
       INSERT INTO @retContactInformation
         SELECT   @ContactID, @FirstName, @LastName,
                  @JobTitle,@ContactType ;
       END ;
     RETURN ;
 END ;
 GO
```

Listing 1-7: The `ufnGetContactInformation` function, reformatted according to the formatting guidelines presented in this chapter.

Summary

Before you start on a new database application project, it is well worth your time to consider all the layout and naming issues that have to be covered as part of the project, and finding ways of automating the implementation of a standard, where possible, and providing consistent guidelines where it isn't. Hopefully this chapter has provided useful guidance in both cases.

For further reading on this topic, try the links below.

- *Transact-SQL Formatting Standards (Coding Styles)* (HTTP://TINY.CC/IC7SE) – Rob Sheldon's popular and thorough description of all the issues you need to cover when deciding on the way that SQL code should be laid out.

- *SQL Code Layout and Beautification* (WWW.SIMPLE-TALK.COM/SQL/T-SQL-PROGRAMMING/ SQL-CODE-LAYOUT-AND-BEAUTIFICATION/) – William Brewer's sensible take on the subject, from the perspective of a programmer.

- *ISO/IEC 11179* (HTTP://METADATA-STDS.ORG/11179/) – the international standard for vocabulary and naming conventions for IT data.

- *Joe Celko's SQL Programming Style* (HTTP://TINY.CC/337PL) – the first book to tackle the subject in depth, and still well worth reading. You may not agree with all he says, but reading the book will still improve your SQL Coding, as it is packed with good advice.

Chapter 2: Documenting your Database

One can sympathize with anyone who is responsible for making sure that a SQL Server database is properly documented. Generally, in the matter of database practice, one can fall back on a reasonable consensus position, or "best practice." However, no sensible method for producing database documentation has been provided by Microsoft, or, indeed, properly supported by the software tools that are available. In the absence of an obvious way of going about the business of documenting routines or objects in databases, many techniques have been adopted, but no standard has yet emerged.

You should never believe anyone who tells you that database documentation can be entirely generated from a database just by turning a metaphorical handle. Automatic database generators can help a bit, but they cannot absolve the programmer from the requirement of providing enough information to make the database intelligible and maintainable; this requires extra detail. The puzzle is in working out the most effective way of providing this detail.

Once you have an effective way of providing details, with your database code, about the tables, views, routines, constraints, indexes, and so on, how do you extract this documentation and then publish it in a form that can be used?

Why Bother to Document Databases?

When you're doing any database development work, it won't be long before you need to seriously consider the requirement for documenting your routines and data structures. Even if you are working solo, and you operate a perfect source-control system, it is still a requirement that kicks in pretty soon, unless you have perfect recall. Many times, I've sat down in front of some convoluted code, asked the rhetorical question, "God, what idiot wrote this code?" only to find out it was me, some time in the past. By documenting, I don't just mean the liberal sprinkling of inline comments to explain particular sections of code. If you are coordinating a number of programmers on a project, then it is essential to have more than this; you'll require at least an explanation of what it does, who wrote it or changed it, and why they did so. I would never advocate presenting the hapless code-refactorer with a sea of green, but with a reasonable commentary on the code to provide enough clues for the curious. I'd also want examples of use, and a series of assertion tests that I can execute to check that I haven't broken anything. Such things can save a great deal of time.

Where the Documentation Should Be Held

Most database developers like to keep the documentation for a database object together with its build script, where possible, so that it is easy to access and never gets out of synchronization. Certain information should be held in source control, but only sufficient for the purposes of continuous integration and generating the correct builds for various purposes. This is best done by an automatic process from the main source of the documentation. This primary source of the essential documentation should be, in effect, stored within the database, and the ideal place is usually within the source script. Source control cannot take away this responsibility from the developer. In any case, source control, as devised for procedural code, doesn't always fit perfectly with database development. It is good practice to store the individual build scripts in source control, and this is essential for the processes of configuration management, but it doesn't provide everything that's required for the day-to-day work of the database developer.

The obvious place to hold documentation is in a comment block in the actual text for routines such as stored procedures, rules, triggers, views, constraints, and functions.

This sort of comment block is frequently used, held in structured headers that are normally placed at the start of a routine, but acceptable anywhere within it. Microsoft had an attempt at a standard for doing it. Some SSMS templates have headers like the one shown in Listing 2-1.

```
- - ================================================
- - Author:        <Author,,Name>
- - Create date:   <Create Date, ,>
- - Description:   <Description, ,>
- - ================================================
```

Listing 2-1:   A standard SSMS code header.

However, they are neither consistent not comprehensive enough for practical use. These headers would have to conform to a standard, so that routines can be listed and searched. At a minimum, there should be agreement as to the choice of headings. The system should be capable of representing lists, such as revisions or examples of use. Many different corporate-wide standards exist, but I don't know of any common shared standard for documenting these various aspects. Many conventions for "structured headers" take their inspiration from JavaDocs, or from the XML comment blocks in Visual Studio. Doxygen is probably one of the best of the documenters designed for C-style languages like C++, C, IDL, Java, and even C# or PHP.

The major difficulty that developers face with database documentation is with tables, columns, and other things that are not held in the form of scripts. You cannot store documentation for these in comment blocks: you have to store them in extended properties. We'll discuss this at length later on in this chapter.

Wherever they are stored, these headers require special formatting, because the information is really hierarchical. Microsoft uses XML-formatted headers with Visual Studio. I know of people who have experimented with YAML and JSON headers with homebrew methods of extracting the information. Most of these scripts extract structured headers from T-SQL routines, automatically add information that is available within the database such as name, schema, and object type, and store them in an XML file. From there on, things get murky.

What Should Be In the Documentation?

We want at least a summary of what the database object does, who wrote and revised it, when, why, and what they did, even if that "who" was yourself. For routines, I suspect that you'll also need a comprehensive list of examples of use, together with the expected output, which can then become a quick-check test harness when you make a minor routine change. This information should all be stored in the database itself, close-coupled with the code for the routine. Headers need to support extensible lists, so you can make lists of revisions, parameters, examples of use, and so on.

How Should the Documentation Be Published?

There is no point in keeping all this documentation if it cannot be published in a variety of ways. There are many ways that development teams need to communicate, including intranet sites, PDF files, DDL scripts, DML scripts, and Help files. This usually means extracting the contents of structured headers, along with the DDL for the routine, as an XML file and transforming that into the required form. Regrettably, because there are no current standards for structured headers, no existing SQL Documenter app is able to do this effectively. Several applications can publish prettified versions of the SQL code, but none can directly use such important fields of information as summary information or examples of use. We don't have the database equivalent of Sandcastle, which takes the XML file and generates a formatted, readable, Help file. However, one can easily do an XSLT transformation on the XML output to provide HTML pages of the data, all nicely formatted, or one can do corresponding transformations into a format compatible with Help-file documentation systems.

What Standards Exist?

In this section, we'll consider some of the Standards for documentation, namely XMLDOCS, JSON, and YAML, which we might wish to consider implementing in our database documentation.

XMLDOCS

Let's firstly have a look at the equivalent standard for C#, VB.NET, and F#. The compilers for these languages can extract strings tagged with "well-formed" XML markup that are in special comment lines (/// for C# and ''' for Visual Basic) or in a special comment block delimited as /** .... **/.

The compilers can add information that it gains by parsing the source file and then placing the result into XML files called XMLDOCS. These are then used for Visual Studio Intellisense and the object browser, and can be imported into applications such as Sandcastle to convert them into Help files. Of course, you can transform an XMLDOCS file into anything you choose with XSL.

Microsoft's XML documentation standard isn't much used outside Visual Studio, and all tools seem to assume that you are writing in a .NET procedural language. The standard has not been adopted with much enthusiasm except for the three items of information (Summary, Params, and Remarks) that are used by Visual Studio.

The basic tags used in XMLDOCS are appropriate for most purposes but, if you are doing your own processing of the results, you can add to them. The three basic tags, as noted above, are the <summary>, <param> and <remarks> tags, all of which are used by Visual Studio if you are programming in a .NET language.

Unlike most forms of structured documentation, XML documentation is usually inserted immediately before the definition of the component that you are documenting.

The rest of the standard tags are listed in Table 2-1.

Tag	Purpose
<c>	Set text within a paragraph in a code-like font to indicate that it is a token.
<code>	Set one or more lines of code or output.
<example>	An example of the routine's use.
<exception>	The errors or exceptions that can be thrown by the code.
<list>	Create a list or table.
<para>	delimits a paragraph within the text.
<param>	Describe a parameter for a routine, procedure, method or constructor.
<paramref>	Identify that a word is a parameter name.
<permission>	Document the security accessibility of a routine or member.
<remarks>	Describe a type.
<returns>	Describe the results, variables, or return value of a routine or method.
<see>	Specify a link.
<seealso>	Generate a *See Also* entry e.g. <seealso cref="MyProcedure"/>.
<summary>	Describe a member of a type.
<typeparam>	The name of the type parameter, with the name enclosed in double quotation marks (" ").
<value>	Describe a property or variable.

Table 2-1:   Standard tags in XMLDOCS.

There is, in addition, one tag, **<include>**, that is actually a directive ,and which refers to another file that describes the types and members in your source code. This can include an XPath spec to explain where in the file the compiler should go to get the information.

Not all these tags require their contents to be filled in, since information such as the parameters and the permissions is easily retrieved. With the Microsoft .NET languages, the compiler will fill in the details that it can. Some of the most useful things you can put into structured headers aren't included because they are made into lists, and XML isn't as suited for lists as JSON or YAML.

The **<LIST>** elements are mostly used for revision/version lists but the format is no good for searching for version numbers, or the details of particular revisions of code.

In order to try to persuade you that this is not a good standard to adopt for documenting SQL Server code, here is a very simple SQL Server function with the barest minimum of documentation. What the function does is unimportant; the point here is to observe the XMLDOCS header.

```sql
IF OBJECT_ID(N'IsSpace') IS NOT NULL
    DROP FUNCTION IsSpace
GO
CREATE FUNCTION dbo.[IsSpace] ( @string VARCHAR(MAX) )
/**
  <summary>IsSpace string Function Returns Non-Zero if all characters in
  @string are whitespace characters, 0 otherwise.</summary>
  <example>
    <code>Select dbo.IsSpace('how many times must i tell you')</code>
  </example>
  <example>
    <code>Select dbo.IsSpace(' <>[]{}"!@#$%9  )))))))')</code>
  </example>
  <example>
    <code>Select dbo.IsSpace(' ????/>.<,')</code>
  </example>
  <returns>integer: 1 if whitespace, otherwise 0</returns>
**/
RETURNS INT
```

```
AS
    BEGIN
        RETURN CASE WHEN PATINDEX(
                '%[A-Za-z0-9-]%', @string  COLLATE Latin1_General_CS_AI
                        ) > 0 THEN 0
                ELSE 1
            END
    END
GO
```

Listing 2-2: A header in XMLDOCS format.

Extracting the XML file from the comments isn't too hard and, once we've got it, we can put it into Sandcastle. What you want to aim for is as shown in Listing 2-3.

```
<?xml version="1.0"?>
<xml>
  <summary>IsSpace string Function Returns Non-Zero if all characters in
  @string are whitespace characters, 0 otherwise.</summary>
  <example>
    <code>Select dbo.IsSpace('how many times must i tell you')</code>
  </example>
  <example>
    <code>Select dbo.IsSpace(' &lt;&gt;[]{}"!@#$%9 )))))))')</code>
  </example>
  <example>
    <code>Select dbo.IsSpace(' ????/&gt;.&lt;,')</code>
  </example>
  <returns>integer: 1 if whitespace, otherwise 0</returns>
</xml>
```

Listing 2-3: Extracting the XML file from the XMLDOCs header.

However, this is just a fragment from the file you need to produce. Notice that you ought to escape certain characters. This makes the translation more complicated.

It isn't hard to see from this why the XMLDOCS convention never really caught on, beyond using the summary tag to generate intellisense. It is awkward. It makes the code hard to read. You are liable to miss important information. More modern approaches to structured text, such as YAML, provide a far easier and more intuitive approach, and allow for a much more versatile way of handling paragraphs of text.

YAML and JSON

It is far better to take a human-oriented approach to headers. Here is a YAML version of the header which is directly equivalent to the XMLDOCS version in Listing 2-2.

```
IF OBJECT_ID(N'IsSpace') IS NOT NULL
    DROP FUNCTION IsSpace
GO
CREATE FUNCTION dbo.[IsSpace] ( @string VARCHAR(MAX) )
/**
summary:    >
                IsSpace string Function Returns Non-Zero if all characters
                in s are whitespace characters, 0 otherwise.
example:
  — code:    Select dbo.IsSpace('how many times must i tell you')
  — code:    Select dbo.IsSpace(' <>[]{}"!@#$%9  )))))))')
  — code:    Select dbo.IsSpace(' ????/>.<,')
returns: 1  if whitespace, otherwise 0
**/
RETURNS INT
AS
    BEGIN
        RETURN CASE WHEN PATINDEX(
            '%[A-Za-z0-9-]%', @string  COLLATE Latin1_General_CS_AI
                            ) > 0 THEN 0
                ELSE 1
            END
    END
GO
```

Listing 2-4:   A comment header in YAML format.

Naturally, we may want several comment blocks and, most likely, we will want them anywhere we choose in our routine. We'll also want inline headers, using the triple-dash rather than the double-dash of inline comments.

Listing 2-5 shows the JSON version, which may answer the question as to why JSON isn't really a better choice.

```
/**
{
  "returns": "1  if whitespace, otherwise 0,"
  "example": [
    {
      "code": "Select dbo.IsSpace('how many times must i tell you')"
    },
    {
      "code": "Select dbo.IsSpace(' <>[]{}\"!@#$%9  )))))))')"
    },
    {
      "code": "Select dbo.IsSpace(' ????/>.<,') "
    }
  ],
  "summary": "IsSpace string Function Returns Non-Zero if all characters
  in s are whitespace characters, 0 otherwise.\n"
}
*/
```

Listing 2-5:   A comment header in JSON format.

YAML is far more usable, but would require processing to turn it into XML, preferably via a relational table. However, it means that other approaches can be modified with little change. JSON code can, for example, normally be digested by a YAML parser.

The SSMS templates need just a slight adjustment in order to adopt the YAML standard (the content between the chevron brackets is filled in by SSMS as part of the templating process and is not part of YAML). So, the standard SSMS header, shown in Listing 2-1, becomes as shown in Listing 2-6.

```
-- -- # ===============================================
-- -- Author:          <Author,,Name>
-- -- Create date:     <Create Date, ,>
-- -- Description:     <Description, ,>
-- -- # ===============================================
```

Listing 2-6: A YAML-compliant header.

Or alternatively, Listing 2-7 will work just as well.

```
/**
# ===============================================
Author:          <Author,,Name>
Create date:     <Create Date, ,>
Description:     <Description, ,>
# ===============================================
**/
```

Listing 2-7: Another YAML-compliant header.

In our example, we have placed the comments in a structured header at the head of the text of the routine.

How Headers are Stored in the Database

Having decided to put headers in using YAML, here is our next problem: only the text for Check constraints, Defaults (constraint or stand-alone), stored procedures, scalar functions, Replication filter procedures, DML triggers, DDL triggers, inline table-valued functions, table-valued functions, and views is retained.

However, when we run a **CREATE TABLE** script, it is not retained. In effect, that source code for tables and columns, as well as indexes is not stored in SQL Server, and so the comments for tables, indexes, and columns are lost. Whereas all .NET objects boil down to code, the same is not true of tables in SQL Server. When you script out a table in SSMS, or via SMO, you'll notice that table build scripts have lost any comments that you put in them.

This may or may not present a problem. It depends on how you develop databases. There are two basic ways of developing databases: one where the script is the primary source, and the other where the database is considered to be the source. If you are doing the former, and you run a fiendishly clever source-control system, then you don't have a problem, but otherwise, you will have to put your structured header in an "extended property" of the table.

The first method of developing databases involves maintaining one or more build scripts which contain all the comment blocks and inline comments. This is used to generate the database, but the process is never reversed. The second method avoids the meticulous source-control systems that the script-based method involved. The current version of the development database effectively becomes the source, and the state of the database is "pulled off" at regular intervals as a build script, using SMO or a third-party tool, such as SQL Compare. Each developer alters a database routine by first scripting off the routine he is working on using SSMS.

If you use the latter method of developing databases then you have to use extended properties to store your header information, rather than storing it with the code itself, in the header.

Extended properties

There are problems in using extended properties as an alternative to headers, because GUIs generally only allow access to the ones that are used by SSMS, and that boils down to one extended property called MS_Documentation. This, by itself, isn't enough. Even if you define extra properties to store different types of information, you still face problems with lists, such as revision lists, since one cannot have more than one instance of any particular extended property. If, therefore, you need to describe the parameters that you pass to routines, give examples of their use, give a revision history of the routine and so on, then it suddenly all gets more difficult unless you store the information in a structure and store that structure in an extended property. In other words, you can use extended properties, but only if you use it merely to contain the structure.

Listing 2-8 shows an example of how you might use extended properties to store table documentation in a build script.

```
CREATE TABLE [dbo].[Person]
    (
      [Person_id] [int] IDENTITY(1, 1)
                        NOT NULL ,
      [Title] [varchar](20) NOT NULL ,
      [FirstName] [nvarchar](50) NOT NULL ,
      [NickName] [nvarchar](50) NOT NULL ,
      [LastName] [nvarchar](50) NOT NULL ,
      [DateOfBirth] [datetime] NULL ,
      [insertiondate] [datetime] NOT NULL ,
      [terminationdate] [datetime] NULL ,
      [Creator_ID] [int] NOT NULL ,
      CONSTRAINT [PK_dbo_Person] PRIMARY KEY CLUSTERED ( [Person_id] ASC )
        WITH ( PAD_INDEX = OFF, STATISTICS_NORECOMPUTE = OFF,
                IGNORE_DUP_KEY = OFF, ALLOW_ROW_LOCKS = ON,
                ALLOW_PAGE_LOCKS = ON ) ON [PRIMARY]
    )
ON  [PRIMARY]
GO
SET ANSI_PADDING OFF
GO
EXEC sys.sp_addextendedproperty @name = N'MS_Description',
    @value = N'primary key for the table', @level0type = N'SCHEMA',
    @level0name = N'dbo', @level1type = N'TABLE', @level1name = N'Person',
    @level2type = N'COLUMN', @level2name = N'Person_id'
GO
EXEC sys.sp_addextendedproperty @name = N'MS_Description',
    @value = N'Creator of the record', @level0type = N'SCHEMA',
    @level0name = N'dbo', @level1type = N'TABLE', @level1name = N'Person',
    @level2type = N'COLUMN', @level2name = N'LastName'
GO
```

```
EXEC sys.sp_addextendedproperty @name = N'MS_Description',
    @value = N'Date the record was created (automatic)',
    @level0type = N'SCHEMA', @level0name = N'dbo', @level1type = N'TABLE',
    @level1name = N'Person', @level2type = N'COLUMN',
    @level2name = N'insertiondate'
GO
EXEC sys.sp_addextendedproperty @name = N'MS_Description',
    @value = N'Date for the termination of the record',
    @level0type = N'SCHEMA', @level0name = N'dbo', @level1type = N'TABLE',
    @level1name = N'Person', @level2type = N'COLUMN',
    @level2name = N'terminationdate'
GO
EXEC sys.sp_addextendedproperty @name = N'Documentation', @value = N'
 summary:   >
            The Person table is used to store the essential datails
            that we store on an individual for which there is a one-to-one
            correspondence with the person. (assuming that an individual has
            only one name.
 Revisions:
 — version: 1
        Modification: Created table
        Author: Phil Factor
        Date:   24/11/2009
 — version: 2
        Modification: Added the creator ID for the record for audit.
        Author: Phil Factor
        Date:   28/11/2009
 ', @level0type = N'SCHEMA', @level0name = N'dbo', @level1type = N'TABLE',
    @level1name = N'Person'
GO
EXEC sys.sp_addextendedproperty @name = N'MS_Description',
    @value = N'The identifier of a person', @level0type = N'SCHEMA',
    @level0name = N'dbo', @level1type = N'TABLE', @level1name = N'Person'
GO
ALTER TABLE [dbo].[Person]
  ADD  CONSTRAINT [DF_Person_Title]  DEFAULT ('') FOR [Title]
GO
ALTER TABLE [dbo].[Person]
   ADD  CONSTRAINT [DF_Person_Title]  DEFAULT ('') FOR [Title]
GO
ALTER TABLE [dbo].[Person]
  ADD  CONSTRAINT [DF_Person_FirstName]  DEFAULT ('') FOR [FirstName]
GO
ALTER TABLE [dbo].[Person]
```

```
   ADD   CONSTRAINT [DF_Person_NickName]   DEFAULT ('') FOR [NickName]
GO
ALTER TABLE [dbo].[Person]
   ADD   CONSTRAINT [DF_Person_creator]   DEFAULT (USER_NAME()) FOR [LastName]
GO
ALTER TABLE [dbo].[Person]
 ADD   CONSTRAINT [DF_Person_insertiondate]   DEFAULT (GETDATE()) FOR
                                                     [insertiondate]
GO
```

Listing 2-8:   Storing documentation for tables in extended properties.

Now, we are able to attach documentation to all our database objects. With extended properties, you can now document almost any conceivable database object, except:

- full-text objects

- objects outside the database scope, such as HTTP end points

- unnamed objects such as partition function parameters

- certificates, symmetric keys, asymmetric keys, and credentials

- system-defined objects such as system tables, catalog views, and system stored procedures.

That's quite sufficient for me, anyway.

Why didn't I use MS_Description? We need some way of distinguishing ordinary comments and structured headers. I'm always loath to use MS_Description for special purposes because there is always someone, me in this case, who is considering whether to use it for something else.

Get Information Out of Headers

Now, how about getting information from our structured headers? Before we think about parsing the structured information, we have to consider how to extract the extended properties. These were originally accessible only via a rather awkward function called `fn_listextendedproperty`. Mercifully, Microsoft added a system catalog view called `sys.extended_properties` that is much easier to use. The extended properties that we have called "documentation" in the current database can be extracted for all our tables by means of the SQL shown in Listing 2-9.

```sql
SELECT   SCHEMA_NAME(tbl.schema_id) AS [Table_Schema] ,
         tbl.name AS [Table_Name] ,
         p.value
FROM     sys.tables AS tbl
         INNER JOIN sys.extended_properties AS p ON p.major_id = tbl.object_id
                                                 AND p.minor_id = 0
                                                 AND p.class = 1
WHERE    p.name LIKE 'Documentation'
ORDER BY [Table_Schema] ASC ,
         [Table_Name] ASC
```

Listing 2-9:   Extracting documentation from tables.

And you can do the same for the columns with code such as that shown in Listing 2-10.

```sql
SELECT   SCHEMA_NAME(tbl.schema_id) AS [Table_Schema] ,
         tbl.name AS [Table_Name] ,
         clmns.name AS [Column_Name,
         CAST(p.value AS SQL_VARIANT) AS [Value]
FROM     sys.tables AS tbl
         INNER JOIN sys.all_columns AS clmns ON clmns.object_id = tbl.object_id
         INNER JOIN sys.extended_properties AS p ON p.major_id = clmns.object_id
                                                 AND p.minor_id = clmns.column_id
                                                 AND p.class = 1
WHERE    p.name LIKE 'Documentation'
ORDER BY [Table_Schema] ASC ,
```

```
        [Table_Name] ASC ,
        [Column_ID] ASC ,
        [Name] ASC
```

Listing 2-10: Extracting documentation from columns.

For the rest of our database objects and routines, we can extract the contents of the header in a number of different ways. Listing 2-11 shows a stored procedure that does the job for any header. It will extract all headers in a routine, wherever they are in the code, and will add all the inline header material. It will work for any type of header that conforms to the /*** ... */ (block comment) and − − − (inline) convention.


```
CREATE PROCEDURE Header
    @RoutineCode VARCHAR(MAX) ,
    @header VARCHAR(MAX) OUTPUT
/** summary:    >
    .  takes a routine's definition and extracts all header information from it,
       including inline header information
Revisions:
 — version     : 1
    Modification: Created the procedure
    Author      : Phil Factor
    Date        :   15/12/2009
 — version     : 2
    Modification: Added mod to allow for nested comment blocks.
    Author      : Phil Factor
    Date        : 16/12/2009
example:
 — code: >
      Declare @Definition varchar(Max)
      Declare @Header Varchar(max)
      SELECT @Definition=Definition
      FROM sys.sql_modules AS sm
      JOIN sys.objects AS o ON sm.object_id = o.object_id
      where OBJECT_NAME(sm.object_id) = 'header'
      Execute header @Definition, @Header output
      Select @Header
returns:      the header block as an output variable
 */
AS
```

53

```
    DECLARE @parser TABLE
        (
          TheOrder INT PRIMARY KEY ,
          TheChar CHAR(1) ,
          [State] VARCHAR(12) ,
          Lookback VARCHAR(3) ,
          Lookahead VARCHAR(3) ,
          [output] VARCHAR(3)
        )
--fill the parser table with each character in turn
    INSERT  INTO @parser
          ( theOrder ,
            thechar ,
            lookback ,
            lookahead
          )
          SELECT  number ,
                  SUBSTRING(@RoutineCode, number, 1) ,--character
                  SUBSTRING('   ' + @routinecode, number, 3) ,--lookback
                  SUBSTRING(@RoutineCode, number, 3)--lookAhead
          FROM    numbers
          WHERE   number <= LEN(@RoutineCode)
---Dependencies:
-- - number table
    DECLARE @PreviousState VARCHAR(12)
    DECLARE @Output VARCHAR(4)
    DECLARE @State VARCHAR(12)
--select @Routinecode
    SELECT  @PreviousState = 'code' ,
            @State = 'code'
    UPDATE  @parser
    SET - -are we in a string
            @PreviousState = @State ,
            @State = [State] =
                  CASE WHEN @PreviousState <> 'string'--start of a header?
                          AND LookBack = '/**' THEN 'header'
                       WHEN @PreviousState = 'lineheader'--end of lineheader?
                          AND RIGHT(LookBack, 2) = CHAR(13)
                          + CHAR(10) THEN 'code'
                       WHEN @PreviousState = 'header'
                          AND Lookahead LIKE '_*/' THEN 'code'
                       WHEN @PreviousState NOT IN ( 'string',
                                                    'header' )
                          AND LookBack = '---'
```

```
ALTER PROCEDURE ExtractDocumentation
/**
summary:    >
    Gets the source of every routine in the database and extracts the header
    files from them, and then parses the YAML file to extract a relational table
    with all the information.
Revisions:
 — version    : 1
    Modification: Created the procedure
    Author      : Phil Factor
    Date        : 01/10/2010
example:
 — code: >
returns:  >
    The documentation table
*/
AS
    DECLARE @documentation TABLE
        (
        [object_type] VARCHAR(32) ,
        [schema] SYSNAME ,
        [object_name] SYSNAME ,
        [sequence_ID] INT ,
        [path] VARCHAR(255) ,
        [attribute] VARCHAR(255) ,
        [sequence] VARCHAR(255) ,
        [value] VARCHAR(MAX)
        )--the table to take the documentation items
    DECLARE @allObjects TABLE
        (
        TheID INT IDENTITY(1, 1) ,
        [object_type] VARCHAR(32) ,
        [schema] SYSNAME ,
        [object_name] SYSNAME ,
        [definition] VARCHAR(MAX)
        )- — the table containing all the objects
    DECLARE @Definition VARCHAR(MAX) ,
        @Header VARCHAR(MAX) ,--what is in the header information
        @Object_name SYSNAME ,--the object name
        @schema SYSNAME ,--the schema
        @Object_type VARCHAR(32) ,--the type of object
        @ii INT ,--iteration counter
        @iiMax INT — -max value of iteration counter
    INSERT  INTO @AllObjects
```

```
            ( [object_type] ,
              [schema] ,
              [object_name] ,
              [definition]
            )
            SELECT   REPLACE(SUBSTRING(v.name, 5, 31), 'cns', 'constraint') ,
                     object_schema_name(o.object_ID) ,
                     OBJECT_NAME(o.object_ID) ,
                     definition
            FROM     sys.sql_modules sm
                     INNER JOIN sys.objects AS o ON sm.object_id = o.OBJECT_ID
                     LEFT OUTER JOIN master.dbo.spt_values v - -to get the type of
object
                     ON o.type = SUBSTRING(v.name, 1, 2) COLLATE database_default
                        AND v.type = 'O9T'
    SELECT   @ii = MIN(TheID) ,
             @iiMax = MAX(TheID)
    FROM     @allObjects
    WHILE @ii <= @iiMax
        BEGIN
            SELECT   @Object_Type = [object_Type] ,
                     @Schema = [schema] ,
                     @Object_name = [object_name] ,
                     @Definition = [definition]
            FROM     @allObjects
            WHERE    TheID = @ii
            EXECUTE header @Definition, @Header OUTPUT
            INSERT   INTO @Documentation
                     ( [object_type] ,
                       [schema] ,
                       [object_name] ,
                       [sequence_ID] ,
                       [path] ,
                       [attribute] ,
                       [sequence] ,
                       [value]
                     )
                     SELECT   @Object_type ,
                              @Schema ,
                              @Object_name ,
                              [sequence_ID] ,
                              [path] ,
                              [attribute] ,
                              [sequence] ,
```

```
                          [value]
               FROM    YAMLtoTable(@header)
          SELECT  @ii = @ii + 1
      END
  SELECT  *
  FROM    @documentation
```

Listing 2-12: Publishing documentation to a table.

The routines for getting comments from the extended properties of tables, columns and indexes are very similar, so I won't repeat them here.

Now we have all the information, we can convert it to XML (using a `WITH XML SELECT` statement) and pass it to Sandcastle, or we can produce HTML documentation directly from it. At last, we have the documentation neatly filleted up in the place where a dyed-in-the-wool database programmer likes it best: in a table.

Conclusion

It isn't surprising that the proper documentation of database code has been so neglected by Microsoft or the third-party tool providers. The existing standards of procedural languages are clumsy to use, and the tools that are developed for them cannot be used for database scripts.

YAML, which has always seemed like a solution looking for a problem, has emerged as a perfect means of embedding readable, structured, hierarchical information into the script of database objects. Even if the methods of converting this information into Help text or intranet sites is currently slightly awkward, the method is useful, as it is easy to scan when inspecting the code itself.

Chapter 3: Change Management and Source Control

With this chapter, we begin our exploration of the processes, tools and practices that are required in order to allow a team, or even several teams, of developers to work together to deliver to production, successfully and smoothly, an application and its database.

The purpose of change management is to protect the integrity of the database design throughout the development process, to identify what changes have been made, when, and by whom and, where necessary, to undo individual modifications. A source control system is typically the critical application around which a change management regime is structured, and this is a requirement for any team development project.

In this chapter, we will explore:

- development environments that are necessary, as an application and its database make their way from initial development through to production

- an overview of source control for databases, including coverage of source control models and systems, and the challenges of managing database objects in source control

- how to get your database objects into source control, via scripting or by using Red Gate SQL Source Control

- managing data in source control, and how to synchronize the data needed for the application to run (lookup tables, metadata, and so on).

With all this in place, we will move on, in Chapter 4, to see how to automate the deployment of a database, including necessary data, from one environment to another.

The Challenges of Team-based Development

The journey of a team-developed application and its database, from initial development to successful deployment to production, involves many stages, including, but not limited to, the following:

- initial development and unit testing of code on local sandbox servers

- strict use of source control to store and version control individual code modules

- use of Continuous Integration (see Chapter 4) to perform regular builds in a test environment, to find out how the small units work when put together

- a way to automate the build and deployment process, including a reliable way to push schema and data changes, from one environment to the next, for testing, staging, and so on.

All of this requires mechanisms for establishing multiple development platforms, sandboxes, integration environments, local servers, and more. Each of these can then lead to multiple testing servers, performance testing, Quality Assurance, financial test, and user acceptance test. Ultimately, it all comes together to go out to a production server.

Regardless of the specific development methodology employed (ITIL, Scrum, etc.) it is vital that a process is put in place to manage all these people, their code, and the environments. In support of this process, tools will be needed in order to automate builds and deployments because, with this many people and this many environments, attempting to deploy manually would be a time-consuming, error-prone exercise in frustration. The goal of the process is to enable large teams of developers to work on the same project, at the same time, without stepping on each other's toes.

If all this isn't enough, the very purpose of having a database, keeping data, storing it, retrieving it, and presenting it to the user, means that you can't just throw away yesterday's database. It has data. That data is kept for a reason. It may be vital financial information or it may be very simple lookup data that helps you maintain consistency.

Regardless, it needs to be kept around and that makes the job of building databases even harder. You have to be able to retain data even as you make changes to the underlying structure. You may need to move data with the deployment of new versions of the database. You'll probably need a mechanism to make one database look like another without performing a backup and restore but, instead, performing a deployment of code, structure, and data. You're going to want to automate all this as well.

Fortunately, there are a number of tools available that can help you manage your code and deploy multiple versions of the database to any number of systems, with varying degrees of automation. There are tools and methods for putting database code, objects, and data into source control so that these database specific objects can be managed just like the developers manage their application source code. Best of all, many of these tools work together and can be automated in such a way that you arrive at a place where you automatically deploy different versions of your database to different servers in a timely manner, freeing you up to work on performance tuning.

The key to achieving successful team and cross-team development is to implement a process and to follow that process with a great deal of discipline. The military has a saying, "Slow is smooth, and smooth is fast." No one wants a slow development process, but a rough-and-tumble development process with lots of errors, a great deal of friction and rework, one that is not smooth, will not be fast. Better to concentrate on making your process smooth, and fast will follow.

Environments

In very small shops, it's possible to develop directly against your production server. It's not smart, but it's possible. However, as the importance, to the company, of your production data grows, and the number of people and number of steps within your development process expands, you'll find it increasingly important to have multiple layers of servers between your production and development systems. Not all of these environments are required for every development process. in addition, some environments can serve multiple purposes, depending on the stringency of your process, the number of teams involved, and the business requirements you're striving to meet. With this many servers, the migration problem becomes clear: you need a lot of change scripts; hence the need for automation.

In order to support team development in any application that persists information to a relational database system, you will need somewhere to host the database server. SQL Server can be run on large or small systems, and within virtual environments. I'm not going to spend time specifying when, or if, you need a physical or virtual server for these environments, or what size of environment you'll need. That's going to vary widely, depending on the applications you're developing, the processes you implement, the amount of money you're willing to spend, and any number of other variables. Instead, I'll focus here on the purposes to which a given server may be dedicated in order to achieve a goal, within the process of developing your application. Just remember, once you define the needs and purposes of the servers within your process, use them in a disciplined manner, in order to ensure the smoothness of your development process.

For most development, in order to provide a mechanism for testing prior to deployment, you should have at least three basic environments:

- a development environment where you can make mistakes without hurting your production system.
- a testing environment to ensure that anything you're releasing into the wild of production will work correctly.
- a production system where the data that supports your company will live.

Development environments

There are two common models for organizing database development:

- **dedicated**, where each developer has their own local copy of the database
- **shared**, where each developer works on the same, central copy of the database.

With a local server, a developer has a lot more flexibility, and can try things out without affecting the rest of the team. However, integration can be problematic. In a shared server environment, integration becomes more fluid, but changes by any individual developer or development team can seriously impact others. I'm going to assume a situation where both models are in use, in order to maximize flexibility without compromising the importance of integration.

Sandbox (local server)

The first place where most development will occur is on a sandbox server. This is usually, but not necessarily, a full instance of a database server running locally on the developer's machine or, possibly, in a private server environment. The sandbox server is meant to be a playground, a place where developers and designers can try things out, even break things. It's the one place where just about anything goes. However, all the fun and games in the sandbox server should remain there. No code and no structures should be moved off a sandbox server unless they've gone through some type of local testing, frequently referred to as a unit test. Once a piece of code has passed a unit test (see Chapter 5) it can be moved into whatever type of source control is being used.

Security on the sandbox should allow the developer at least database owner (dbo) access to the databases on which they're working. If the sandbox is located locally, you can probably go ahead and let them have system administrator (sa) privileges.

Common server

When working with a team of developers it's usually necessary to have, in addition to the sandbox server, a common, shared work space for database work. That way, the new column you've added, or the new procedure your co-worker has built, will be immediately available to other developers in the team. If you're using Red Gate SQL Source Control (covered later), the need for a common server is greatly diminished; since the tool integrates the source control system directly into SSMS, each team member can simply get the latest changes from the **Get Latest** tab.

I've known cases where multiple teams develop against a single common server, but this only really works if there are few, if any, dependencies between the code bases. Otherwise, as changes get made by one team, they'll break the code of the next team, which can lead to a lot of frustration and, even worse, slow down development.

Direct development against the common server should be expected and planned for. As with the sandbox, no code should be moved off the common server until it has passed a unit test and, if necessary, a more extended test between multiple teams if there are dependencies (integration testing will be covered shortly).

In terms of security, an individual or team should only have access to the database or schema for which they're responsible. If certain developers are responsible for the whole database, then they will probably require dbo privileges. Where possible, however, you should control access at a more granular, object level. If a developer is responsible only for creating stored procedures, then his or her privileges should be limited to just those objects, and the right, for example, to create tables, should be denied.

Testing, staging and production environments

At various stages during development, the application and database code must be subject to rigorous testing to make sure, not only that it is functionally correct, but also that the database conforms to user and business requirements, deploys smoothly, and so on. This requires the creation of multiple environments, including integration, testing, and staging.

Integration server

When multiple developers or teams are working on various different parts of an application, and there is a great deal of dependency between these parts, then it's a good idea to build an integration server.

The integration server presents a controlled environment where code that has already gone through initial testing can be combined with other, tested, parts of the application under development. Integration testing is a means of ensuring that tightly-coupled applications are validated before being sent to a Quality Assurance team.

No direct development should be allowed on the integration server. You should only allow a deployment directly from source control, so that the server is always in a known state. This will enable your development teams to establish that their application, or part of the application, works with a specific version of any number of other applications and components. It provides a foundation for further development. Deployments to this server could be performed on demand, or according to an agreed schedule

Security should be fairly clamped down, allowing developers only read access or access through an application's limited-privilege role. Developers should not be allowed to modify structures directly on this server as this will lead to inconsistent test results, which will cause rework and friction between the teams, and will slow down development.

Continuous integration server

When there are a lot of dependencies between teams or applications, it might be a good idea to check those dependencies a lot more frequently, maybe even constantly. This is the purpose of a continuous integration (CI) server. With a CI server, you'll want to automate a build based, either on code being checked into source control, or on a regular, but frequent schedule. The key word to associate with a CI server is "automation." You need to set up automatic deployment and automatic testing, so that you can validate the build and deployment without involving a single human being. This provides a solid early warning system for integration issues. The CI process is discussed in more detail in Chapter 4.

Security shouldn't be a problem on a CI server, because no one from a development team should be allowed access to it.

Quality Assurance

Quality Assurance (QA) is a standard practice whereby, as each new build is deployed, the general quality of the code is repeatedly validated through a combination of automated and manual testing. The QA process usually includes verifying that the code meets the documented business requirements and Service Level Agreements (SLAs). Deployments to a QA server are either done on an ad hoc basis, as milestones within the code are met, or on a scheduled basis, so that QA is constantly checking the status of the code.

Deployments are based on a known version of the code, and can take the form of differential (incremental) builds, or full builds. In a differential build, only the code or structures that have changed are deployed; in a full build, all of the code, including the database, is completely replaced each time.

The importance of repeatable tests in a QA environment suggests the need for realistic test data, as supplied by data generation tools such as the Data Generator in Visual Studio Team System Database Edition, or SQL Data Generator from Red Gate.

Security in a QA system should be more stringent than in most development systems. In order to ensure that the tests are valid, changes can't be introduced. This means that developers and QA operators should not have the ability to manipulate objects. You may, however, want to allow them to manipulate data.

Performance testing

The performance testing environment is sometimes combined with QA, but this is generally inadvisable. Separating performance testing from the more general business testing of QA allows for more flexibility in both testing processes.

The idea of a performance test is not to carefully simulate a production load, although that is a part of the process. Instead, you want to measure performance under an ever-increasing load, as measured in transactions per second, user connections, data volume, and other metrics. You want to see, not only how the application behaves under load, but also where and how it breaks. This can be a time-consuming process when done properly, which is one of the main reasons why it needs to be separated from the standard QA process. In order to provide a reliable set of test results, deployments should be from a version or label within source control, as described in more detail later, in the *Source Control* section.

Security on the performance testing server can be somewhat flexible, but again, once testing starts, you don't want changes introduced. It's probably better to treat it like a QA system and not allow data definition language (DDL) operations against the databases on the server.

User Acceptance Testing

User Acceptance Testing (UAT) is a lot like QA testing but, whereas QA is focused on careful verification of the quality of code, UAT involves business operators and end-users manually testing the system to ensure it performs in ways they anticipated.

The UAT process can be combined with QA, but QA is sometimes on a faster schedule, and UAT can take a long time, so having a separate environment is useful. Security should be clamped down on a scale similar to that in your production system. No direct access to manipulate the data outside of what is provided through application, and certainly no DDL, should be allowed.

Staging

On the staging server, we perform a final check for our application's deployment process, to ensure that it will run successfully in production. As such, the staging server should be a mirror of the production environment. This doesn't mean it has to be the same size machine, with as much memory and CPU horsepower. It does mean, though, that the staging server must host an exact copy of the production database, and must exactly mimic the production server configuration and environmental settings. If the production server is configured as a linked server, for example, this configuration must be replicated on the staging server; all ANSI settings, which may affect the way your code is deployed, must be identical.

You need to treat any errors occurring during a deployment on a staging system as a failure of the entire deployment. Do not simply try to fix the error in situ and proceed with the deployment. Instead, reset the server so that it is once more a copy of your production system (e.g. by using a backup and restore, or Red Gate's SQL Compare and Data Compare), fix the error in the deployment, and retry the entire process from scratch.

Once a successful deployment, from a known state in source control, is completed, no other changes to code should be allowed before you run the deployment on production. Security should be as tight as on a production system. No direct DML and no DDL.

Production

The production system represents the culmination of all your application's hopes and dreams. Deployment should be from the same source that was just successfully deployed to staging. Again, security should be clamped down in order to protect the integrity of the company's data.

Source Control

A database application development project depends on the successful coordination of the application and database development efforts. It is essential to be able to keep the scripts together so that any working build can be reproduced. To do this, we need to be able to tie database changes to the code changes to which they relate. The way to do this is to check them into source control as a part of the same changeset transaction. This makes it far easier to make consistent builds and deployments.

As discussed earlier, there are several points in the development life cycle, such as for integration testing, QA testing and so on, where a consistent working build must be readily available. For databases, there must be a correct version of the build script, not just for the database structure and routines, but also for key "static" data and configuration information. Everything that goes towards the build must be in source control, including configuration files, and it should be possible to build the entire application from these scripts.

Use of a source control system has long been an established part of the development process for application code but not, sadly, for database code. This is largely because, unlike application code, database code is all about persistence. You can't simply recompile the database into a new form. You must take into account the data and structures that already exist. Mechanisms for automating the process of getting a database into source control, and deploying it from that location, have either been manual or home-grown.

In either case, database source control processes have traditionally been problematic and difficult to maintain.

Recently, a number of tools, such as Red Gate's SQL Source Control (and SQL Compare) and Microsoft's Visual Studio Database Projects have sought to make it much easier to manage database code in a source control system, and to automate the deployment of databases out of source control. This means that checking your database into a source control system can, and should, be a fundamental part of your processes.

Source control features

Source control provides several important solutions to almost all development processes, including:

- ability to share code, allowing multiple people/teams to access pieces of code, or a database, at the same time

- a way to manage and protect the code generated

- a way to version each piece of code, so that a history of changes can be kept

- a way to version, or label, whole sets of code, so that you can deploy from a known state, or revert to a previously known state

- facilitation of change management, so that new software or new functionality is carefully tracked and approved.

As this suggests, every source control system will provide a means by which a developer can retrieve a particular version of a given piece of code, and a way to put the changed code back into the system, thus creating a new version of the code. When a developer accesses a piece of code, depending on the source control system used, he or she will get either shared or exclusive access to the code. Shared access is common in source control systems, such as Subversion, that employ an "optimistic" approach to concurrent access, while exclusive access to the code is the "pessimistic" approach used, for example, by Microsoft's Visual SourceSafe.

A good source control system should have a mechanism in place for merging multiple changes to the same code. In other words, if more than one developer has worked on the same procedure, a mechanism must exist for reconciling their individual changes. Furthermore, in order to support multiple development streams (for example, one stream writing service patches for code already in production, while another is creating all new functionality for the system) the source control system should allow developers to create branches of the codebase for testing or for releases. The alterations in the branches can then be merged back into the main trunk of development, although this is sometimes a difficult process requiring careful planning.

Versioning databases

The location of the database within source control is important. If you create your own separate storage location, then the vital coordination between the database and the application is lost, or left to the mercy of manual processes. Instead, the database should be made an integral part of the larger project or solution in which the application is stored. This ensures that when a label or branch is created in the application, the database is labeled or branched in exactly the same way.

While code frequently has versioning built into the executables, databases don't automatically receive a versioning system as they are created or updated. A method of labeling the database itself should be incorporated into the source management process.

One popular, though rather messy, solution is to insert rows into a version table, but this requires maintaining data, not simply working with code. A better approach is to use extended properties within SQL Server. Extended properties can be applied to most objects within the database and, by applying and updating these property values as appropriate, it is possible to version, either the database as a whole, or each of the individual objects. Best of all, this can be automated as part of the build and deploy process, so that the source control versions or labels are automatically applied to the values on the extended property.

Optimistic versus pessimistic source control

There are a couple of prevailing models for managing code within source control. The older method, used by tools such as Microsoft VSS, is a pessimistic process, wherein the developer takes an exclusive lock on the code in question through a process known as a check-out. While a piece of code is checked out, other developers can read the code, but they cannot edit it themselves. When the original developer is done, the code is checked back in to VSS and is now available for other developers to use.

Most developers prefer a more flexible, optimistic approach to source control, as offered by modern source control systems, such as Subversion or Microsoft's Team Foundation Server. Instead of an exclusive lock, a developer just retrieves a copy of the code and begins to edit. Other developers are free to also start working with the same code. When any developer is done with the work, the code is merged back into source control and committed. This allows for more than one developer to work on any given piece of code, but still manage the changes so that no one's work is inadvertently overwritten and lost.

Source control systems

There are source control systems available from a large number of vendors, as well as several open source options. The two source control systems currently supported by Red Gate SQL Source Control are Microsoft's Team Foundation Server (TFS) and the open source Subversion (SVN). Microsoft still has available Visual SourceSafe (VSS) but that is being retired and will no longer be supported.

While TFS and SVN work in similar ways, there are distinct differences, and you may find one or the other better suited to your particular system. Table 3-1 outlines some of the fundamental differences between the two products.

Feature	TFS	SVN
Branching	Strong support for creating branches and merging them back together.	Strong support for creating branches and merging them back together.
Labeling	Fundamental behavior allows for multiple labels of individual files or entire projects.	Fundamental behavior allows for labels of individual files or entire projects.
Merge	Works in either traditional VSS mode of exclusive check-outs or within the Edit/Merge methods of modern source control systems.	Works within Edit/Merge method of modern source control systems. Some weakness in tracking merge history.
Offline editing	TFS does not work well in an offline state.	SVN can work in an offline state, with the ability to retrieve a set of code, disconnect from the server to work and then reconnect later to merge the changes.
Multi-platform support	This is available through third-party plug-ins at additional cost.	Multi-platform support is the fundamental foundation of SVN. Clients can be in any OS connected to a server in any OS.

Feature	TFS	SVN
Work integration	TFS is intended as an enterprise development management tool, of which source control is just one aspect. It exposes multiple tools and processes for managing development teams, projects, problem tracking and integration.	SVN is a source control system and does not provide this type of processing.
Integration with SQL Server	SQL Server is a fundamental piece of TFS, so the software available for SQL Server management such as Reporting Services or Integration Services is available for working with TFS.	SVN manages data in a proprietary (open source) format. Tools are available, but a learning curve will be associated with each one.

Table 3-1:   A comparison of the SVN and TFS source control systems.

While SVN does offer support for working offline, some of the newer "distributed" source control systems, such as Git and Mercurial, aim to make this much easier.

Git, in particular, has been gaining traction. Whereas traditional source control systems, such as SVN and TFS, store data as a series of files and change sets, Git uses the concept of **snapshots**. At each commit, Git takes a snapshot of the state of all of the files in the project, and stores a reference to this snapshot. The entire project history is stored on a developer's local database, so virtually all operations can be performed locally, offline. The idea behind Git is that it is built "from the ground up" to handle branching and merging. An excellent resource for learning more about Git is Scott Chacon's online book, Pro Git (HTTP://PROGIT.ORG/BOOK/).

Ultimately, the source control system you use isn't nearly as important as the fact that you do need to start managing your databases through source control.

Database objects in source control

Changes made to an application during development result directly in a change to the underlying code file. These source files can be kept in source control so that each revision to a file is retained. This process does not interrupt or modify the developer's "interactive" development model, whereby a developer works directly with his or her code, within Visual Studio, with direct access to syntax checking, debugging tools, and so on.

While one would like to extend the "interactive" model to databases, allowing developers to work directly with the databases, in SSMS, while still maintaining a history of changes in the source control system, there are complicating factors. The most obvious difficulty is that DML and DDL queries modify the current state of a database, so there are no files being changed and there is essentially no source code to control.

Developers can periodically script out the database objects they have changed but, in the absence of third-party tools, it is very hard to maintain a proper incremental history of changes, packaging up a specific database version becomes difficult, and discrepancies are common between the "working" database and what's in source control.

This is the reason why most home-grown solutions for source controlling databases have, of necessity, adopted an "offline" development model whereby, rather than working directly with the database, you work directly with the scripts, in source control, which are then applied to a database. As long as all developers rigorously adopt the approach of never editing a database object directly within SSMS, but instead updating a script in source control, then maintaining change history is easier, and one can be confident that what's in source control should accurately represent the "truth" regarding the current state of the database.

Nevertheless, there are many drawbacks to the offline model. It is disruptive, and the biggest obvious disadvantage is that, in working with scripts rather than a database, you lose the benefits of immediate syntax checking. If you are just working with a script, completely independent of the database, it is possible, even likely, that you will introduce syntax errors. To check the syntax of an offline script, it must be run against a database to make sure that the latest version of the scripts, in source control, will build a functional database. Additional processes must be in place to ensure that objects are scripted in dependency order and referential integrity is maintained, and that changes made by teams of developers can successfully be merged.

The tools available to help manage databases in source control adopt different models. Visual Studio Team System uses the offline model and builds in features to help overcome the issues above. Conversely, Red Gate's SQL Source Control integrates your source control system directly with SSMS in order to allow developers to continue using the interactive development model, working with an "online" database. It automates the source control of object creation scripts, alerting users to differences between the database and source control versions, and making it simpler to commit changes to source control.

The model and tools you choose may vary, depending on the skill set and preferences of your team. Most DBAs I know are very comfortable within SSMS and are much less so in other development environments, such as Visual Studio. However, for many of the developers I know, the opposite is true, and these developers can take advantage of the enhanced text editing offered by tools like Visual Studio. Likewise, if you've come to rely on luxuries such as intellisense and syntax checking when writing database code, then the online model will be very attractive. However, if you have learned how to work with T-SQL in such a way that you're able to write scripts to create database objects much faster than is possible through a GUI, then the offline model may work better for you.

Whether you use an online or offline development method with your database, the key point is that you need to deploy databases out of source control. You need to establish this as a discipline, in order to be able to automate your processes. You'll find that, far from slowing down development, deploying from source control will, in fact, speed it up, because you'll be dealing with fewer errors in deployment.

Getting your database objects into source control

If following the offline model, or if using the online model but without full integration between SSMS and your source control system, then the first step is to add the database objects to the source control system. In other words, the most basic building blocks of the database objects, the T-SQL scripts, need to be checked individually into whatever source control system is being used. With those individual scripts, the database T-SQL code can be managed through the source control processes. To properly manage a database in a team environment, you'll need to break down the scripts into the smallest possible component parts, preferably one script per database object, and then store these scripts in your source control system, usually with separate folders for each type of object, for various types of reference data, and so on.

```
SVN
    MyProject
        Databases
            MyDatabase
                Database
                Tables
                Procs
                Functions
            Data
                Procs
                Tables
                TestData
            ReleaseScripts
...<etc.>...
```

Listing 3-1: Database file layout in source control.

You will need to take into account that either the objects you're creating won't exist in your database, or that they do exist and you're making changes to them. I usually find the best way to solve this, if you're not using a tool to perform the integration with source control for you, is to use scripts that DROP and then CREATE the objects. In this manner, you can always be sure the objects will be built. If you just use ALTER commands in your scripts, you may not get all the objects into the database.

If you use Red Gate's SQL Source Control tool, the need to script out your objects as a separate step is removed. Over the coming sections, we'll take a look at a few ways to generate scripts separately, either via a command line or a GUI, and then at how it works using SQL Source Control.

Scripting a database using Powershell/SMO

Getting your scripts output from the database can be a tedious task. The best way to script out your database objects is through automation and, in this example, we'll show how to do this using an SMO/Powershell script. The full script is available with the code download for this book, but Listing 3-2, for which we thank Allen White (HTTP://SQLBLOG.COM/BLOGS/ALLEN_WHITE/DEFAULT.ASPX), shows the basic details. It takes three parameters, the instance name for the server to which you want to connect, the name of the database that is going to be scripted out, and the base directory for the location of the script files. It will create a directory there, with the name of the target database, and then script the objects within, with a separate folder for each type of object.

```
#DBscripting.ps1
#Script all the objects in the specified database
# Backs up user databases
# Get the SQL Server instance name, database and base directory from the command
line
param(
  [string]$inst=$null,
  [string]$dtbase=$null,
  [string]$base=$null
```

```
  )
# Load SMO assembly, and if we're running SQL 2008 DLLs load the SMOExtended and
SQLWMIManagement libraries
$v = [System.Reflection.Assembly]::LoadWithPartialName( 'Microsoft.SqlServer.SMO')
if ((($v.FullName.Split(','))[1].Split('='))[1].Split('.')[0] - ne '9') {
   [System.Reflection.Assembly]::LoadWithPartialName('Microsoft.SqlServer.
SMOExtended') | out-null
   [System.Reflection.Assembly]::LoadWithPartialName('Microsoft.SqlServer.
SQLWMIManagement') | out-null
   }
# Handle any errors that occur
Function Error_Handler {
   Write-Host "Error Category: " + $error[0].CategoryInfo.Category
   Write-Host " Error Object: " + $error[0].TargetObject
   Write-Host " Error Message: " + $error[0].Exception.Message
   Write-Host " Error Message: " + $error[0].FullyQualifiedErrorId
   }
Trap {
   # Handle the error
   Error_Handler;
   # End the script.
   break
   }
# Connect to the specified instance
$s = new-object ('Microsoft.SqlServer.Management.Smo.Server') $inst
# Connect to the specified database
$db = $s.Databases[$dtbase]
$dbname = $db.Name
# Create the Database root directory if it doesn't exist
if (!(Test-Path - path "$base\$dbname\"))
   {
   New-Item "$base\$dbname\" - type directory | out-null
   }
$homedir = "$base\$dbname\"
# Instantiate the Scripter object and set the base properties
$scrp = new-object ('Microsoft.SqlServer.Management.Smo.Scripter') ($s)
$scrp.Options.ScriptDrops = $False
$scrp.Options.WithDependencies = $False
$scrp.Options.IncludeHeaders = $True
$scrp.Options.AppendToFile = $False
$scrp.Options.ToFileOnly = $True
$scrp.Options.ClusteredIndexes = $True
$scrp.Options.DriAll = $True
$scrp.Options.Indexes = $True
```

```
$scrp.Options.Triggers = $True
# Script any DDL triggers in the database
$db.Triggers | foreach-object {
    if($_.IsSystemObject — eq $False) {
        $trg = $_
        if (!(Test-Path — path "$homedir\DatabaseTriggers\"))
            {
            New-Item "$homedir\DatabaseTriggers\"
 — type directory | out-null
            }
        $trgname = $trg.Name
        $scrp.Options.FileName =
                    "$homedir\DatabaseTriggers\$trgname.sql"
        $scrp.Script($trg)
        }
    }
# Script the tables in the database
$db.Tables | foreach-object {
    if($_.IsSystemObject — eq $False) {
        $tbl = $_
        if (!(Test-Path — path "$homedir\Tables\"))
            {
            New-Item "$homedir\Tables\"
 — type directory | out-null
            }
        $tblname = $tbl.Name
        $scrp.Options.FileName =
                        "$homedir\Tables\$tblname.sql"
        $scrp.Script($tbl)
        }
    }
# Script the Functions in the database
<….SNIP….>
```

Listing 3-2: Scripting out database objects using Powershell.

With the **DBScripting.ps1** script, you can very quickly generate a set of scripts for your database. Further, with this type of automation, you can adjust the mechanism to better fit your needs to ensure that all your databases are scripted in the same way.

Red Gate SQL Source Control

SQL Source Control integrates directly into SSMS and is specifically designed to synchronize databases and source control. This tool essentially removes the need to generate a set of files on the file system as a part of moving the database objects into source control. Of course, this step still happens, but the tool does it automatically behind the scenes.

SQL Source Control uses SSMS as a front end that directly links a database and its objects into files within source control. In database terms, this is online database development, meaning changes to structures or SQL code are made directly in a live database, rather than to scripts.

In this example, we will place the `AdventureWorks` database into source control, so developers can begin working on it. This example uses:

- the Subversion source control system

- the Tortoise SVN client for Subversion

- SQL Source Control.

There are two stages to source controlling a database with SQL Source Control. First, we need to link the database to source control, and then commit the database objects.

Linking associates the database with a location in source control. That location must be an existing, empty folder. We can create a folder in SVN, and link the database to that location as shown below.

1. In a Windows Explorer window, right-click, and from TortoiseSVN select Repo-browser:
   The URL dialog box is displayed.

2. In the URL dialog box, type or paste the URL for your repository, and click **OK**.

3. The Repository Browser is displayed:
   In the Repository Browser, in the left pane, select the folder in the repository where you want to source control the database. Then right-click and select **Create folder**:

4. On the Create Folder dialog box, specify a name for the folder, and click **OK**.

5. Right-click the new folder, and select **Copy URL to clipboard**.

One member of the team, with SQL Source Control running within SSMS, can now simply select a database that is not yet under source control, click on **Create new link to source control**, select the source control system (SVN in this case) and enter the repository URL defining where within that system the database will be created. Once the **Create Link** button is pressed, all the objects are marked as changed ,and they are then ready to be checked into a structure within source control. In SQL Source Control you can click on the **Commit Changes** tab. It will then display the objects that SQL Source Control is capturing, ready for moving into source control. You can add comments and click on the **Commit** button, shown in Figure 3-3. That will then move all the objects into source control.

Other members of the team can then link their own local copy of the database to the source controlled database to get all the latest objects.

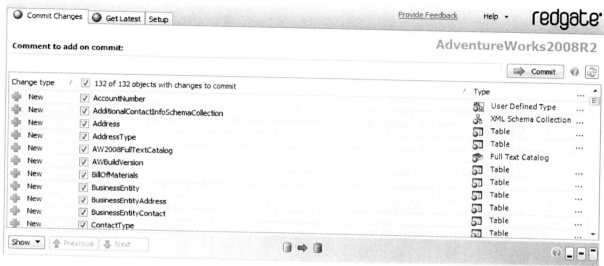

Figure 3-3:   Committing database objects to source control with SQL Source Control.

Red Gate SQL Compare

If you are not using SQL Source Control, an alternative is to script out the database using Red Gate's SQL Compare tool. At its most basic, SQL Compare is a utility for directly comparing the structure of one database against another, then generating a script that reflects the difference between the databases, in order to make one database look like another.

Building straight from one database to another doesn't allow for source control or a lot of process automation, but SQL Compare also allows you to create a script folder, in which it can generate the scripts needed to recreate the database and its objects. These scripts can then be put into source control, and SQL Compare can compare the scripts to a live database, and create a synchronization script to update that database.

The basic steps for the initial generation of the scripts are:

- select **Script Folder** as the Source, on the New Project screen
- click on the shortcut **Create Schema Scripts...**
- connect to the database, and choose a name and location for the scripts
- click the **Create Scripts Folder** button.

It will use the database that you defined as the source and will reverse engineer each of the objects out to a file. The files, unlike the output from SSMS, will be categorized and placed into a nice neat set of folders as shown in Figure 3-1.

Figure 3-1:   Script folder output from SQL Compare.

With the database objects separated into scripts, and the scripts neatly categorized, you can check these objects into the source control program of your choice to begin managing the deployments.

should elect to **Script to file**, select the **File per object** radio button, determine the output path for the scripts and then click on the **Finish** button to generate the scripts.

You'll end up with a rather disorganized folder full of scripts that you can check into your source control system. The only problem is that there's no easy way get these scripts back together to build your database. It's possible to run the scripts, but they won't run in the correct order, so you'll end up with lots of dependency errors.

You'd need to build some mechanism for taking all the individual scripts, determine what has been changed and then generate a synchronization script, **a script that reflects only the changed objects,** to deploy to each environment.

Managing data in source control

Getting control of the code, the object definitions, is only part of what makes up a database; there is also the data that is a part of any database. I'm not talking about the standard business data generated by users interacting with the application, but the metadata needed for the application to run. This data includes things like lookup tables, metadata, data that defines behavior, and so on. This data also has to be managed as part of any deployment. It can be maintained manually through scripts, or by storing in a database, but there are also tools for managing data, similar to those tools used to manage code.

Authoritative source database

Data can't really be checked into a source control system unless you export it as scripts but then, depending on how much data you have, you could overwhelm your source control system. If you have a small set of data, you can script out the insert statements, or use `sqlcmd` to export the data to a set of files and check these into source control. However, if you have large sets of data, this might not be a viable option. Instead, a good method is to create an authoritative source database; a database you would treat like a production system, where you maintain what your source data should look like. You can add effective dates, expiration dates, and flags to determine if a piece of data is ready for a production rollout. A basic lookup table, consisting of an ID/Value pair, would look something like the one in Listing 3-3.

```
CREATE TABLE dbo.IvLookup
    (
        ID INT NOT NULL IDENTITY(1,1) ,
        IvValue NVARCHAR(50) NOT NULL ,
        EffDate DATETIME NOT NULL ,
        ExpDate DATETIME NULL ,
        ProductionReady BIT NOT NULL ,
        IsDeleted BIT NOT NULL ,
        AppLabel NVARCHAR(30) NOT NULL ,
        PRIMARY KEY CLUSTERED ( ID )
    );
```

Listing 3-3: A lookup table in the authoritative source database.

The data stored in a table, following this approach, allows for a number of control points to help dictate which data is ready for use in various environments. The `ID` and `IVvalue` columns for the lookup information are the easiest to describe. These would be artificial keys and associated values that provide the lookup information. The effective and expiration dates, `EffDate` and `ExpDate`, can be used to return only data that is active within a given time period. The bit fields `ProductionRead` and `IsDeleted` can be used to mark a value as being either ready for release to production, or logically deleted. Logical deletion is the best way to maintain data integrity and yet remove lookup values from active lists within the application. By labeling the software version that last updated the value, `AppLabel`, the data can be associated with a particular rollout, especially when the deployments are incremental, meaning that we are only deploying changes rather than performing a complete redeployment of a database.

Summary

Change management in development can be very difficult, and in database development it can be extremely hard, especially when multiple teams are involved.

Having the right processes in place, and sufficient environments to support those processes, is a large step towards taming team-based database development. Once you've established these processes and moved your code into source control, you will need to work on automating as many of the deployments to all these new environments as you can, in order to make the processes repeatable and easy to maintain.

Chapter 4: Managing Deployments

In Chapter 3, we discussed the need to establish a range of development and testing environments; a series of gates through which your application and database must pass, on their way to production. With your database, plus reference data, stored safely in source control alongside your application, what's required next is a consistent and reliable mechanism by which to deploy a given version of the application and database to each environment.

In this chapter, I'm going to show how two different tool sets – Microsoft's Visual Studio 2010 Premium edition and Red Gate's source control and schema comparison tools – can be used to manage a set of deployments.

Deployment Schemes

When managing deployments, the word that cannot be repeated often enough is **discipline**. You need to make sure that everyone involved is aware that the source of your code is in your source control system. Don't let any database or set of scripts outside of source control become the mechanism for deployment. All deployments come from source control. That means that all code changes go into source control.

You also need to be somewhat draconian in ensuring that the various environments don't bleed into each other; for example, only perform quality assurance in that environment, and don't let developers begin experimenting with code in that environment.

Your exact deployment scheme will vary, depending on your deployment environments, but the general practices remain the same. In this chapter, I'll be using the scheme illustrated in Figure 4-1.

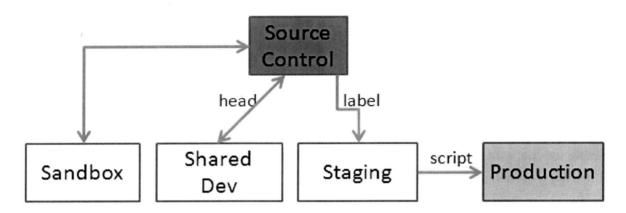

Figure 4-1: Example deployment scheme.

As illustrated in this figure, we have:

- a local sandbox server where any changes at all can be made, all of which must be checked into source control

- a shared development (alternatively, integration testing) environment where only unit tested and confirmed changes should be deployed; deployments are scheduled, or performed on demand, from the source control "head," also known as the "tip," i.e. the latest version of the files in source control

- all deployments to Staging will be from a label within source control

- following a complete successful deployment to Staging, the build script can be run on the production server.

With that set of servers and general processes in mind, I'll start the process with Microsoft Visual Studio, and then move on to show how it's done with Red Gate SQL Source Control.

Visual Studio 2010 Premium tools

Visual Studio 2010 Premium, still commonly known among most DBAs and developers by its previous name of Visual Studio Team System Database Edition, or VSTS:DB, provides a suite of tools for database development and deployment that allows direct integration into some form of source control system (usually Microsoft's Team Foundation Server).

Over the coming sections, I'll demonstrate how to use these tools to take an existing database project and deploy it to each environment.

Sandbox

The individual developers can do what they need to do in their sandbox, but have to check everything into source control and then subject it to the approved build processes supplied for all the other environments.

To deploy to your sandbox server, you could use the plain, unadorned database project in VSTS:DB. Unfortunately, in an environment where you're sharing this project with lots of people, this would require each developer to go through the rather tedious process of checking the project out, editing the configuration for working locally on their system, and then checking it back in, so it can be deployed to their sandbox server, and so on. Instead, we'll configure a mechanism that allows deployment to any sandbox server, and then use similar mechanisms for the other deployments.

To begin this process, you need to ensure that the database project includes only those objects that are going to be common to all environments. This means that the project can't include special logins for the sandbox or any SQL Server roles for the Staging environment, or production users.

99

After paring down the database project (here called **MyApp**) in this fashion, save it as part of your solution. You'll also need to create a server project (**Sandbox**), specific to the sandbox environment, which contains any of the special logins and roles needed to support your application, and which would not be available in the MyApp database project.

You'll then need to create a third, compound project (**Sandbox_MyApp**), which brings together the database project and the server project, and is what will be deployed. These three projects, created within a solution, would look as shown in Figure 4-2.

Figure 4-2:   Three projects visible in the Visual Studio Solution Explorer.

Within the compound project, you need to create references to the database and server projects, so expand the Sandbox_MyApp project, right-click on the **References** folder and select **Add Database Reference**. Select the **MyApp** project from the window (shown in Figure 4-3) and click OK. Repeat the process with the sandbox server project.

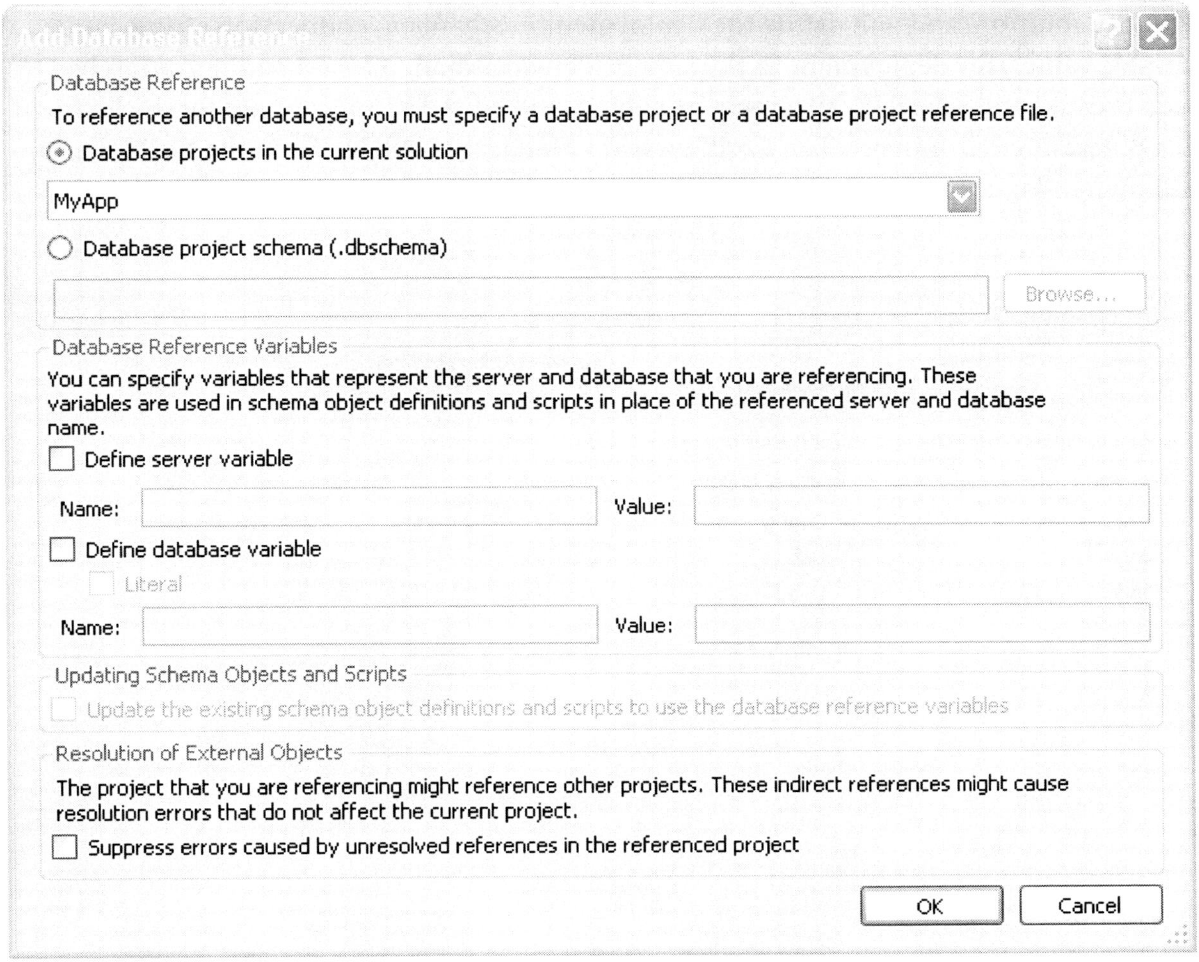

Figure 4-3: The Add Database Reference window.

There are a number of options that allow granular control over how projects are built and deployed. I'm going to focus on the most direct mechanism for deployment within your team environment, so I won't discuss them here, but it's worth noting that VSTS:DB aims to support a wide range of different deployment processes.

The next step is to create a custom **configuration** for the project. This will be stored with the solution, and will define the deployment mechanism, connection string, and variable values, for deployment to the sandbox environment. Once a configuration has been created and saved, it can simply be copied, and edited as appropriate for deployment to a different environment. The Configuration Manager (available from the **Build** menu) is shown in Figure 4-4-

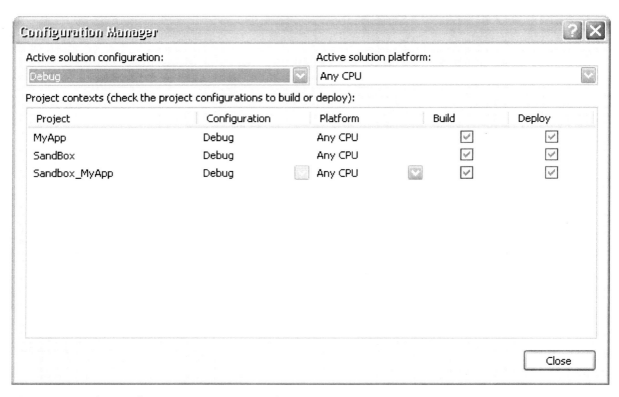

Figure 4-4: The Configuration Manager Window.

To create a new configuration for deploying the MyApp database to the sandbox server, click on the **Active solution configuration** drop-down, select <**New**>, and give it a sensible name (e.g. Sandbox). Once created, the new configuration can be selected from the drop-down, and you can modify the deployment options for the projects that will be built and deployed from that configuration. So far, we only have the three projects but, even here, I would recommend that the **Deploy** check box be deselected for the sandbox server project, so that it will be built and available to the `Sandbox_MyApp` project, but won't be deployed to your server. Once you're finished, click on the **Close** button.

At the top of the standard editing screen in Visual Studio, in the default toolbar, you should now see your configuration in the configuration selection drop-down. The next step is to make sure that all the projects will deploy to the correct server. With the new `Sandbox` configuration selected, open the **Properties** window of the `MyApp` project and navigate to the **Deploy** tab, as shown in Figure 4-5. Notice that you can modify the **Deploy action** so that you either create a script and deploy it to the database, or just create a script. For the sandbox server, we'll build and deploy. To deploy to the sandbox server, simply click on the **Edit...** button next to the **Target Connection** and set up the connection string.

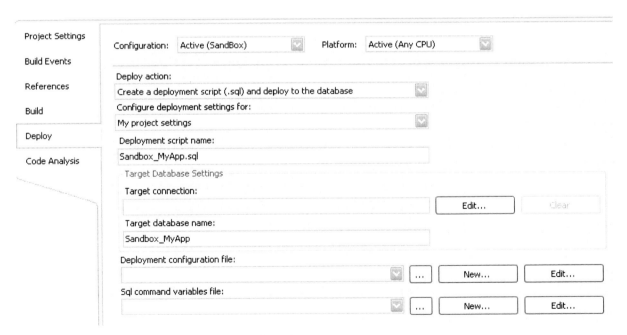

Figure 4-5:   MyApp Properties on the Deploy tab.

You'll need to open the properties for all the projects and set the connection string for each one. Once you've completed these edits and saved the solution, you're done, and the `Sandbox_MyApp` project is ready for deployment. Simply check the latest code out of source control, set the configuration to the server to which you want to deploy, and run the deploy process.

Shared development

At some point, you'll have new functionality completed in your sandbox environment. You'll have synchronized it with source control, and possibly applied a label or some other determined version. It's now time to make sure your code works properly with the code developed by the rest of your team, prior to releasing it to the Staging team. In this example, I've referred to this environment as the shared development (or common server) environment, to make it clear that you may expect changes to the code base in this environment.

This deployment is usually scheduled, but could be on demand, depending on your processes and the needs of the development project. In either case, your goal is an unattended, automated install, rather than something that requires a lot of manual effort.

To deploy to the integration server, you need to set up a new server project (`Development`) and a new compound project (`Development_MyApp`) within the solution. Once these are completed, you can create custom security logins for the server project. You can also add environment-specific roles and privileges to the compound project, independent of the server roles and privileges, if needed.

With the projects created, you can then create a new `Development` solution configuration, as described previously. This time, you'll have five projects in the solution, as shown in Figure 4-6.

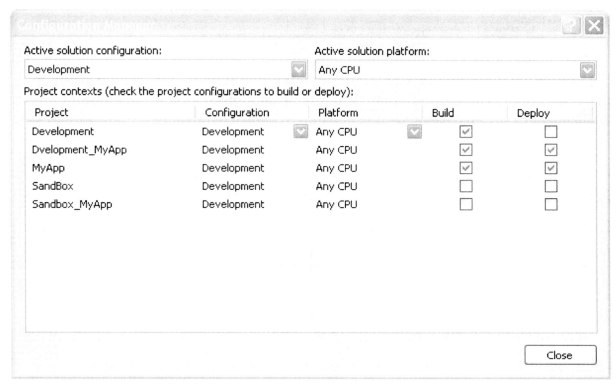

Figure 4-6: Configuration Manager with the `Development` projects added.

Note that for the `Development` project, I've deselected the `SandBox` and `Sandbox_MyApp` projects for both **Build** and **Deploy** so that these projects are ignored during a deployment to the shared development environment. Be sure to edit the connection strings for the new projects, and then you're ready for deployment.

As noted earlier, however, we want to automate these deployments, which is easily achieved with VSTS:DB. By using the command-line utilities, we can run the deployments from other applications, for example, scheduling applications like Windows Scheduler or SQL Agent, and we can use, from the command line, the projects we just created . The process for automation will be two steps. First, we need to get the code out of TFS, using the **tf.exe**, as shown in Listing 4-1.

```
tf get MyApp /version:MyLabel /all
```

Listing 4-1: Getting a labeled code version out of TFS.

Second, we use the **msbuild.exe**, available with Visual Studio, to deploy this solution in the same way as developers would deploy their solutions. The command line for deployment to shared development would look as shown in Listing 4-2.

```
Msbuild /target:Deploy /p:Configuration=Development Development_MyApp.proj
```

Listing 4-2: Deploying to development using MSBuild.

It's fairly simple to understand what's happening.

- The **/target** is telling the build process what to do, namely create the T-SQL script for deployment and deploy the database. You could use **/target:SQLBuild** if you were only interested in generating a script.

- The **/p** is setting the configuration parameter, which is set to **Development**.

- The final argument defines the project to be deployed, **Development_Myapp.proj.**

You can also use the command line to modify projects through the use of custom parameters, rather than setting up projects and configurations. This makes your solution a bit cleaner to look at, not having all the clutter of multiple projects and configurations, and somewhat easier to work with. This is done by defining parameters within the **.sqlcmdvars** file on the **Deploy** screen. You can use those variables within the code using SQLCMD syntax, and then refer to them in the command line. Using this approach means that you don't have a lot of visual control over what gets deployed, so you'll need to keep very good records of what each of the individual batch files you were forced to use for deployment does. I prefer the visual approach.

Through SQL Source Control, you can obtain previous versions, or labeled versions for deployment within your database, but you can't apply labels, merge, shelf, or perform any number of other source control operations. You will need to go directly to your source control environment to perform these actions.

Shared development environment

The scripts checked into source control by SQL Source Control can be retrieved directly from your source control system and simply run as is, but the object dependency chain isn't going to be maintained.

Probably the best method to get the database deployed to an environment where you expect further development to take place on the code base is the one described in the previous section. However, an alternative approach, and one that is suitable for moving to an integration environment where further changes to the code can't be made, is to use Red Gate's SSMS Integration Pack, which enables Red Gate's SQL Compare to work within SSMS. To manually deploy a new database to the development environment, right-click on the database in source control. In the context menu select **Schema Compare/ Deploy** and, from the pop-up menu, **Set As Source**. This will open the SQL Compare set up window within SSMS, and define the source-controlled database to be the source for the compare operation.

You can choose to deploy the latest version (referred to as the "head" or tip") or use SQL Source Control's history window to select a version or labeled version of the database within source control. On the right-hand side of the screen you can select a server to which to deploy the database. The server must be one that is currently connected within SSMS. The final screen will look something like Figure 4-10.

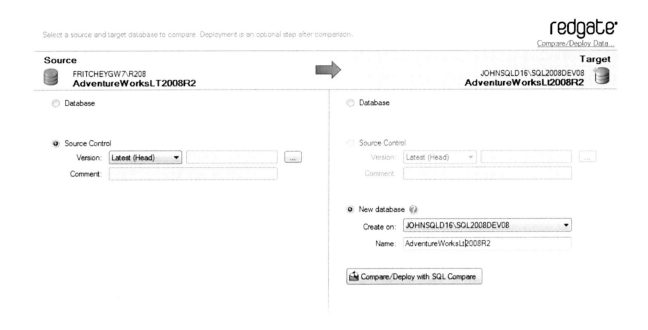

Figure 4-10: Ready to deploy a new database.

To configure the deployment, simply click on the **Compare/Deploy with SQL Compare** button, which will launch SQL Compare. Jump to the **Options** tab and you'll see two sections: **Behavior** and **Ignore**. The **Behavior** section allows you to change the way that SQL Compare performs the comparison, or the way it formats the scripts resulting from the comparison. Most of these settings are dependent on the needs of your system and, possibly, business policies within your company, and I won't address them here. One change from the default that I do recommend is that you enable the option **Add database USE statement**. This will add a statement at the top of the scripts generated to point the script at the appropriate database when you run the script automatically.

The next section, **Ignore**, is where you can control which objects from the database are included or excluded from the comparison process and from the resulting scripts. There is a full set of default options already enabled or disabled. You'll want to validate that these options will work within your environment. It's worth noting, however, that in order to automate this process across multiple databases (covered shortly), changes will need to be made to the defaults in this section. One change that will be necessary is to tick the U**sers' permissions and role memberships** box because the users assigned to the database and the roles they are associated with will change from one environment to the next. Next, again to preserve data and settings, you need to ignore **Identity seed and increment values**.

After setting up all the options, run the comparison, and you'll be presented with a screen showing the various database objects that match, exist only one database or the other, or exist in both but are different. You can scroll through these lists and identify individual objects that you'd like to see synchronized between the two sources, the script, and the database.

Once this is accomplished, click on the **Save** button and give the comparison a name. The default will be "MyApp v MyApp" but since all the comparisons for this application will be between the same databases, using this naming standard would be counterproductive. A better approach would be to use the application or database name and the target environment (e.g. `Development_AdventureWorks2008R2`). This is possible because, in all our compare projects, the source will be the same, our scripts as stored in source control. Further, instead of just storing this compare project in its default folder, it would be a very good idea to check it into source control as well. This way, any of the other developers can automate the use of the compare project to build their sandbox servers, without having to go through all the trouble of setting it up manually.

Finally, you can simply use Red Gate SQL Compare Pro and the command line, **sqlcompare.exe**, to create a completely automated method for deploying the database. The basic command-line syntax for comparing and deploying the database would look as shown in Listing 4-4.

```
Sqlcompare /scr1:"C:\source\AdventureWorksLt2008R2" /db2:AdventureWorksLt2008R2 /
s2:FRITCHEYG1XP\GF2008 /Sync
```

Listing 4-4:   A basic command line "compare and deploy."

This very simple command will work but, in order to set the options in the same manner as we did for the GUI project, the command line will need to look like Listing 4-5.

```
Sqlcompare /scr1:"C:\source\AdventureWorksLt2008R2" /db2:AdventureWorksLt2008R2 /
s2:FRITCHEYG1XP\GF2008 /Sync /o:Default,if,iip,ist,iup,iu
```

Listing 4-5: A command line "compare and deploy" with options.

It looks a bit alien at first but, once you break it down, it makes sense and corresponds very closely to what we did inside the GUI:

- **/scr1** – this command-line switch sets the Scripts Folder as a source

- **/db2** and **/s2** are the database and the server it lives on, respectively

- **/Sync** is the command to synchronize everything, meaning deploy the changes to the database

- **/o** corresponds to the options settings that we chose, the defaults plus, ignore fill factor (if), ignore identity properties (iip), ignore statistics (ist), ignore user properties (iup) and ignore users (iu).

To completely automate this process, including retrieving the versions out of source control, you'll need to create a batch file in DOS or PowerShell or whatever you use for scripting to the command line. If you check this Powershell (say) script into source control along with the database objects, you can ensure that all developers on the team are building their database in the same way.

This batch file will perform the following series of commands:

- run SQL Compare to build all the code into the database (see Listing 4-5)

- run SQL Data Compare to move the lookup data into the database (if any)

- apply security settings for the development environment.

To synchronize lookup data, you can use the SQL Data Compare command-line interface, as shown in Listing 4-6.

```
Sqldatacompare /pr:"c:\source\AdventureWorks2008Lt2008R2\dev.sdc" /sync
```

Listing 4-6:   Synchronizing lookup data using the SQL Data Compare command line.

Finally, you'll probably want to create specific security settings within the development environment. I won't specify what these settings might be; you just need to create a script with the appropriate security within your environment. Once you have the script you can use the SQL Server command-line utility, SQLCMD.EXE, to run the appropriate script, as demonstrated in Listing 4-7.

```
Sqlcmd —S FRITCHEYG1XP\GF2008 —E —i DevSecurity.sql
```

Listing 4-7:   Applying security settings.

All these command can be run, one after the other, in a single batch script to recreate a development database. The batch file can be executed as needed, or according to some sort of scheduling. Almost exactly the same process can be used for the staging and production servers, with only a couple of minor changes.

Staging and production

When dealing with a three-tier development and deployment process, such as the one we're working with here, the Staging server acts in a dual role, as a test bed and as a staging environment. Deployments to this server will always be based on a known starting point, usually represented by the production system itself, but possibly from scratch for new applications. You should always deploy to the Staging server using the same approach as for your production machine, as a method of testing that production deployment. I recommend that, after a set of tests are done in Staging, prior to a new deployment to the server, you reset it so that it looks like the production machine, whether that means removing database changes or removing the database entirely.

This database may also have data in place that must be retained, something that you may not always have to worry about in development. Because the Staging server is the last stop before the production system, you'll want to create a deployment script and test it, not simply synchronize the data and structures. Finally, the builds for the Staging system should be from a labeled version within source control, not the tip.

Taking all this into account, the command-line process changes to the following:

- retrieve your code from source control
- run SQL Compare and output to a script file
- run SQL Data Compare and output to a script file
- manually test the script files.

The process of getting code from source control from the label varies only very slightly to the process of getting it from the tip, so I won't cover it again. It's just important that you always deploy from a known state to a known state, so that you recreate the Staging database and your deployment script as often as you need during the testing phases of your development and deployment life cycle.

Running SQL Compare and SQL Data Compare to output to a T-SQL script instead of syncing directly to the database only requires a slight change to the process, as illustrated in Listing 4-8 for SQL Compare.

```
Sqlcompare /scr2:"C:\source\MyApp" /db1:MyApp /s1:FRITCHEYG1XP\GF2008 /sf:"staging_
build.sql" /o:Default,if,iip,ist,iup,iu
```

Listing 4-8: Applying security settings.

Instead of using the switch `/sync`, the switch `/scriptfile`, or `/sf`, is used to generate T-SQL output from the compare process.

This will generate the SQL statements necessary to upgrade the database to match the source control version, but won't run it automatically. You should run this build script manually, and verify that it works and that it will run exactly the same way on production.

If there are errors, you need to take the disciplined approach of refreshing the Staging system prior to rerunning the script. This can be as simple as running a restore from the production system, or it might involve running a series of deployment scripts to rebuild the Staging system to a known state. Regardless, if the scripts generated from the compare fail in any way, you need to reset the Staging system, then rerun the scripts until you know for sure that they'll run flawlessly in production.

Once you've got the script tested in Staging, you can check it in to source control, wait for the scheduled production deployment, and then just run the script; no edits or manual labor needed. This reduces the chance of errors slipping into production.

Automating Builds for Continuous Integration

In any database application where the database and the application are likely to develop simultaneously, our ultimate goal with deployments is to make the process so easy and fast that it can be adapted into a continuous integration process.

In the previous section, we've discussed various tools, such as MSBuild, SQL Source Control, SQL Compare, SQL Data Compare and Powershell, which can be used in this automation process. In this section, we'll take a somewhat more detailed look at how this might be tailored towards continuous integration.

What is continuous integration?

To ensure that everything works together, the code and related resources in a development project should be frequently integrated, so that all developers are working with code that is as near as possible to the contents of the existing code repository, and this code is committed so as to ensure it produces a stable build that will then be tested. The process, which is repeated until all tests are passed, is the continuous integration process.

Code changes are checked into source control regularly and any conflicts are resolved at that time. If there are any significant changes, this will trigger an automated build, with unit tests, and rapid feedback to the developers to fix problems. This process ensures that a stable current build is consistently available, and if a build fails, it is fixed rapidly and retested.

A continuous integration server uses a build script to execute a series of commands that build an application. Generally, these commands will clean directories, run a compiler on source code, and execute unit tests. However, build scripts can be extended to perform additional tasks, such as deploying the application or updating a database with SQL Compare.

The continuous integration process minimizes the task of integration because the extent of the task increases by a greater magnitude than the delay between builds. It is now an established development practice.

If the continuous integration process is done well, it is possible to deploy the working application onto a new machine automatically from a recent build without manual intervention, excepting stable things such as third-party components that are too complicated to install automatically.

Example: deploying to test

In this example, we have deployed to our development environment a `WidgetDev` database, using the method described earlier for deploying to a sandbox server using Red Gate SQL Source Control.

Changes have been made to the schema and data of the database, and these changes are committed to source control (in the scripts folder `WidgetDevScripts` of SVN). When development changes are sufficient to trigger a build, the database is to be deployed to the testing database, `WidgetTest`.

Data synchronization may fail if the schemas are not identical, so the schema changes are deployed first. This example deploys the schema and static data of `WidgetDev` to the testing server `WidgetTest`, and creates reports as part of the build process. To automate the deployment, save the command lines shown in Listing 4-9 as a `.bat` file, and run it as part of the build process.

```
cd C:\program files\subversion\bin
svn checkout http://<repository location>/WidgetDev
"C:\Scripts\WidgetDevScripts"
cd "C:\Program Files\Red Gate\SQL Compare 8"
sqlcompare /scr1:"C:\Scripts\WidgetDevScripts" /db2:WidgetTest
/o:Default
/Report:"C:\SchemaDiffReport.html"
/ReportType:Interactive
/ScriptFile:"C:\SchemaSyncScript.sql"
/sync
cd "C:\Program Files\Red Gate\SQL Data Compare 8"
sqldatacompare /scr1:"C:\Scripts\WidgetDevScripts" /db2:WidgetTest
/o:Default
/Exclude:table:WidgetPurchases
/ScriptFile:"C:\DataSyncScript.sql"
/sync /v > C:\DataDeploy.txt
```

Listing 4-9: Automating deployment to the test environment.

Where:

- **svn checkout** is the Subversion command that creates a local copy of the latest source control version of the database

- **http://<repository location>/WidgetDev** is the URL for the database in your Subversion repository

- **"C:\Scripts\WidgetDevScripts"** is the file path for the directory where the local copy will be created

- **/scr1:"C:\Scripts\WidgetDevScripts"** specifies WidgetDevScripts as the source

- **/db2:WidgetTest** specifies WidgetTest as the target

- **/o:Default** specifies that the default options will be used for comparison and synchronization

- **/sync** synchronizes the data sources, making WidgetTest the same as WidgetDevScripts

- **/v > "C:\SchemaDeploy.txt"** directs detailed command-line output describing the schema synchronization to a file

- **/v > "C:\DataDeploy.txt"** directs detailed command-line output describing the data synchronization to a file

- **/Report** generates a report of the schema differences and writes it to the specified file

- **/ReportType** specifies the format of the report, in this case, a detailed interactive HTML format

- **/ScriptFile** saves a copy of the SQL script used to migrate the changes

- **/Exclude:table:WidgetPurchases** excludes WidgetPurchases; all other tables will be deployed.

Creating test data

While our example discusses the deployment of existing test data, it is also possible to create realistic test data using Red Gate's SQL Data Generator. You can set up a SQL Data Generator project specifying details of the target database, what kind of data to generate, and so on. To generate data at build time, you can run that SQL Data Generator project from the command line, as demonstrated in Listing 4-10.

```
sqldatagenerator /Project:"C:\Deployment\TestData.sqlgen"
/Out:"C:\Deployment\DataGenerationReport.txt"
```

Listing 4-10: Generating test data.

Here, `TestData.sqlgen` is a SQL Data Generator project file, and the `/Out` switch writes a summary of the data generated to the file `DataGenerationReport.txt`

Automation with MSBuild, NAnt, and Powershell

The previous example uses MS-DOS batch scripting to run SQL Compare and SQL Data Compare. Although this has the benefit of being supported by all versions of Windows, it does not integrate elegantly with contemporary build systems. Checking the script files into and out of source control using the command line requires additional scripting, and lacks flexibility. The following examples cover some more customizable and powerful technologies.

Using MSBuild

MSBuild was released with Visual Studio 2005, and is now one of the most popular build scripting systems. Using it, you can quickly get started building your application. Although MSBuild is commonly used with Team Foundation Server, it can be used by any continuous integration server, or directly from the command-line interface. For more information, see the MSBuild documentation (HTTP://MSDN.MICROSOFT.COM/EN-US/LIBRARY/WEA2SCA5.ASPX).

Deploying to test using MSBuild

The complete script used in this example can be found in the downloadable .zip file for this book, as the file: `DeployToTest.msbuild`.

The simplest way to integrate SQL Compare with MSBuild is to use the built in **Exec** task to execute command lines similar to those described in Listing 4-9. Although the results are identical, you can take advantage of the MSBuild infrastructure, and information such as whether the build was successful, and where files have been checked out to. The MSBuild target shown in Listing 4-11 executes SQL Compare, using a scripts folder as the source.

```
<Target Name="Deploy" DependsOnTargets="Build">
<!- — Sync from scripts to Database — ->
<Exec Command='SQLCompare.exe /scripts1:"$(CheckoutPath)\SqlCompareDB" /
Server2:"$(TargetServer)" /db2:"$(TargetDatabase)" /synchronize'
WorkingDirectory="C:\Program Files\Red Gate\SQL Compare 8" IgnoreExitCode="true" />
</Target>
```

Listing 4-11: The MSBuild target.

The target for synchronization is then set using properties at the top of your build file (see Listing 4-12). The properties specify that the target server is called **SQLStaged**, the target database is `Northwind`, and the SQL Compare script folder is checked out to the directory `C:\VSSGet`.

```
<PropertyGroup>
<TargetServer>SQLStaged</TargetServer>
<TargetDatabase>Northwind</TargetDatabase>
<CheckoutPath>C:\VSSGet</CheckoutPath>
</PropertyGroup>
```

Listing 4-12: Setting the target server using MSBuild file properties.

These options can also be specified as arguments when you execute the MSBuild script, allowing for more flexibility, as demonstrated in Listing 4-13.

```
MSBuild DeployToTest.msbuild /p:TargetServer=SQLStaged
```

Listing 4-13: Specifying options on the fly.

This command executes the build script which, in turn, executes SQL Compare with the appropriate settings. This can be integrated into a larger build file that also handles build and deployment.

Given the power of MSBuild, many people have created additional tasks as part of the MSBuild Community Tasks project (HTTP://MSBUILDTASKS.TIGRIS.ORG/). For example, to check out from Visual SourceSafe you could include the snippet shown in Listing 4-14.

```
<VssGet UserName="Deploy"
Password="test"
LocalPath="$(CheckoutPath)"
Recursive="True"
DatabasePath="C:\Visual SourceSafe\srcsafe.ini"
Path="$/"
Writable="true" />
```

Listing 4-14: Checking out from VSS.

However, most continuous integration servers will do this for you as part of their build process, before executing your build script.

Combining these methods, you can check out the latest version of your scripts and execute SQL Compare to update your database with a single command. The same approach can be taken with SQL Data Compare. This is demonstrated in the next section, using NAnt.

Using NAnt

NAnt is a popular alternative to MSBuild, with similar syntax. For more information, see the NAnt home page (HTTP://NANT.SOURCEFORGE.NET/).

Here, instead of synchronizing from a scripts folder, the NAnt script in Listing 4-15 synchronizes from another database. This is useful if many developers are working on a shared central database, and you want to deploy its static data.

```
<exec program="c:\program files\red gate\SQL Compare 8\SQLCompare.exe"
commandline="/f /v /server1:${sqlcompare.server1} /server2:${sqlcompare.server2} /
database1:${sqlcompare.database1} /database2:${sqlcompare.database2} /synchronize"
resultproperty="execReturnCode"
failonerror ="false"/>
```

Listing 4-15: Synchronizing from a live database using NAnt.

Listing 4-16 shows the four different properties that define the synchronization.

```
<property name="sqlcompare.server1" value=.""/>
<property name="sqlcompare.server2" value="SQLStaged"/>
<property name="sqlcompare.database1" value="Northwind"/>
<property name="sqlcompare.database2" value="Northwind"/>
```

Listing 4-16: Setting the source and target databases.

The script can then be executed via NAnt with build command shown in Listing 4-17.

```
NAnt.exe — buildfile:nant.build
```
Listing 4-17: The NAnt build command.

The complete script used in this example can be found in the downloadable .zip file, as the file: `nant.build`

Using Powershell

Powershell is an advanced command-line and task-scripting tool. It allows you to write custom scripts that solve everyday problems, such as synchronizing your database. For example, the following two snippets of code are Powershell methods which synchronize databases. Listing 4-18 synchronizes the schemas.

```
Function SqlCompare
{
param($Server1, $Database1, $Server2, $Database2)
$Command = '&"C:\Program Files\Red Gate\SQL Compare 8\sqlcompare.exe" /Server1:' +
$Server1 + ' /database1:' + $Database1 + ' /server2:' + $Server2 + ' /database2:' +
$Database2 + ' /synchronize'
Invoke-Expression $Command
}
```
Listing 4-18: Synchronizing database schemas using Powershell.

Listing 4-19 synchronizes the data.

```
Function SqlDataCompare
{
param($Server1, $Database1, $Server2, $Database2)
$Command = '&"C:\Program Files\Red Gate\SQL Data Compare 8\sqldatacompare.exe" /
Server1:' + $Server1 + ' /database1:' + $Database1 + ' /server2:' + $Server2 + ' /
database2:' + $Database2 + ' /synchronize'
Invoke-Expression $Command
}
```

Listing 4-19: Synchronizing the data using Powershell.

The advantage of having these commands as methods is that you can store them in a Powershell script file. That file can be included in any subsequent Powershell script or at the interactive console, in order to perform the synchronization, as shown in Listing 4-20.

```
.\SqlCompare.ps1
SqlCompare '.' 'NorthwindDev' '(local)' 'Northwind'
SqlDataCompare '.' 'NorthwindDev' '(local)' 'Northwind'
The complete script used in this example can be found in the downloadable .zip file
, as the file: SQLCompare.ps1
```

Listing 4-20: Automating the synchronization.

Automation with CruiseControl

In addition to the techniques discussed, there are a few dedicated continuous integration tools and frameworks, which you might consider. Once such is CruiseControl.NET (HTTP://SOURCEFORGE.NET/PROJECTS/CCNET/).

From the CruiseControl configuration file, we can use the SQL Compare command line to deploy the scripts folder held in the source control system to a real database. The full CruiseControl configuration file is included with the code download, but the key snippet is shown in Listing 4-21. It assumes the professional edition of SQL Compare, since using the command line and using a script folder are both professional features.

```
<exec>
  <executable>
   C:\Program Files (x86)\Red Gate\SQL Compare 8\SQLCompare.exe
  </executable>
  <buildArgs>
   /scripts1:AdventureWorksDatabase /server2:(local)\sql2008
               /database2:ContinuousIntegration /synchronize
  </buildArgs>
  <successExitCodes>0,63</successExitCodes>
</exec>
```

Listing 4-21: The CruiseControl configuration file (extract).

The script is reasonably straightforward. Firstly, the **<executable>** element defines the location of the SQL Compare exe.

The **<buildArgs>** element identifies the source scripts in source control, and the target database to synchronize. Essentially, CruiseControl will check out a copy of everything in source control to a directory, and this is then used as the source. You need to ensure that the place in the source control repository that CruiseControl checks out contains both the application code and the database scripts folder. The directory of the database scripts folder needs to be specified as **/scripts1**. This example also assumes that the target continuous integration database will be on a local instance called **sql2008** and that the database is called **ContinuousIntegration**. Clearly, these easily can be changed, if required.

Finally, it assumes that Windows authentication will be used to log in to the SQL server instance. If you need to use SQL authentication, then just amend the script to add **/username2** and **/password2**.

CruiseControl considers it to have successfully deployed if the exit code is either 0 or 63. The SQL Compare command line sets the exit code to 0 if everything went OK, and it sets the exit code to 63 if the scripts folder and the database were identical to begin with. This would happen if only the application code had been changed, for example.

Conclusion

The tools and methods discussed in this chapter are not the only possible ways to get this difficult job done. Instead, these topics have been presented to you as tools that you can put into your toolbox. You may not need all of them, you may need different ones but, as your deployments change, and the applications you're developing morph, you may need to make use of processes, methods and tools such as those which were discussed here. Always look for opportunities to automate the deployment process. Regardless of the mechanisms you use to deploy your database, remember that the most important job you have is protecting the production system from data loss. Make sure that the processes you develop and use reflect that goal.

Chapter 5: Testing Databases

Consider how you generally handle a fairly typical request for an application or a database change: you make a change, then you manually test a few usage scenarios and deploy it. It has taken you the whole day, the boss is happy, and you move on to the next thing. Soon, however, a particular user (the one that always works in mysterious ways and find the strangest bugs) happens to create a situation in which, as a result of your nice change, a completely different part of the application blows up. Suddenly, fixing the other parts of your application that were broken by your one little change has taken up a whole week's worth of work.

We've all been there at one time or another and, sooner or later, it becomes clear that the most obvious answer to the question of "Why test a database?" is that you can't afford not to. With tests, we can verify that our product does what it was intended to do. By having tests in place, we can identify bugs quicker, and spend less time on fixing those bugs that do occur, since we have a safety net that tells us if our change broke anything else down the line.

Testing also provides the ability to track changes in the behavior of application and database code over time. We write tests to verify the behavior of our objects; as the behavior changes, so do the tests. Therefore, if we store these tests in our source control system, we get a history of how tests have changed over time and, therefore, how application/database behavior has changed.

In this chapter, we'll discuss the essential aspects of database testing, covering the types of testing that must be performed, the tools and techniques needed for successful testing, and a series of unit testing examples, demonstrating how to test the data interface, schema, and specific objects, such as tables, views, stored procedures, and functions.

All the examples use the NUnit testing tool, so basic familiarity with this tool is required, if you wish to work through the examples.

Why Test a Database?

Despite the importance of testing, it is still a relatively underemployed practice in the world of IT. I learned during my B.Sc. that testing is an integral part of long-established sciences such as Electrical Engineering, and is taught right from the beginning, as a fundamental part of the discipline. With age comes wisdom; computer programming is a relatively young branch of science and, in general, not that mature. Of course, electrical engineers know that failing to test can have disastrous consequences. If, for example, a transformer wasn't properly tested before being put into production, it could simply break down or explode. While explosions are rarer in database applications, the same basic principles apply: by testing, we can lessen the occurrence of failures.

In recent years, application testing has successfully gained momentum with the advent of test-driven development (TDD), but database testing still seems to be lagging behind. This is a pity, because effective testing of the database is even more critical than effective testing of the application, for one simple reason: databases outlive most applications by a factor of 5 to 10, depending on the application type. The best examples are banks and historical databases, most of which are already over 20 years old, while the applications running off of them come and go.

In short, it's essential that, as developers, we carry out the tests that *prove* that our databases will work as expected.

Essential Types of Database Testing

In some ways, database testing is very similar to general application testing. The terminology used, and the types of tests we need to undertake, are pretty much the same. In each case, we need to perform both black – and white-box testing. In each case, we need to perform small, fast, unit tests as well as more time-consuming integration tests, and so on.

However there are quite a few differences, too. For example, when testing applications, we test their "schema" (such as public properties and methods) at compile time. An application won't even compile if its schema changes. With databases, we have to explicitly test for schema changes.

Furthermore, the tools we use for testing application objects don't always translate easily to testing databases. When testing applications, we can use mock objects to simulate real objects, with complex dependencies, thus simplifying test implementations and reducing the test run time. When testing databases, "mocking" is harder. For example, say we have two tables connected by a **FOREIGN KEY** constraint, and we're trying to delete a row from the parent table. There's not really a way to mock this; we test either the whole context or nothing.

We'll explore these and other issues, such as achieving repeatability with data-driven tests, as we progress through the chapter.

Black-box and white-box testing

There are two basic types of testing that are universal to any system, computer or otherwise: black-box and white-box testing.

Black-box testing tests the functionality of a component. Tests are written based on application requirements and specifications, which describe the expected output values for a range of given input values, and with no knowledge of the internal structure of the tested component.

We input some data into the tested component and, based on what the component does, it outputs some data. We know what output values to expect for any given input values, a property of any deterministic system, so we can supply a range of valid and invalid input values, and test that the component returns the expected output value in each case.

Black-box tests have to cover the whole spectrum of possible input values, paying special attention to the edge cases. Improper testing of edge cases is a common cause of crashes when the application goes live, and there have been many times when this has led to component crashes. One common mistake I've seen is a failure to test the behavior of a C# list when it has not been initialized (it results in a Null reference exception). The database equivalent would be having a stored procedure that has to return a single row, and not testing what happens when it returns more than one row, or even an empty result set.

Black-box testing helps us verify that any refactoring (i.e. internal change to a component) hasn't changed the expected input/output behavior. Without them we can't be really sure, and we may only find out when the component is part of the wider code base, when the problem will be much, much harder to track down. For example, let's say we wish to refactor a database table; we split it into two new tables, and give both tables new names. By adding a view with the original table name, we should be able run our black-box test exactly as we did before, and receive exactly the same result. If the black-box test fails, after the change, then we haven't just refactored the component; we've added new functionality.

White-box tests, by contrast, have full knowledge of the component internals, and will test to ensure that the various methods work as expected, abnormal runtime conditions are handled gracefully, and so on. When we refactor a component, in other words, alter its internal behavior, we will *always* cause some existing white-box tests to fail. If we don't, then we haven't really refactored the component. Returning to the previous table-splitting example, we would expect such a refactoring to break several of our white-box tests. These failed tests will have to be updated to reflect our refactoring.

Later in the chapter, when we explore how to test different parts of the database, we'll consider how both black-box and white-box testing plays a part in this process.

Unit testing

Unit tests can be considered both white – and black-box testing, depending on how we use them. Suppose we're writing a library that will use a third-party tool to access data. In this case, unit tests are considered white-box when we're testing our own code, and black-box when we're testing only the third-party library behavior. Unit tests are multi-user by default, so User1's execution of a test shouldn't affect User2's execution of the same test.

Unit tests are small, fast and independent tests and should be designed to verify only a "single piece" or unit of the application. In database testing, the definition of a unit can vary depending on the testing context. If we have two tables, connected by referential constraints, but we're testing the results returned only from the parent table, then a unit is just the parent table. If we're testing the deletion of data from the parent table then a unit means both tables, since we have to specify what happens to child rows when a parent is deleted.

When unit testing an application and its database, I try to decouple the two as far as possible, in order to simplify the database testing process. For example, by use of a mock object framework and, and by applying principles such as Inversion of Control and Dependency Injection to the application design, we can create mock objects that simulate the real database access interface, and we can test the database access part of the application without actually connecting to the database. In this way, a test that would take 2 seconds to run, because it had to connect to the database, can be reduced to milliseconds. Over a large number of tests, this can save a lot of time.

Mock objects, frameworks, etc.

Further discussion of these, and related topics, is out of scope for this book, but do look them up online. This Wikipedia website is a good place to start: HTTP://EN.WIKIPEDIA.ORG/WIKI/ LIST_OF_MOCK_OBJECT_FRAMEWORKS.

I tend to introduce the database as late as possible into the testing scheme, and I've found that the best way to unit test a database is to have separate read and write test scenarios. This way we get the database version of "separation of concerns," and it makes defining the testing context much simpler and easier.

For read tests, we have to create some kind of test data. One tool that can help here is Red Gate's SQL Data Generator (see later). This way, we have to generate the known test data only once and perform our tests on it. For write tests, we don't really have to touch the already generated data at all. We can write tests that always insert or update new, random data.

Integration and acceptance testing

Integration and acceptance testing are performed later in the development lifecycle and, whereas unit testing looks at individual components, each of the former involves full system testing.

We use unit tests to test small pieces (units) of code, but we use integration tests to test how those small units work when put together. Writing integration tests isn't that much different from writing unit tests; we can still use NUnit to put together code that integrates different parts of the application.

However, whereas in unit tests we might use mock objects instead of connecting to a database, in integration tests we're testing the real interaction between the application and the database. Think of a system that has a front end that connects to a web service, which connects to the database, and to the mail server to send email notifications. Throw in some BizTalk integration, and so on, and we have a complex system. While we can test each part of the system by itself, with integration testing we're testing how they're communicate with each other. Integration testing is usually automated, and methods of automation, as part of a continuous integration process, are discussed in Chapter 4.

Acceptance testing tests how the application will be used by the end user and is usually performed by the Quality Assurance (QA) people. The two types of testing are very similar, but whereas integration testing is automated, acceptance testing is mostly performed by hand.

Stress testing databases

One mistake I see being made over and over again is testing a database application with only a few hundred rows in each of the base tables, or failing to test the behavior of the application under conditions of high concurrent access, when database resources (CPU, I/O, memory) may become stretched.

Performance seems fine, and the application goes to production, only to come crashing down when the tables grow larger, or when the database load increases. On one particular third-party application I worked with, we started experiencing time-outs after one table reached 20,000 rows in size. I'm sure that application was "tested" only for 100 or so rows before being deployed. It took quite a while to find out what the problem was and how to solve it, and that time cost a lot of money. Don't make the same mistake.

Database stress testing is usually performed towards the end of the development cycle (though sometimes it is started earlier), and some shops perform it in parallel with user acceptance testing.

To ease the process of database stress testing, Microsoft has created a tool called **SQLIOSim** that tests your IO disk subsystem for performance problems. It simulates SQL Server read/write activity on a disk subsystem, without the need to install SQL Server. Another useful Microsoft tool is **OStress**; it is part of the RML utilities for SQL Server, and it will run SQL scripts we provide over multiple connections, simulating multiple users, in order to determine how SQL Server will respond under heavy load conditions.

Error testing

Not many developers or database administrators think much about testing for returned errors, beyond making sure that the `customErrors` setting in the `web.config` (if it's a web application) is working properly, so that the application does not return the full error, but redirects to a custom error page.

However, error testing is useful, especially if you use your own custom error messages, stored in the database. With the introduction of **TRY...CATCH** blocks in SQL Server 2005, the use of custom error messages is becoming more prevalent, so testing them can provide great value. After all, exceptions are as much a part of your application's inner workings as any other part of the code.

Error testing is done in the same way as other types of test. For example, if we have a stored procedure that returns a specific error under certain conditions, then we call the stored procedure from our test and check that we get back the correct type of error. Usually we check the error number, because the actual error text can be localized.

Essentials for Successful Database Testing

There are a few essentials we must have in place, before even starting to think about doing serious database testing.

The right attitude

Most developers perform some kind of testing on their code. As described earlier, in a small developer-only company, a typical scenario might be that the developer writes (or modifies) the code, runs a few manual tests covering the use cases that spring to mind, and moves on.

However, the chances are high that you're not following a rigorous, automated, test-driven development (TDD) approach. The lure of the "we don't need automated testing" company mentality is strong. It's like an eternal calling from the dark side. I've succumbed to it more than once. Don't be like that. Resist it with all your might! The usual reasons given for avoiding a rigorous approach to testing are:

- we're on a deadline and this will take too much time

- we write good code

- we can't afford to spend more money for tests.

So how do we deal with this sort of opposition from the management and coworkers? It turns out that handling coworkers is easy. All we need to do is apply a little gentle peer pressure. For example, I always write tests that cover the code base on which I'm working. When something breaks in the future (notice that I say "when" not "if") I can simply run the tests and prove that the problem lies elsewhere.

The important part is to not insult our coworkers in the process of proving their fallibility. Accepting fault and responsibility isn't a human virtue that always comes easily, but it is a necessary virtue of the professional developer and, hopefully, you're working with professionals. If you're not, then it's probably better to hurt their feelings a bit.

Convincing managers is somewhat more difficult. By testing our code thoroughly, we are substantially reducing future costs associated with bug fixing, refactoring, and so on, at the expense of a smaller increase in development cost. Unfortunately, another common human trait is to place extreme emphasis on current costs, while displaying rather poor judgment when it comes to evaluating possible future costs.

For most managers, it's all about "now" and "how soon." The faster we deliver something, the better. The usual rebuttal to the request to set up a proper testing environment is: "Code this now, so we have version X out the door, and we'll fix the bugs later." I understand this position. It's normal and quite necessary to get products out quickly and stay ahead of the market, but we, as developers, have to walk the fine line between just making it work, and making it work with fewer bugs to fix later.

An alternative to sacrificing proper testing in to properly evaluate just how many new features a product needs. When discussing the new feature list, ask the end-user if everything listed is really required right now; the answer is usually "No." The golden rule of new releases is *fewer features, but all working well*. It is important to have this mindset, as it can help bridge the gap between what developers need and what managers want.

If your coworkers and managers still aren't convinced, show them the article called *On the Effectiveness of a Test-first Approach to Programming*, published in the IEEE *Transactions on Software Engineering* journal in March, 2005. It describes how practicing a form of test-driven development caused the developers to have "better task understanding, better task focus, faster learning, lower rework effort, etc..." If nothing else convinces them, I really hope this will. If it doesn't, maybe it's time to update your résumé.

A test lab

Having got "buy-in" from coworkers and management, the first thing you'll need is a test lab. If you don't have spare physical machines, set it up with virtual ones. There are plenty of virtualization options out there, the most popular being Virtual PC and Hyper-V from Microsoft, VMWare from VMWare, and VirtualBox from SUN.

The good thing about virtual machines is that you can copy them. Build a full-featured virtual disk, then copy it as many times as you need to different virtual machines, to accommodate the various stages of development testing, or simply as backups if existing machines crash. This way, you can easily test different hardware set-ups, perhaps varying the distribution of RAM or CPU across the machines until you find the optimum configuration.

One thing we have to look out for is real physical RAM usage; a physical machine must have plenty of RAM. Also note that, by "going virtual" on a single physical machine, we can't really test well for performance problems. For that we would still need a physical machine, configured to match the production server as closely as possible. If that's not possible, try at least to mimic the "work : computing power" ratio that is used on the production machine. For example, if a production machine with 100 units of computing power performs 1,000 units of work, then try to configure the test machine such that it has 10 units of computing power for 100 units of work. A unit of work can be CPU power, transactions/sec, RAM, disk speed, and so on. It depends on what we're testing. Configuring a test machine proportionally is not ideal, but we can get valid results from performance testing in this way.

Source control

Source control, as described in Chapter 3, lets us track changes made to the application code, the database schema and the actual tests, over time. If we have all three of these stored in the source control system, we can get the exact snapshot of the system at any point in time, and can, for instance, correlate changes made to tests, with changes made to the application or database.

Source control is vital for managing multiple concurrent versions of a database application. For example, let's say we may have versions for the working production system, plus one for an ongoing development project. However, due to some policy change, we're then asked to make an urgent change to the production system, separately from the new development project. With source control, this can be achieved easily by forking the deployed production version from source control, making a change, and then redeploying it.

There are plenty of source control systems out there, from Microsoft's Team Foundation Server (TFS) to well-established Open Source tools such as SubVersion (SVN), as well as newer, distributed source control systems such as Git and Mercurial.

I take quite a hard-line stance on the use of source control in application development, to the point that, if your company isn't using source control at all, I suggest you either lobby hard for it, or leave.

If you use it for application code but not for tracking database changes, then work to change this; gradually introduce database testing into your development processes. Today, you can't be a professional IT company without serious source control management.

Database schema change management

In an ideal world, the production environment is always a subset of the QA environment which, in turn, is a subset of the test environment. In other words, the newest version of the application and database will be the ones in the test environment, and the oldest versions will be the ones in production.

Unfortunately, we're not living in an ideal world and, more often than we'd like to admit, the "quick and painless" changes creep up into production, usually because it's considered a low-risk change that the customer needs "yesterday," and so there is no time to push it through testing and QA. I've seen this happen more than once. To alleviate this problem (somewhat) you need to have some way of comparing database schemas, to make sure that any ad hoc changes made to production are reflected in the development and test environments.

A good tool to help you deal with this, as well as with the more general requirement to push schema changes from one environment to the next (see Chapter 3), is Red Gate's SQL Compare although, if you're tight on cash, there are free alternatives, albeit with far fewer options.

Semi- or fully-automated deployment

Anything we can do as developers to simplify the code migration process, and so boost confidence in the code base, is worthwhile. The ideal is a single process that automatically deploys database DDL changes to the target database, builds the application, runs the application and database tests, and deploys everything to the QA environment. If code doesn't compile or tests fail, we know that code won't be deployed. At this point, we use a rollback script to return the system to its original state, and we try again.

If fully-automated deployment is not possible, then having a semi-automatic build/deploy process is better than nothing, as it at least means that we can pinpoint problems faster. A typical semi-automatic build/deploy process will compile and test the application, but stop short of then pushing it on, to production or QA. Someone then has to come and press a button to continue with the deployment.

One of the barriers to fully-automated deployment is the use of tools which lack a command-line executable, which is usually the case with free tools. As the build process becomes more complex, it's worth investing in better tools that seamlessly integrate into it.

If you don't have this process automated at all, I urge you to look into continuous integration tools for your platform. There are many out there, with CruiseControl.NET forming a good free alternative (covered in more detail in Chapter 4). Although some might be a bit complex to install, it's worth it in the long run.

A testing tool

Having set up the test lab, source control, schema management, and auto deployment, it's time to think about how to actually write the tests. My tool of choice is NUnit (HTTP:// WWW.NUNIT.ORG) which, along with similar tools such as xUnit or MBUnit, requires the test code to be written in a .NET language such as C# or VB.NET. An alternative approach is a unit testing tool such as TSQLUnit (HTTP://SOURCEFORGE.NET/APPS/TRAC/ TSQLUNIT/), which allows tests to be written in T-SQL. When testing databases, this may feel like a good fit, but it's a tool I've tried and now avoid, mainly because it violates my "Don't store any unnecessary objects in SQL Server" principle.

Every extra object means more space is taken up; not just space on disk, but memory space for associated execution plans and cached data pages. Sure, those can be flushed, but this just means extra work for the database engine.

For these reasons, I think that tests have no place in a database and, in any event, I find that tests written in .NET are far easier to manage and run.

A data generation tool

Testing often requires a database to be populated with known test data. It is not always appropriate to use production data in a development environment, and manually creating test data can be a monotonous, time-consuming task.

One solution to this problem is to use a tool such as SQL Data Generator (SDG) to help create realistic test data. It has a simple graphical user interface that allows you to choose the type of data you want to generate for each table and column, and it automatically assigns a generator to each column based on its table name, column name, data type, and length. If the column has constraints, SDG uses these to set the generator parameters for the column (you can change the generator used by a particular column later, if required).

Alternatively, you can create your own regular expression, or import data from an existing table.

Crucially, you can save your data generation settings as a SDG project file (.sqlgen). This project file can be used with the SDG command line interface, as shown in Listing 5-1.

```
cd "c:\program files (x86)\red gate\sql data generator 1"
sqldatagenerator /project:"c:\<location>\Project.sqlgen"
```

Listing 5-1: The SDG command line utility.

You can then create a method in your unit test that uses the project via the command-line interface to generate the data you require. For example, the C# code in Listing 5-2 defines a `DataGenerator.PopulateData()` method, which can then be used in a test by supplying the name of a .sqlgen project file.

```
{
  internal class DataGenerator
  {
    /// <summary>
    /// Use SDG to populate a table from a project file.
    /// </summary>
    /// <param name="projectFilename"></param>
    static internal void PopulateData(string
                                             projectFilename)
    {
      //Generate the data into Person.Contact table
      ProcessStartInfo startInfo = new ProcessStartInfo();
      //Point at the SQL Data Generator application
      startInfo.FileName = @"C:\Program Files\Red Gate\
              SQL Data Generator1\SQLDataGenerator.exe";
      //Specify the SDG project file to use
      startInfo.Arguments =
          string.Format(@"/project:""C:\DB Unit Testing
              Demo\DataGenerator\{0}""," projectFilename);
      startInfo.CreateNoWindow = true;
      startInfo.UseShellExecute = false;
```

```
    //Start the process with the info we specified and
    // wait for SDG to finish
    using (Process dataGeneratorProcess =
                          Process.Start(startInfo))
    {
      dataGeneratorProcess.WaitForExit();
    }
  }
 }
}
```

Listing 5-2: Automating data generation with the SDG command line.

How to Test Databases

In this section, we'll discuss some important considerations that are specific to running database tests, then we'll move on to present some examples of how to unit test various features of a database system.

Reverting the database state

Unit tests are, by definition, single units of work, so they should not be dependent on test execution order, or on shared "state" between different tests (i.e. one test expecting to use data from another test). If we do have these kinds of tests, they cannot be counted as unit tests, because they're not standalone units of code.

When performing single unit tests we should, with a little planning, rarely need to revert the data to its original state after each test finishes (and we should never change the database schema in testing). Avoiding the need to revert database state during unit tests is discussed in more detail later in this chapter, in the section, *Simplifying unit tests*.

However, when performing a series of concurrent tests, during integration and acceptance testing, reverting the database state may well be necessary. In such cases there are two possible approaches:

- one big test method that executes the whole integration procedure we're testing, essentially stringing together many unit tests, and reverting the data at the end of the method

- multiple smaller tests, with each test providing the data for the next test to use.

I've successfully used both techniques, and I don't have a strong preference for either one.

There are four ways to revert the database to its original state after each test, as described in the following sections.

Use transactions

We can put a test into a transaction and roll it back when it finishes. This is a good option for really simple tests, and most unit tests should be simple.

However, integration tests can comprise multiple unit tests, and unit tests usually have the transaction begin/commit in the **SetUp** and **TearDown** parts of the NUnit framework, which execute before and after every test. This makes reverting data using transactions unsuitable for composing integration tests, and is why we have to look for another solution for all but the simplest unit tests.

Use the NDbUnit framework

The NDbUnit (HTTP://CODE.GOOGLE.COM/P/NDBUNIT/) framework allows us to revert the database into a previous state, using a .NET Dataset for the table definition and XML files for test data. However, it is a bit of work to set up, as can be seen from the

QuickStart guide on the projects webpage at HTTP://CODE.GOOGLE.COM/P/NDBUNIT/WIKI/
QUICKSTARTGUIDE.

Do a backup/restore

In SQL Server 2000, I've used this approach with a lot with success. After every test, a
backup would be restored, and the database would be in the same state as before the test.
The downside is that backup/restore takes time, and is useful only for single-user testing
because restoring prevents other users from accessing the database. It works well, though,
for the overnight automated integration tests.

Use database snapshots

With SQL Server 2005, and later (Enterprise and Developer editions only, unfortunately)
we can use database snapshots to revert the data. We simply create two C# functions, as
shown in Listing 5-3; one to create a database snapshot before the test, and one to revert
back to the snapshot after the test, and so put the data back into the pre-test state.

I've started using this technique a lot, because it's simple, it's faster than backup/restore,
and our tests only need to call two functions; one call to `CreateDatabaseSnapshot`
before the test, and one call to `RevertDatabaseFromSnapshot` after running the test,
or group of tests.

```csharp
// sample use:
// CreateDatabaseSnapshot("testdb," "testdb," @"c:\testdb_ss.ss");
private void CreateDatabaseSnapshot(string databaseName,
                                    string databaseLogicalName,
                                        string snapshotPath)
{
    using (SqlConnection conn = new SqlConnection("server=MyServer;
database=master; trusted_connection=yes;"))
    {
```

```
        string sql = "CREATE DATABASE " +
            Path.GetFileNameWithoutExtension(snapshotPath) +
            " ON ( NAME = " + databaseLogicalName +
            ," FILENAME = '" + snapshotPath + "' )" +
            " AS SNAPSHOT OF " + databaseName + ";";
        using (SqlCommand cmd = new SqlCommand(sql, conn))
        {
            try
            {
                // command timeout set to 1000 seconds
                cmd.CommandTimeout = 1000;
                conn.Open();
                Console.WriteLine("CREATE SNAPSHOT: " +
                    cmd.ExecuteNonQuery().ToString());
            }
            catch (Exception ex)
            {
                Console.WriteLine(ex.Message);
                throw;
            }
        }
        conn.Close();
    }
}
// sample use:
// RevertDatabaseFromSnapshot("testdb," "testdb_ss");
private void RevertDatabaseFromSnapshot(
                                string databaseName,
                                string snapshotName)
{
    using (SqlConnection conn = new SqlConnection("server=MyServer;
database=master;
            trusted_connection=yes;"))
    {
        string sql = "RESTORE DATABASE " + databaseName +
                " FROM DATABASE_SNAPSHOT = '" +
                    snapshotName + "';" +
                    "DROP DATABASE " + snapshotName + ";";
        using (SqlCommand cmd = new SqlCommand(sql, conn))
        {
            try
            {
                cmd.CommandTimeout = 1000;
                conn.Open();
```

```
            Console.WriteLine("REVERT SNAPSHOT: " +
                    cmd.ExecuteNonQuery().ToString());
        }
        catch (Exception ex)
        {
            Console.WriteLine(ex.Message);
            throw;
        }
      }
    }
}
```

Listing 5-3: C# code to create a database snapshot and restore the database from a database snapshot.

Simplifying unit tests

With unit tests, we're testing database access methods, which can be stored procedures, direct **SELECT** statements, views, and so on. By adopting a particular approach to this testing, involving the separation of read and write tests, we can avoid the need to revert the data to its original state after each test, and so simplify our testing substantially.

In the early days of database testing, it was common to create some random test data, insert that data and run a bunch of read and write tests on that data to see if we'd get the correct results back. This meant that we needed to revert the data using one of the techniques discussed in the previous section, such as wrapping each test within **BEGIN** and **ROLLBACK TRANSACTION** statements, or by restoring database snapshots for groups of tests. In essence, we were testing our databases using the object-oriented testing mindset, which was to create and destroy objects in each test, and it was leading to cumbersome testing. Luckily, we didn't need to change our approach completely, only adjust it a bit.

By separating out read and write tests, we can simplify our testing considerably. With read tests, we only test that the database object is returning the correct data, based on some known conditions. Rather than insert fresh data as part of each test, we started using auto-generated data that was preloaded into the database. We knew what the generated data looked like and, because our tests were read only, we didn't have to do any data reverts. An added bonus was the fact that by preloading the generated data we would, in effect, be testing the data bulk load process, so solving two problems at once.

With the read test problem solved, let's tackle the write tests. A thing to remember about databases is that rows in a table are independent of each other. By adding new rows we can't somehow "break" existing ones. With that in mind, it becomes clear that, even for write tests, we may not need data reverts. For each write test, we can create a small sample of random test data (10–50 rows). Generating such small data samples is fast and should not present a problem. Our test will then do any updates or deletes on those generated rows. If we need to insert more rows, we simply generate new test data.

It is important to remember to run write tests under the same isolation level as will be used when the modifications run in production. This way, we can find if any code causes strange, unwanted behavior. For example, imagine we have a `SELECT` statement with a `NOLOCK` hint on it. This statement can now read a row that has been modified in another, still-running, transaction. We get the modified row, but the other transaction rolls back to the old row values. We now have invalid data in our returned result set. If this happens, our test should fail and give us information about what to fix.

So, by asking ourselves fundamental questions regarding whether or not data reversion was really necessary, we were able to greatly simplify our unit tests.

Testing existing databases

We would all prefer to work all the time on cool new projects, but the reality is that most of our time is spent "fixing" existing (bordering on legacy) databases. In my experience, existing databases usually suffer from two major problems:

- there are no tests of any kind (if there are, consider yourself lucky)

- there is no documentation describing the various ways in which the database integrates with the outside world.

As a result, we invariably have to spend considerable time getting to know the database and its various interactions with the outside world, before we can even begin writing any tests.

A good first step is to use a database documenting tool, such as Red Gate's SQL Doc, to generate a description of the database and its schema. The second step is to understand what kinds of queries are run against the database. We can capture a typical query workload by using the SQL Server Profiler tool and filtering on the relevant database ID or name. The trace duration will depend on what the database is used for and when, and may vary from an hour to a day, or longer. For example, if we have a heavy OLTP load for one hour per day, it's pointless to run the trace for the whole day. On the other hand, if we have a load that is equally distributed over the whole day, then we have to trace the whole day's activity.

Step three is to talk to the people who use all of the applications that connect to the database, and get their input regarding the business requirements and how they use the database. Once we have all this info, we can start writing tests that cover as much of the necessary functionality as possible.

With this information in place, testing an existing database becomes similar to testing a new database. We create a new database with the same structure, import random or production test data, create read and write tests based on the feedback we received from our enquiries, and we're set to go.

Unit Testing Examples: Testing Data and Schema Validity

Realistically, it is never possible to test every aspect of a database's usage, much as we may strive towards that goal; time, knowledge, and other constraints always intervene.

That's why we have to make compromises. We have to get to know the systems that use our database, and evaluate their priority for testing. For example, testing the database interface is high priority because of security concerns, while testing smaller, monthly ETL jobs might be of lower priority. By prioritizing, we can make an informed decision what to give more attention to, and what is more important to test in the long run.

As noted earlier, my advice is not to store and run tests within the database. Databases are components themselves, and the first rule of testing says, "Don't litter the components with code that tests those components." We don't deploy tests into our production environment, right? All of the following examples use NUnit to create and run the tests, and the `AdventureWorks` database is used in all examples. Code for disposing connections, commands and other objects is omitted for brevity, but you can view it in the accompanying code download.

Bear in mind that we are testing the behavior of the database objects – in other words, the data and schema validity, not the performance of these objects. Performance testing is a whole separate art form, a full discussion of which is outside the scope of this chapter.

Testing the database interface

The term "interface" isn't one commonly used in the database world but, of course, each data access point represents an interface to the database, and any table, view, UDF (User Defined Function) or stored procedure that is accessible from outside the database to an end-user, is an access point.

Security theory teaches us that the best way to create a controllable environment is to minimize the "surface area" of possible attacks, and one of the ways to do this with a database is to deny access to everything, then selectively grant access to the minimal set of stored procedures, views, and possibly UDFs, as required by a given role.

Another good strategy is to categorize objects into schemas, which allows us to control access to groups of database objects with one security setting, using roles, rather than having to grant or deny access rights to every single object. Take a look at the **AdventureWorks** database, for an example of how schemas can be used. It has various schemas to which we can grant or deny access via a certain role; we have a **Person** schema that can be accessible only to HR people, a **Sales** schema that is only accessible to marketing people, and so on.

Having defined our database interface as objects visible to the outside world, we have to test to make sure that the structure of this interface is what we expect it to be, and to clarify to whom the different parts of the interface are accessible.

Note that we're not testing the returned data, only the characteristics of the interface. We can do this with a very useful SQL command, called **SET FMTONLY**, which can help us greatly with interface testing. This command instructs SQL Server to return only metadata regarding the object, and no data. So, for example, a **SELECT** query against a table in the **AdventureWorks** database would, after issuing **SET FMTONLY ON**, return only column information, and no rows of data. By doing this, interface tests become read tests and don't need any data.

Listing 5-4 shows an interface test in action. First we create a stored procedure named **spTestInterface** that we have to test, and which returns three result sets. Next, the unit test consists of a method, **Test_interface_spTestInterface**, which executes this stored procedure with **SET FMTONLY ON**, so forcing the stored procedure to return empty result sets. Then we test all of the returned column names and column ordinal numbers against our expected values.

```sql
- - interface stored procedure to test
CREATE PROC spTestInterface
    @AllContactsCount INT = NULL OUTPUT
AS
    SELECT TOP 10
            AddressID ,
            AddressLine1
    FROM     Person.Address
    SELECT TOP 10
            ContactID ,
            FirstName ,
            LastName
    FROM     Person.Contact
    SELECT   @AllContactsCount = COUNT(*)
    FROM     Person.Contact
GO
```

```csharp
// C# Test in NUnit
[Test]
public void Test_interface_spTestInterface()
{
    // for simplicity assume we have
    // a valid connection already opened.
    SqlCommand cmd = new SqlCommand("," conn);
    // we have to do it like this because of
    // the FMTONLY option.
    // We can't just say it's a sproc.
    cmd.CommandText = "SET FMTONLY ON;
                exec spTestInterface @AllContactsCount out;";
    cmd.Parameters.Add("@AllContactsCount," SqlDbType.int);
    cmd.Parameters["@AllContactsCount"]
        .Direction = ParameterDirection.Output;
    DataSet ds = new DataSet();
    ds.Load(cmd.ExecuteReader(),
            LoadOption.OverwriteChanges,
            "Address," "Contact");
        Assert.IsTrue(cmd.Parameters.Contains("@AllContactsCount"),
                "No parameter @AllContactsCount found.");
    // test columns of the Address table
    DataColumn dc = ds.Tables["Address"]
                        .Columns["AddressId"];
    Assert.AreEqual(dc.Ordinal, 0,
            "Column AddressId has wrong ordinal.");
    Assert.AreEqual(dc.DataType, typeof(int),
            "Column AddressId has wrong data type.");
```

153

```
    dc = ds.Tables["Address"].Columns["AddressLine1"];
    Assert.AreEqual(dc.Ordinal, 1,
            "Column AddressLine1 has wrong ordinal.");
    Assert.AreEqual(dc.DataType, typeof(string),
            "Column AddressLine1 has wrong data type.");
    // test columns of the Contact table
    dc = ds.Tables["Contact"].Columns["ContactId"];
    Assert.AreEqual(dc.Ordinal, 0,
                    "Column ContactId has wrong ordinal.");
    Assert.AreEqual(dc.DataType, typeof(int),
            "Column ContactId has wrong data type.");
    dc = ds.Tables["Contact"].Columns["FirstName"];
    Assert.AreEqual(dc.Ordinal, 1,
            "Column FirstName has wrong ordinal.");
    Assert.AreEqual(dc.DataType, typeof(string),
            "Column FirstName has wrong data type.");
    dc = ds.Tables["Contact"].Columns["LastName"];
    Assert.AreEqual(dc.Ordinal, 2,
            "Column LastName has wrong ordinal.");
    Assert.AreEqual(dc.DataType, typeof(string),
            "Column LastName has wrong data type.");
    // here you can test other
    // conditions like column lengths etc...
}
```

Listing 5-4: Test in C# to test interface for a simple stored procedure with two result sets and an output parameter.

Testing the database schema

Testing the database schema can be viewed as part white-box and part black-box testing, although I prefer to think of it in terms of white-box testing, because we've already tested the exposed database interface as a black box.

Schema testing means we're testing the actual database structure. One of the cast-iron rules of an RDBMS is that we must be able to query the schema using the same language that we use to query the data, i.e. SQL. We do this by running queries against the INFORMATION_SCHEMA views, which hold information about the database structure (these views are covered in more detail in Chapter 8). Testing the schema thus becomes simply a matter of writing proper SQL statements to interrogate those views, and checking that the results are as we expect. Some of the things we're testing for are described below.

- Is column data type and size what our application expects?

- Are appropriate PRIMARY KEY and FOREIGN KEY constraints defined?

- Do appropriate DEFAULT and CHECK constraints exist, and do they restrict the column data appropriately?

- Is nullability of columns as expected?

Database schema testing is read-only testing, so it never changes the schema and, again, does not require us to test the data returned. Consider, for example, the testing of constraints. Since SQL Server guarantees the constrained data to be valid, we can simply test the constraints directly, then assume that no data will be ever outside of the constraints, thus removing the need to test referential integrity, default values, and so on. For example, if our schema tests confirm that a DEFAULT constraint exists, with the appropriate default value, then there is no need to test for values that do not comply with that constraint. Why test something we know is guaranteed anyway, right?

However, bear in mind that SQL Server does allow non-trusted constraints; any new data will comply with the constraint, but existing data may not. It's worth testing the schema for the existence of any non-trusted constraints.

Schema testing on new databases

When developing a new database, there is little to be gained from testing the schema before a stable version 1.0 is achieved. Before v1.0, the database structure is still volatile, as development and redesign take place. For v1.0, I assume a version that is stable enough that the application development can be started.

Listing 5-5 shows how to perform schema tests on the table, `Person.Address`, and the `CHECK` constraint, `CK_Contact_EmailPromotion`, by querying the `INFORMATION_ SCHEMA` views.

The `Schema_Person_Address` test method compares the value for the column name, ordinal position, data type, default value, nullability, and maximum numbers of characters, to the expected value, for every column in the `Person.Address` table.

The `Constraint_CK_Contact_EmailPromotion` test method verifies the `CHECK` constraint by comparing the returned expression to the expected values that the constraint should allow.

```
[Test]
public void Schema_Person_Addres()
{
    // for simplicity assume we have a valid connection already opened.
    SqlCommand cmd = new SqlCommand("," conn);
    cmd.CommandText = @"SELECT COLUMN_NAME,
                            ORDINAL_POSITION, DATA_TYPE,
                            COLUMN_DEFAULT, IS_NULLABLE,
                            CHARACTER_MAXIMUM_LENGTH
                    FROM    INFORMATION_SCHEMA.COLUMNS
                    WHERE     TABLE_SCHEMA = 'Person'
                            AND TABLE_NAME = 'Address'";
    DataSet ds = new DataSet();
    ds.Load(cmd.ExecuteReader(), LoadOption.OverwriteChanges, "ColumnData");
    DataRow row = ds.Tables["ColumnData"].Rows[0];
    // Skipped rows are similar to the ones shown.
    // No need to include them in the example.
    // test schema data for column AddressID
    Assert.AreEqual(row["COLUMN_NAME"].ToString(),
            "AddressID,"
            "Column has wrong COLUMN_NAME.");
    Assert.AreEqual(row["ORDINAL_POSITION"], 1,
            "Column has wrong ORDINAL_POSITION.");
    Assert.AreEqual(row["DATA_TYPE"].ToString(), "int,"
            "Column has wrong DATA_TYPE.");
    Assert.AreEqual(row["COLUMN_DEFAULT"], DBNull.Value,
            "Column has wrong COLUMN_DEFAULT.");
```

```
Assert.AreEqual(row["IS_NULLABLE"].ToString(), "NO,"
        "Column has wrong IS_NULLABLE.");
Assert.AreEqual(row["CHARACTER_MAXIMUM_LENGTH"],
        DBNull.Value,
        "Column has wrong CHARACTER_MAXIMUM_LENGTH.");
// test schema data for column AddressLine2
row = ds.Tables["ColumnData"].Rows[2];
Assert.AreEqual(row["COLUMN_NAME"].ToString(),
        "AddressLine2,"
        "Column has wrong COLUMN_NAME.");
Assert.AreEqual(row["ORDINAL_POSITION"], 3,
        "Column has wrong ORDINAL_POSITION.");
Assert.AreEqual(row["DATA_TYPE"].ToString(),
        "nvarchar,"
        "Column has wrong DATA_TYPE.");
Assert.AreEqual(row["COLUMN_DEFAULT"], DBNull.Value,
        "Column has wrong COLUMN_DEFAULT.");
Assert.AreEqual(row["IS_NULLABLE"].ToString(), "YES,"
        "Column has wrong IS_NULLABLE.");
Assert.AreEqual(row["CHARACTER_MAXIMUM_LENGTH"], 60,
        "Column has wrong CHARACTER_MAXIMUM_LENGTH.");
// test schema data for column rowguid
row = ds.Tables["ColumnData"].Rows[6];
Assert.AreEqual(row["COLUMN_NAME"].ToString(),
        "rowguid,"
        "Column has wrong COLUMN_NAME.");
Assert.AreEqual(row["ORDINAL_POSITION"], 7,
        "Column has wrong ORDINAL_POSITION.");
Assert.AreEqual(row["DATA_TYPE"].ToString(),
        "uniqueidentifier,"
        "Column has wrong DATA_TYPE.");
Assert.AreEqual(row["COLUMN_DEFAULT"].ToString(),
        "(newid()),"
        "Column has wrong COLUMN_DEFAULT.");
Assert.AreEqual(row["IS_NULLABLE"].ToString(), "NO,"
        "Column has wrong IS_NULLABLE.");
Assert.AreEqual(row["CHARACTER_MAXIMUM_LENGTH"],
        DBNull.Value,
        "Column has wrong CHARACTER_MAXIMUM_LENGTH.");
// test schema data for column ModifiedDate
row = ds.Tables["ColumnData"].Rows[7];
Assert.AreEqual(row["COLUMN_NAME"].ToString(),
        "ModifiedDate,"
        "Column has wrong COLUMN_NAME.");
```

```csharp
        Assert.AreEqual(row["ORDINAL_POSITION"], 8,
                "Column has wrong ORDINAL_POSITION.");
        Assert.AreEqual(row["DATA_TYPE"].ToString(),
                "datetime,"
                "Column has wrong DATA_TYPE.");
        Assert.AreEqual(row["COLUMN_DEFAULT"].ToString(),
                "(getdate()),"
                "Column has wrong COLUMN_DEFAULT.");
        Assert.AreEqual(row["IS_NULLABLE"].ToString(), "NO,"
                "Column has wrong IS_NULLABLE.");
        Assert.AreEqual(row["CHARACTER_MAXIMUM_LENGTH"],
                DBNull.Value,
                "Column has wrong CHARACTER_MAXIMUM_LENGTH.");
}
[Test]
public void Constraint_CK_Contact_EmailPromotion()
{
        // for simplicity assume we have a
        // valid connection already opened.
        SqlCommand cmd = new SqlCommand(",", conn);
        cmd.CommandText = @"SELECT CHECK_CLAUSE
                            FROM
                            INFORMATION_SCHEMA.CHECK_CONSTRAINTS
                            WHERE  CONSTRAINT_SCHEMA = 'Person'
                                AND CONSTRAINT_NAME =
                                'CK_Contact_EmailPromotion'";
        DataSet ds = new DataSet();
        ds.Load(cmd.ExecuteReader(),
                LoadOption.OverwriteChanges,
                "CheckConstraints");
        DataRow row = ds.Tables["CheckConstraints"].Rows[0];
        Assert.AreEqual(row["CHECK_CLAUSE"].ToString(),
            "([EmailPromotion]>=(0) AND [EmailPromotion]<=(2)),"
                "CK_Contact_EmailPromotion has invalid value.");
}
```

Listing 5-5:   Test in C# for table schema and a check constraint value.

Testing tables, views, and UDFs

Tables, views, and UDFs are all tested in the same manner, namely by directly executing T-SQL queries against them. In each case, we are testing the validity of the returned data so, in that sense, this is pure black-box testing.

We're basically testing that any changes made to these database objects, such as adding or removing joins to views, or changing some business logic in a UDF, haven't changed the expected result.

These tests should be run under the same isolation level as the application will use, and we need to perform both read and write tests against these objects, since they can be used to modify data, as well as read it. Scalar UDFs fall into the read-test category, since we can't insert data through a scalar UDF.

Included in the write-testing of tables, is the testing of triggers. A trigger cannot be fired directly; it is executed as part of a table modification procedure. Therefore, our write tests on the tables must consider the effects of any triggers that may be fired, and may modify other tables as a result. Each of these "secondary" tables is added to the unit that we must test. Overuse of triggers can greatly widen our testing scope and make the tests huge, bulky, and impractical.

Listing 5-6 shows three test methods; a table read test, along with write tests for a table and a view, as shown here.

- **Table_single_line_read_from_Person_Address** method – returns the first row from the `Person.Address` table, ordered by `AddressId` column, and checks its value against our known values.

- **Table_single_line_insert_into_Person_Address** method – inserts a single new row into the `Person.Address` table and tests if the inserted values match to our known values. For example, if we had a trigger on the `Person.Address` table that would change `ModifiedDate` column to remove the time portion, it would make our test fail.

- **View_single_line_insert_into_Person_vStateProvinceCountryRegion** method – inserts one row into the `Person.vStateProvinceCountryRegion` view. The view is a join between a parent and a child table (see the `AdventureWorks` database for details) and we're inserting data into the child table. Lastly, we're comparing inserted rows with the known values.

```
[Test]
public void Table_single_line_read_from_Person_Address()
{
    // Load test data before doing read tests!
    // for brevity's sake we'll use the
    // existing data in AdventureWorks database
    SqlCommand cmd = new SqlCommand("," conn);
    cmd.CommandText = @"SELECT TOP 1 AddressID,
                               AddressLine1, AddressLine2,
                               City, StateProvinceID,
                               PostalCode
                        FROM Person.Address
                        ORDER BY AddressID";
    DataSet ds = new DataSet();
    ds.Load(cmd.ExecuteReader(),
            LoadOption.OverwriteChanges,
            "ReadData");
    DataRow row = ds.Tables["ReadData"].Rows[0];
    Assert.AreEqual(row["AddressID"], 1,
        "Inserted value different from expected value.");
    Assert.AreEqual(row["AddressLine1"], "1970 Napa Ct.,"
        "Inserted value different from expected value.");
    Assert.AreEqual(row["AddressLine2"], DBNull.Value,
        "Inserted value different from expected value.");
    Assert.AreEqual(row["City"], "Bothell,"
        "Inserted value different from expected value.");
    Assert.AreEqual(row["StateProvinceID"], 79,
        "Inserted value different from expected value.");
    Assert.AreEqual(row["PostalCode"], "98011,"
        "Inserted value different from expected value.");
}
[Test]
```

```
public void Table_single_line_insert_into_Person_Address()
{
    // for simplicity assume we have a
    // valid connection already opened.
    SqlCommand cmd = new SqlCommand(",", conn);
    string randomNumber = new Random(DateTime.Now
                                            .Millisecond)
                    .Next(10, 1000).ToString();
    DateTime date = DateTime.Parse(DateTime.Now
                    .ToString("yyyy-MM-dd HH:mm:ss.ff"));
    // insert a random row and use output
    // so we don't have to do a read
    cmd.CommandText = @"INSERT INTO Person.Address(
                        AddressLine1, AddressLine2,
                        City, StateProvinceID,
                        PostalCode, ModifiedDate)
                OUTPUT  inserted.*
                VALUES  ('Test Address Line 1 " +
                            randomNumber + @"',
                        'Test Address Line 2 " +
                            randomNumber + @"',
                        'Test City " +
                            randomNumber + "', 79,
                        '98011', '" +
        date.ToString("yyyy-MM-dd HH:mm:ss.ff") + "')";
    // insert and return inserted data
    DataSet ds = new DataSet();
    ds.Load(cmd.ExecuteReader(),
        LoadOption.OverwriteChanges,
        "InsertedData");
    DataRow row = ds.Tables["InsertedData"].Rows[0];
    Assert.AreEqual(row["AddressLine1"].ToString(),
        "Test Address Line 1 " + randomNumber,
        "Inserted value different from expected value.");
    Assert.AreEqual(row["AddressLine2"].ToString(),
        "Test Address Line 2 " + randomNumber,
        "Inserted value different from expected value.");
    Assert.AreEqual(row["City"].ToString(),
        "Test City " + randomNumber,
        "Inserted value different from expected value.");
    Assert.AreEqual(row["StateProvinceID"], 79,
        "Inserted value different from expected value.");
    Assert.AreEqual(row["PostalCode"].ToString(), "98011,"
        "Inserted value different from expected value.");
```

```
        Assert.AreEqual(row["ModifiedDate"], date,
            "Inserted value different from expected value.");
}
[Test]
public void View_single_line_insert_into_Person_vStateProvinceCountryRegion()
{
    // for simplicity assume we have a
    // valid connection already opened.
    SqlCommand cmd = new SqlCommand("," conn);
    // CountryRegionCode is 3 chars long
    // so generate at maximum a 3 digit number
    string randomNumber = new Random(DateTime.Now
                                        .Millisecond)
                    .Next(0, 999).ToString();
    // we can insert into the view
    // as long as we insert into a single child table.
    // Look at the code for vStateProvinceCountryRegion
    // in AdventureWorks database for the view definition
    cmd.CommandText = @"insert into
                    Person.vStateProvinceCountryRegion
                    (CountryRegionCode, CountryRegionName)
                    output inserted.CountryRegionCode,
                        inserted.CountryRegionName
                    values ('" + randomNumber + @"', '" +
                        randomNumber + @" Country')";
    // insert and return inserted data
    DataSet ds = new DataSet();
    ds.Load(cmd.ExecuteReader(),
            LoadOption.OverwriteChanges,
            "InsertedViewData");
    DataRow row = ds.Tables["InsertedViewData"].Rows[0];
    Assert.AreEqual(row["CountryRegionCode"], randomNumber,
        "Inserted value different from expected value.");
    Assert.AreEqual(row["CountryRegionName"],
        randomNumber + " Country,"
        "Inserted value different from expected value.");
}
```

Listing 5-6:   Test in C# for table read/write and a view data insert.

Testing stored procedures

Stored procedures are a bit trickier to test than other database objects. They can return multiple result sets, have multiple, optional input and output parameters, and often contain complex logic that does both reads and writes.

If a stored procedure is read only, or write only, then we can test it in the same way as other objects. However, those stored procedures that perform both functions need a special testing process. Like tables, views, and UDFs we also have to test stored procedures inside the same type of a transaction that the application will use in production. For example, if an application uses SERIALIZABLE transaction isolation level, then we should test the stored procedure with the same transaction isolation level.

Listing 5-7 shows a test case for a complex stored procedure that combines read and write operations. First we create our complex stored procedure, smartly named spComplexProc. It selects data from the Person.Address table, inserts it into a temporary table, and then inserts those rows, with some changes, back into the Person. Address table. Lastly, it returns the last modified address, as of the same time on the previous day.

The test code starts a transaction, calls the stored procedure, compares the returned results with expected values, and then reverts the data to its original state, by rolling back the transaction.

```
- - create our complex stored procedure
CREATE PROCEDURE spComplexProc @addressId INT
AS -  - copy the data from the input addressId
    SELECT   AddressLine1 ,
             AddressLine2 ,
             City ,
             StateProvinceID ,
             PostalCode
    INTO     #temp
    FROM     Person.Address
```

```
    WHERE     AddressID = @addressId
- - Duplicate half of the retrieved row
- - This is the "complex" part. What matters is that
- - the stored procedure combines reads and writes
- - and it can't be split into
- - a read-only and write-only scenario
    INSERT   INTO Person.Address
             ( AddressLine1 ,
               AddressLine2 ,
               City ,
               StateProvinceID ,
               PostalCode
             )
    OUTPUT   inserted.AddressID ,
             inserted.AddressLine1 ,
             inserted.AddressLine2 ,
             inserted.City ,
             inserted.StateProvinceID ,
             inserted.PostalCode
             SELECT  'New AL 1' ,
                     'New AL 2' ,
                     City ,
                     StateProvinceID ,
                     PostalCode
             FROM     #temp
- - return last modified addresses before
- - yesterday at the same time as now
    SELECT TOP 1
             AddressID ,
             AddressLine1 ,
             AddressLine2 ,
             City ,
             StateProvinceID ,
             PostalCode ,
             ModifiedDate
    FROM     Person.Address
    WHERE    ModifiedDate < GETDATE() - 1
    ORDER BY ModifiedDate DESC
GO
// Test code in C#
[Test]
public void Complex_stored_procedure_data_spComplexProc()
{
```

```
// for simplicity assume we have a
// valid connection already opened.
SqlCommand cmd = new SqlCommand("spComplexProc," conn);
cmd.CommandType = CommandType.StoredProcedure;
// add parameter values
SqlParameter param = new SqlParameter("@addressId,"
                                        SqlDbType.int);
param.Value = 1;
cmd.Parameters.Add(param);
// the end call is "spComplexProc 1"
DataSet ds = new DataSet();
// assume that the application is running the stored
// procedure in ReadCommitted isolation level
using (SqlTransaction tx =
        conn.BeginTransaction(IsolationLevel.ReadCommitted))
{
    cmd.Transaction = tx;
    ds.Load(cmd.ExecuteReader(),
            LoadOption.OverwriteChanges,
            "InsertedData," "DayBeforeData");
    // test inserted data
    DataRow row = ds.Tables["InsertedData"].Rows[0];
    Assert.AreEqual(row["AddressLine1"], "New AL 1,"
      "Inserted value different from expected value.");
    Assert.AreEqual(row["AddressLine2"], "New AL 2,"
      "Inserted value different from expected value.");
    Assert.AreEqual(row["City"], "Bothell,"
      "Inserted value different from expected value.");
    Assert.AreEqual(row["StateProvinceID"], 79,
      "Inserted value different from expected value.");
    Assert.AreEqual(row["PostalCode"], "98011,"
      "Inserted value different from expected value.");
    // test the day before data
    row = ds.Tables["DayBeforeData"].Rows[0];
    // the expected values are existisng values
    // in the AdventureWorks database
    Assert.AreEqual(row["AddressID"], 28975,
      "Returned value different from expected value.");
    Assert.AreEqual(row["AddressLine1"],
      "9777 Mozden Lane,"
      "Returned value different from expected value.");
    Assert.AreEqual(row["AddressLine2"], DBNull.Value,
      "Returned value different from expected value.");
```

```
      Assert.AreEqual(row["City"], "Puyallup,"
        "Returned value different from expected value.");
      Assert.AreEqual(row["StateProvinceID"], 79,
        "Returned value different from expected value.");
      Assert.AreEqual(row["PostalCode"], "98371,"
        "Returned value different from expected value.");
      Assert.AreEqual(row["ModifiedDate"],
        DateTime.Parse("2004-07-31 00:00:00.000"),
        "Returned value different from expected value.");
      tx.Rollback();
  }
```

Listing 5-7:   Test in C# for a complex stored procedure.

Testing authentication and authorization

When testing authentication, we're testing whether or not a user can connect to a SQL Server instance. When testing authorization we're testing to which database objects a user has access, in the database.

Sadly, many developers completely overlook the testing of authentication and authorization. This is usually because only one account is used for all SQL access and, unfortunately, that account is often **sa**, which has complete control over the SQL Server instance. It is quite common for web applications to use a single account for all database access and, in such cases, there is little to be done in the way of testing. All we can do is avoid using the **sa** account in favor of an account with fewer privileges.

Testing authentication and authorization for desktop enterprise applications can, however, be a lot more complex. It is common for users in the Windows domain to connect to the SQL Server using their own domain account. Users in an enterprise environment are grouped into roles, and each role can access a certain schema or tables in a database. Testing this access can be of great importance when auditing, or when tight security has to be implemented.

Listing 5-8 shows how to test that a valid and authorized user (I've used **sa** in this case, purely for convenience) can access a given SQL Server instance, and specific database, and shows how to test the way in which invalid access attempts are handled.

```
[Test]
public void Authentication_is_valid_for_SA()
{
    conn = new SqlConnection(@"Data Source=yourSQLServer;
                                User Id=sa;
                                Password=saPassword;");
    // if this errors out we know that there's
    // a problem with the authentication for SA
    // since it should've connected OK.
    conn.Open();
    conn.Dispose();
}
[Test]
public void Authentication_is_invalid_for_LoginA()
{
    // LoginA must NOT exist.
    string loginName = "LoginA";
    try
    {
        conn = new SqlConnection(
        @"Data Source=yourSQLServer;
        User Id=" + loginName + @"; Password=saPassword;");
        // if it opens the connection ok then it's an error
        // and the test fails
        conn.Open();
        Assert.Fail(loginName +
                " successfully connected. It shouldn't.");
    }
    catch (SqlException ex)
    {
        // Error text depends on instance language, error
        // number doesn't
        // 2 possible errors due to login problems,
        // so if it's any other throw it.
        if (ex.Number != 233 && ex.Number != 18456)
            throw;
    }
```

```
        finally
        {
            conn.Dispose();
        }
}
[Test]
public void Test_authorizatrion_to_AdventureWorks_is_valid_for_SA()
{
    conn = new SqlConnection(@"Data Source=yourSQLServer;
                        Initial Catalog=AdventureWorks;
                        User Id=sa; Password=saPassword;");
    // if this errors out we know that there's
    // a problem with the authentication for SA
    // since it should've connected OK.
    conn.Open();
    conn.Dispose();
}
[Test]
public void Authorization_to_AdventureWorks_is_invalid_for_LoginA()
{
    // LoginA MUST exist but have no privileges
    // to the AdventureWorks database
    string loginName = "LoginA";
    try
    {
        conn = new SqlConnection(@"
                        Data Source=yourSQLServer;
                        Initial Catalog=AdventureWorks;
                        User Id=" + loginName + @";
                        Password=saPassword;");
        // if it opens the connection ok, it's an error
        conn.Open();
        Assert.Fail(loginName +
                " successfully connected. It shouldn't.");
    }
    catch (SqlException ex)
    {
        // error text depends on instance language error
        // number doesn't
        if (ex.Number != 4060)
            throw;
    }
```

```
    finally
    {
        conn.Dispose();
    }
}
```

Listing 5-8:   Test in C# for a successful and unsuccessful authentication for a login and successful and unsuccessful authorization for a user.

Summary

This chapter aimed to provide a broad overview of database testing, with some specific examples of how you'd go about unit testing various aspects of a database.

Testing in general is way, way underused in software development. However, a time comes when one has to seriously change one's views on how to deliver software. Unfortunately, that time usually comes when one is faced with an already deployed application and a "simple bug fix" is wreaking havoc in other parts of the application without knowing why. By covering why you should even begin testing, how to deal with management opposition, and setting up the testing environment, and by showing you the tools and methodologies to use, I hope this will help to make your first steps much easier than mine were.

If you're still not convinced, this is why you should embrace testing: **"Amateurs work until they get it right. Professionals work until they can't get it wrong."** By testing, you're just being professional, that's all.

When (and not if) you start implementing testing in your environment, I hope this chapter will be your introduction into the whole new world of development.

Chapter 6: Reusing T-SQL Code

Often, we have code that works perfectly well for a particular purpose, and then we find that another member of the team needs to implement some very similar functionality in another database. It is very tempting to just copy the code, adapt it to meet the new requirements, and then deploy this slightly modified code. However, every time we copy-and-paste code in this manner, we are exposed to the following risk: the requirements change, and we fail to change the code in both places.

Whenever evidence of repetition is found in the code base, the team should seek to refactor, so that the code to tackle a given problem or enforce a given rule is implemented in one place only. In other words, common logic should be refactored into a single reusable code unit, in the form of a constraint, stored procedure, trigger, user-defined function (UDF), or index. Whichever approach is used, in each particular case, this proper form of code reuse reduces the possibility of bugs and is a vitally important part of team development, and a good example of a defensive approach to database programming.

Unfortunately, many developers find it difficult to choose the correct implementation for the given requirement; in this chapter, I will offer some useful pointers as to the approach that will lead to the most defensive, and therefore robust, code. We must, as always, benchmark our solutions because the one that most conveniently promotes reuse is not necessarily the one that will perform the best.

Specifically, this chapter will cover:

- why copy-and-paste will get you into trouble

- how proper code reuse will help

- using views to encapsulate simple queries

- using UDFs to encapsulate parameterized queries; and why UDFs may sometimes be preferable to stored procedures for this requirement

- potential performance issues with UDFs

- using constraints, triggers and filtered indexes to implement business logic in one place.

The Dangers of Copy-and-Paste

The biggest problem with copy-and-paste as a means of solving a set of similar problems is that, of course, it leads to code duplication. In turn, this means that we need to maintain multiple copies of essentially the same code, but with each copy subtly modified to suit a particular need. The real danger arises when requirements change, and we need to make sure that this is reflected, not just in the original code, but in all the subsequent copies. We can easily demonstrate this risk with an example. Listing 6-1 creates the **Sales** table and loads it with some test data.

```
CREATE TABLE dbo.Sales
    (
      SalesID INT NOT NULL
                    IDENTITY
                    PRIMARY KEY ,
      StateCode CHAR(2) NOT NULL ,
      SaleDateTime DATETIME NOT NULL ,
      Amount DECIMAL(10, 2) NOT NULL
    ) ;
GO
SET NOCOUNT ON ;
DECLARE @d DATETIME ,
  @i INT ;
SET @d = '20091002' ;
SET @i = 0 ;
WHILE @i < 40
  BEGIN ;
    INSERT  INTO dbo.Sales
            ( StateCode ,
              SaleDateTime ,
              Amount
```

```
                )
          SELECT 'CA' ,
                @d ,
                case WHEN @d <'20091001' THEN 5000000
                     ELSE 5000
                  END
          UNION ALL
          SELECT 'OR' ,
                @d ,
                case WHEN @d <'20091001' THEN 1000000
                     ELSE 1000
                  END ;
     SELECT  @d = DATEADD(day, -1, @d) ,
             @i = @i + 1 ;
   END ;
```

Listing 6-1:   Creating the Sales table and populating it with test data.

Listing 6-2 shows the stored procedure, SelectTotalSalesPerStateForMonth, which returns the **total** sales per state for a given month.

```
CREATE PROCEDURE dbo.SelectTotalSalesPerStateForMonth
   @AsOfDate DATETIME
AS
  SELECT  SUM(Amount) AS SalesPerState ,
          StateCode
  FROM    dbo.Sales
-- month begins on the first calendar day of the month
  WHERE SaleDateTime >= DATEADD(month,
                                DATEDIFF(month, '19900101',
                                         @AsOfDate),
                                '19900101')
        AND SaleDateTime <= @AsOfDate
  GROUP BY StateCode ;
```

Listing 6-2:   The SelectTotalSalesPerStateForMonth stored procedure.

At the time we developed this code, our understanding of a report "for a given month" is one that covers the period of time from the first calendar day of the month until the day we run the report. For this purpose, our stored procedure serves the customers' needs well, and we soon receive a request for a similar report, returning the **average** sales per state, for a given month. Note that our new report is required to use the same definition of "for a given month."

It is very tempting to just copy the existing `SelectTotalSalesPerStateForMonth` procedure, and replace `sum` with `avg` to meet the new requirements, as shown in Listing 6-3.

```sql
CREATE PROCEDURE dbo.SelectAverageSalesPerStateForMonth
  @AsOfDate DATETIME
AS
  SELECT   AVG(Amount) AS SalesPerState ,
           StateCode
  FROM     dbo.Sales
-- month begins on the first calendar day of the month
  WHERE    SaleDateTime >= DATEADD(month,
                                 DATEDIFF(month, '19900101',
                                          @AsOfDate),
                               '19900101')
           AND SaleDateTime <= @AsOfDate
  GROUP BY StateCode ;
```

Listing 6-3:   A simple adaptation of our "total sales" stored procedure allows us to produce an "average sales" equivalent.

In this way, we have completed the task in just a few seconds and, in the short term at least, it will do the job.

Suppose, however, that at some later time the users request to change the definition of "for a given month" to "thirty consecutive calendar days, ending on the day we run the report." Unfortunately, the definition of "for a given month" is implemented twice, both in `SelectTotalSalesPerStateForMonth` and in `SelectAverageSalesPerState-ForMonth`. Even if one and the same person developed them both, it is possible to forget it by the time we need to implement the change. Even if it is clearly documented that

174

both procedures should use one and the same definition, it is still possible that the developer implementing the change has failed to modify both stored procedures in a consistent way.

Suppose, for example, that only the `SelectAverageSalesPerStateForMonth` stored procedure was modified to meet this new requirement. Listing 6-4 shows how it was changed.

```
ALTER PROCEDURE dbo.SelectAverageSalesPerStateForMonth
   @AsOfDate DATETIME
AS
   SELECT   AVG(Amount) AS SalesPerState ,
            StateCode
   FROM     dbo.Sales
-- month means 30 calendar days
   WHERE    SaleDateTime >= DATEADD(day, -29, @AsOfDate)
            AND SaleDateTime <= @AsOfDate
   GROUP BY StateCode ;
```

Listing 6-4:   The modified `SelectAverageSalesPerStateForMonth` stored
procedure, accommodating the new definition of "for a given month."

When we make such changes, it is very easy to forget that we have implemented the definition of "for a given month" in two places. If we update the definition in one place and not the other, we will get inconsistent results, as demonstrated by Listing 6-5.

```
PRINT 'Total Sales Per State For Month:' ;
EXEC dbo.SelectTotalSalesPerStateForMonth
   @AsOfDate = '20091005' ;

PRINT 'Average Sales Per State For Month:' ;
EXEC dbo.SelectAverageSalesPerStateForMonth
   @AsOfDate = '20091005' ;
```

```
Total Sales Per State For Month:
SalesPerState                             StateCode
----------------------------------------- ----------
10000.00                                  CA
2000.00                                   OR

(2 row(s) affected)


Average Sales Per State For Month:
SalesPerState                             StateCode
----------------------------------------- ----------
4630000.000000                            CA
926000.000000                             OR
(2 row(s) affected)
```

Listing 6-5: The stored procedures produce different results.

Clearly the average sales size for the state of California (4,630,000) is many times greater than the total sales for the same state (10,000), which makes no sense at all. In this example, I have deliberately used test data that makes the discrepancy obvious. In general, however, such discrepancies may be more subtle and difficult to spot, so they can lurk around for a long time.

As this example clearly demonstrates, when we cut and paste code, we expose our code to the possibility of bugs if our requirements change, and we fail to change each of the multiple implementations of one and the same logic in exactly the same way. In short, copy-and-paste coding is a direct violation of the DRY (Don't Repeat Yourself) principle, which is so fundamental in software engineering.

The DRY principle...

...was originally stated by ANDY HUNT *see* HTTP://EN.WIKIPEDIA.ORG/WIKI/ANDY_HUNT_(AUTHOR) *and* DAVE THOMAS *see* HTTP://EN.WIKIPEDIA.ORG/WIKI/DAVE_THOMAS_(AUTHOR) *in their book* THE PRAGMATIC PROGRAMMER. *For details, go to* HTTP://EN.WIKIPEDIA.ORG/WIKI/THE_PRAGMATIC_ PROGRAMMER. *I encourage you to read this book; it is very relevant to every programmer.*

The code to implement a given logic should be implemented once, and once only, and reused by all applications that need it. However, of course, due care must be taken when reusing SQL code. Careless reuse of code can lead to maintenance and performance issues, especially when this reuse takes the form of scalar UDFs. We cannot reuse code without first verifying that it runs fast enough. We shall discuss this in more detail later in the chapter.

How Reusing Code Improves its Robustness

Rather than repeat the same logic in multiple places, we need to refactor the common functionality out of our two stored procedures. We can implement the definition of "sales for a given month" in an inline UDF, as shown in Listing 6-6.

```
CREATE   FUNCTION dbo.SalesForMonth (@AsOfDate DATETIME)
RETURNS  TABLE
AS
RETURN
   ( SELECT   SalesID ,
              StateCode ,
              SaleDateTime ,
              Amount
     FROM     dbo.Sales
     WHERE    SaleDateTime >= DATEADD(day, -29, @AsOfDate)
              AND SaleDateTime <= @AsOfDate
   ) ;
```

Listing 6-6:   Implementing the definition of "sales for a given month" in an inline UDF.

This new inline UDF can then be used in both stored procedures.

```
ALTER PROCEDURE dbo.SelectTotalSalesPerStateForMonth
   @AsOfDate DATETIME
AS
   BEGIN
     SELECT  SUM(Amount) AS SalesPerState ,
             StateCode
     FROM    dbo.SalesForMonth(@AsOfDate)
     GROUP BY StateCode ;
   END ;
GO
ALTER PROCEDURE dbo.SelectAverageSalesPerStateForMonth
   @AsOfDate DATETIME
AS
   BEGIN
     SELECT  AVG(Amount) AS SalesPerState ,
             StateCode
     FROM    dbo.SalesForMonth(@AsOfDate)
     GROUP BY StateCode ;
   END ;
```

Listing 6-7: Utilizing the new inline function in our two stored procedures.

After this refactoring, our two stored procedures are guaranteed to have the same definition of "for a given month." We can rerun Listing 6-5 and try them out. If, at some later date, we change the definition of the reporting period again, we will have to modify only one module, `SalesForMonth`.

Can we reuse the definition of the reporting period in other queries against other tables? We can at least try to go one step further, and have one module define our reporting period and do nothing else. As usual, we should verify that the performance is still acceptable. The code in Listing 6-8 shows how to implement the definition of reporting period as an inline UDF.

```
CREATE FUNCTION dbo.MonthReportingPeriodStart
                        (@AsOfDate DATETIME )
RETURNS TABLE
AS
RETURN
  ( SELECT  DATEADD(day, -29, @AsOfDate) AS PeriodStart
  ) ;
```

Listing 6-8: An inline UDF that implements the definition of a reporting period.

We can utilize this inline UDF when we implement the "sales for a given month" functionality.

```
ALTER FUNCTION dbo.SalesForMonth ( @AsOfDate DATETIME )
RETURNS TABLE
AS
RETURN
  ( SELECT  SalesID ,
            StateCode ,
            SaleDateTime ,
            Amount
    FROM    dbo.Sales AS s
            CROSS APPLY
            dbo.MonthReportingPeriodStart(@AsOfDate) AS ps
    WHERE   SaleDateTime >= ps.PeriodStart
            AND SaleDateTime <= @AsOfDate
  ) ;
```

Listing 6-9: Altering `SalesPerStateForMonth` to utilize the new `MonthReportingPeriodStart` function.

You can rerun Listing 6-5 one more time, to verify that both our stored procedures still work correctly.

Alternatively, we can use a scalar UDF to implement the definition of reporting period, as shown in Listing 6-10.

```
-- being defensive, we must drop the old implementation
-- so that reporting periods are implemented
-- only in one place
DROP FUNCTION dbo.MonthReportingPeriodStart ;
GO
CREATE FUNCTION dbo.MonthReportingPeriodStart
                        ( @AsOfDate DATETIME )
RETURNS DATETIME
AS
    BEGIN ;
      DECLARE @ret DATETIME ;
      SET @ret = DATEADD(day, -29, @AsOfDate) ;
      RETURN @ret ;
    END ;
```

Listing 6-10: Scalar UDF which implements the definition of reporting period.

We also have to change our `SalesForMonth` function, so that it utilizes our new scalar UDF, as shown in Listing 6-11.

```
ALTER FUNCTION dbo.SalesForMonth ( @AsOfDate DATETIME )
RETURNS TABLE
AS
RETURN
  ( SELECT  SalesID ,
            StateCode ,
            SaleDateTime ,
            Amount
    FROM    dbo.Sales AS s
    WHERE   SaleDateTime >=
              dbo.MonthReportingPeriodStart(@AsOfDate)
            AND SaleDateTime <= @AsOfDate
  ) ;
```

Listing 6-11: Altering `SalesForMonth` to utilize the new scalar UDF `MonthReportingPeriodStart`.

Note that the new implementation of `SalesForMonth` is simpler than the previous one (Listing 6-9): instead of using the `CROSS APPLY` clause to utilize the inline UDF, we can just invoke the scalar UDF directly in the `WHERE` clause.

In fact, however, the CROSS APPLY version will perform better in many cases. As always when we reuse code, we need to benchmark the performance of each of the possible approaches before making a choice. In some cases, chaining functions can lead to bad performance so, depending on the results of our benchmarking, we might even have to abandon the SalesForMonth and MonthReportingPeriodStart UDFs and return to the simpler function from Listing 6-6.

The basic fact remains, however, that implementing the same logic in multiple places increases the possibility of bugs when our requirements change. Instead, we should aim for sensible code reuse wherever possible, and UDFs are just one of the means to achieve this.

Over the coming sections, we'll discuss other ways in which we can reuse T-SQL code, as dictated by the given circumstances. Overall, reusing code is a very important component of defensive programming, and I cannot emphasize strongly enough how much it can improve the robustness of our code.

Wrapping SELECTs in Views

In some cases, it makes sense to wrap a frequently-used query in a view, as shown in Listing 6-12.

```
CREATE VIEW dbo.TotalSalesByState
AS
SELECT SUM(Amount) AS TotalSales, StateCode
FROM dbo.Sales
GROUP BY StateCode ;
```

Listing 6-12: Wrapping a query inside a view.

You can **SELECT** from views in exactly the same way as you can **SELECT** from tables, so views are very convenient and useful. However, views do not offer the ability to provide parameters to the **SELECT** statements that we are reusing. When this requirement arises, we reuse **SELECT** statements by wrapping them either in stored procedures or in user-defined functions.

As usual, we need to consider performance whenever we choose to use views. Typically views do not cause any performance degradation at all. However, we need to use them in moderation: having to deal with too many layers of nested views may overwhelm the optimizer and cause it to choose a suboptimal plan.

Reusing Parameterized Queries: Stored Procedures versus Inline UDFs

If we want to reuse parameterized queries, it is usually preferable to wrap them in user-defined functions. It is typically less convenient to reuse parameterized queries that are wrapped in stored procedures, as the following examples will demonstrate.

Let's say we have a stored procedure that returns all sales for the month, across all states, as shown in Listing 6-13.

```
CREATE PROCEDURE dbo.SelectSalesForMonth @AsOfDate DATETIME
AS
  BEGIN ;
    SELECT  Amount ,
            StateCode
    FROM    dbo.Sales
    WHERE   SaleDateTime >= DATEADD(day, -29, @AsOfDate)
            AND SaleDateTime <= @AsOfDate ;
  END ;
GO
```

Listing 6-13: A stored procedure that returns all sales for the month.

Hopefully, you spotted the missed opportunity for code reuse in this listing. We should have reused our `MonthReportingPeriodStart` in the `WHERE` clause; I leave this as an exercise for the reader.

We now need to develop a stored procedure that retrieves the total sales **per state** for a given month, and we want to reuse the `SelectSalesForMonth` stored procedure, Although it's possible to do this, we will need to create a table variable or a temporary table with a structure that matches the structure of the result set returned by stored procedure, as shown in Listing 6-14.

```sql
CREATE PROCEDURE dbo.SelectSalesPerStateForMonth
    @AsOfDate DATETIME
AS
    BEGIN ;
        DECLARE @SalesForMonth TABLE
        (
            StateCode CHAR(2) ,
            Amount DECIMAL(10, 2)
        ) ;

        INSERT   INTO @SalesForMonth
                 ( Amount ,
                   StateCode
                 )
                 EXEC dbo.SelectSalesForMonth @AsOfDate ;

        SELECT   SUM(Amount) AS TotalSalesForMonth ,
                 StateCode
        FROM     @SalesForMonth
        GROUP BY StateCode
        ORDER BY StateCode ;
    END ;
GO
```

Listing 6-14: The `SelectSalesPerStateForMonth` stored procedure, which reuses the `SelectSalesForMonth` stored procedure and returns total sales per state for the month.

We can run a smoke test to verify that our two stored procedures work.

```
EXEC dbo.SelectSalesForMonth @AsOfDate = '20091002' ;
EXEC dbo.SelectSalesPerStateForMonth @AsOfDate = '20091002' ;
```

Listing 6-15: Testing the new stored procedures.

So far so good; we have reused the code wrapped in `SelectSalesForMonth` procedure and it works. However, now suppose we want to select the state with the highest total sales for a given month. It looks as if we can simply reuse the `SelectSalesPerState-ForMonth` procedure, again with a slight modification to create a table variable or a temporary table, as shown in Listing 6-16.

```
CREATE PROCEDURE dbo.SelectStateWithBestSalesForMonth
  @AsOfDate DATETIME
AS
  BEGIN ;
    DECLARE @SalesForMonth TABLE
      (
        TotalSales DECIMAL(10, 2) ,
        StateCode CHAR(2)
      ) ;

    INSERT  INTO @SalesForMonth
            ( TotalSales ,
              StateCode
            )
            EXEC dbo.SelectSalesPerStateForMonth @AsOfDate ;

    SELECT TOP (1)
            TotalSales ,
            StateCode
    FROM    @SalesForMonth
    ORDER BY TotalSales DESC ;
  END ;
```

Listing 6-16: Reusing `SelectSalesPerStateForMonth` procedure to get the state with most sales.

Unfortunately, although the procedure creates, it does not work.

```
EXEC dbo.SelectStateWithBestSalesForMonth
  @AsOfDate = '20091002' ;
```

```
Msg 8164, Level 16, State 1, Procedure SelectSalesPerStateForMonth, Line 10
An INSERT EXEC statement cannot be nested.
```

Listing 6-17: An `INSERT...EXEC` statement cannot be nested. Note that the exact error message may vary depending on the version of your SQL Server.

Unfortunately, the `INSERT...EXEC` approach that we used in `SelectSalesPerState-ForMonth` procedure cannot be nested. This is a very serious limitation.

The two inline UDFs shown in Listing 6-18 implement the same requirements. Note that the `TotalSalesPerStateForMonth` function implements the same functionality as our previous `SelectTotalSalesPerStateForMonth` stored procedure.

As per our rules of code reuse, we would only ever implement one or the other, not both, in our solutions.

```
CREATE FUNCTION dbo.TotalSalesPerStateForMonth
  ( @AsOfDate DATETIME )
RETURNS TABLE
AS
RETURN
  ( SELECT   StateCode ,
             SUM(Amount) AS TotalSales
    FROM     dbo.SalesPerStateForMonth(@AsOfDate)
    GROUP BY StateCode
  ) ;
GO

CREATE FUNCTION dbo.StateWithBestSalesForMonth
  ( @AsOfDate DATETIME )
```

185

```
RETURNS TABLE
AS
RETURN
  ( SELECT TOP (1)
          StateCode ,
          TotalSales
    FROM    dbo.TotalSalesPerStateForMonth(@AsOfDate)
    ORDER BY TotalSales DESC
  ) ;
```

Listing 6-18: Implementing the same functionality via inline UDFs.

In contrast to what we saw in Listing 6-17, our attempt to reuse result sets returned from nested inline UDFs works just fine.

```
SELECT * FROM dbo.TotalSalesPerStateForMonth ( '20091002' ) ;
SELECT * FROM dbo.StateWithBestSalesForMonth ( '20091002' ) ;
```

```
StateCode TotalSales
--------- -------------------------------------
CA        140010000.00
OR        28002000.00

(2 row(s) affected)

StateCode TotalSales
--------- -------------------------------------
CA        140010000.00

(1 row(s) affected)
```

Listing 6-19: Testing the inline UDFs.

It is often easier to reuse code when it is wrapped in inline UDFs than when it is wrapped in stored procedures. I should emphasize that I refer only to inline UDFs, not to all three varieties of UDF.

Whenever we are deciding whether to use stored procedures or UDFs, we also need to consider the following:

- `INSERT EXEC` requires you to create a table variable or temporary table before doing the call; stored procedures can have multiple and/or varying result sets, depending on code path, causing all kinds of problems with `INSERT EXEC`

- some functionality, such as data modifications and `TRY...CATCH` blocks, is not allowed in UDFs

- the inline UDF, like a view, is expanded in the execution plan, giving the optimizer the choice to take shortcuts, or even remove joined tables if their columns are not used.

Let's discuss performance considerations and see why it might not be a good idea to use scalar UDFs.

Scalar UDFs and Performance

Hopefully, the examples so far have demonstrated that laying out code in simple reusable modules can simplify maintenance, and reduce the chance of bugs when requirements change.

Although it is clearly vital to write correct, robust code, we must not ignore the issue of performance. The reason is simple: careless code reuse can seriously hurt performance. For example, in some cases scalar UDFs may perform very poorly, and I will provide an example that demonstrates this, for SQL Server 2005 and 2008. Of course, in future versions of SQL Server the relative performance of the different flavors of UDFs may change, so it's essential that you always benchmark the performance impact of code refactoring, and rerun these benchmarks when you upgrade to a new SQL Server version.

For this example, we'll need to create a test table with a reasonable number of rows, so let's first set up a 128K-row helper table, Numbers, as shown in Listing 6-20, which we can use to populate the test table.

These helper tables are a must-have in database development and if you already have your own version that suits the same purpose, then feel free to use that instead.

```
CREATE TABLE dbo.Numbers
  (
    n INT NOT NULL ,
    CONSTRAINT PK_Numbers PRIMARY KEY ( n )
  ) ;
GO
DECLARE @i INT ;
SET @i = 1 ;
INSERT  INTO dbo.Numbers
          ( n )
VALUES  ( 1 ) ;
WHILE @i < 100000
  BEGIN ;
    INSERT  INTO dbo.Numbers
              ( n )
            SELECT  @i + n
            FROM    dbo.Numbers ;
    SET @i = @i * 2 ;
  END ;
```

Listing 6-20: Creating and populating the Numbers helper table.

Next, in Listing 6-21, we create the sample Packages table and populate it using our Numbers helper table.

```
CREATE TABLE dbo.Packages
  (
    PackageID INT NOT NULL ,
    WeightInPounds DECIMAL(5, 2) NOT NULL ,
    CONSTRAINT PK_Packages PRIMARY KEY ( PackageID )
  ) ;
 GO

INSERT  INTO dbo.Packages
        ( PackageID ,
          WeightInPounds
        )
        SELECT  n ,
                1.0 + ( n % 900 ) / 10
        FROM    dbo.Numbers ;
```

Listing 6-21: Create the Packages table and populate it with test data.

Suppose that the cost of shipping for a package is $1 if it weighs less than 5 pounds and $2 if it weighs 5 pounds or more. Listing 6-22 shows how to implement this simple algorithm, both as a scalar and as an inline UDF.

```
CREATE FUNCTION dbo.GetShippingCost
  (
    @WeightInPounds DECIMAL(5, 2)
  )
RETURNS DECIMAL(5, 2)
AS
    BEGIN
      DECLARE @ret DECIMAL(5, 2) ;
      SET @ret = CASE WHEN @WeightInPounds < 5 THEN 1.00
                      ELSE 2.00
                 END ;
      RETURN @ret ;
    END ;
GO

CREATE FUNCTION dbo.GetShippingCost_Inline
  (
    @WeightInPounds DECIMAL(5, 2)
  )
```

```
RETURNS TABLE
AS
RETURN
  ( SELECT  CAST(CASE WHEN @WeightInPounds < 5 THEN 1.00
                      ELSE 2.00
                 END AS DECIMAL(5, 2)) AS ShippingCost
  ) ;
```

Listing 6-22: Calculating the shipping cost using a scalar UDF, `GetShippingCost`, and an inline UDF, `GetShippingCost_Inline`.

Now, we are ready to examine the comparative performance of each function, using the simple benchmark shown in Listing 6-23.

```
SET STATISTICS TIME ON ;
SET NOCOUNT ON ;

PRINT 'Using a scalar UDF' ;
SELECT  SUM(dbo.GetShippingCost(WeightInPounds))
    AS TotalShippingCost
FROM    dbo.Packages ;

PRINT 'Using an inline UDF' ;
SELECT  SUM(s.ShippingCost) AS TotalShippingCost
FROM    dbo.Packages AS p CROSS APPLY
        dbo.GetShippingCost_Inline(p.WeightInPounds) AS s ;

PRINT 'Not using any functions at all' ;
SELECT  SUM(CASE WHEN p.WeightInPounds < 5 THEN 1.00
                 ELSE 2.00
            END) AS TotalShippingCost
FROM    dbo.Packages AS p ;

SET STATISTICS TIME OFF ;
```

Listing 6-23: A simple benchmark to compare the performance of the scalar and inline UDFs vs. the performance of the copy-and-paste approach.

Although both functions implement exactly the same algorithm, the performance is dramatically different. When we run this benchmark on SQL Server 2005 or 2008, the query that uses our scalar UDF runs dramatically slower. Also, in this particular case, the query which uses the inline UDF performs very well, although not as fast as the query that does not use any UDFs at all, as shown in Listing 6-24. Of course, when you run these benchmarks on your system, you may get different results.

```
Using a scalar UDF

...<snip>...

SQL Server Execution Times:
   CPU time = 1531 ms,  elapsed time = 1552 ms.

Using an inline UDF

...<snip>...

SQL Server Execution Times:
   CPU time = 109 ms,  elapsed time = 82 ms.

Not using any functions at all

...<snip>...

  SQL Server Execution Times:
   CPU time = 32 ms,  elapsed time = 52 ms.
```

Listing 6-24: The performance of the query using our scalar UDF is dramatically slower than the performance of other equivalent queries.

I am not saying that using inline UDFs never incurs any performance penalties; blanket statements do not belong in database programming, and we always need to consider the performance of each particular case separately. However, in many cases, inline UDFs perform very well.

Multi-statement Table-valued UDFs

Besides scalar and inline UDFs, there are multi-statement table-valued UDFs. I will not discuss or benchmark them here, because I feel I've already proved the point that we need to consider performance when we refactor code. However, it's worth noting that, in general, while inline UDFs tend to be "performance neutral," scalar and multi-statement ones tend to hurt performance if not used carefully, and should be rigorously tested and benchmarked. Be especially wary of using a multi-statement table-valued UDF in an **APPLY**, since that may force the optimizer to re-execute the UDF for each row in the table the UDF is applied against.

If you are interested in learning about different flavors of UDF, I encourage you to read Books Online and Itzik Ben Gan's T-SQL Programming book (www.amazon.co.uk/Inside-Microsoft-Server-2008-Pro-Developer/dp/0735626022/).

Reusing Business Logic: Stored Procedure, Trigger, Constraint or Index?

There are several ways in which we can choose to implement our business logic. For example, we could use:

- stored procedures

- constraints

- triggers

- unique filtered indexes.

Over the coming sections we'll discuss the sort of situations where each approach may, or may not be appropriate

Use constraints where possible

In many cases, constraints are the easiest and simplest to use. To demonstrate this point, consider the `Teams` table shown in Listing 6-25, with a primary key constraint on the `TeamID` column.

```
CREATE TABLE dbo.Teams
  (
    TeamID INT NOT NULL ,
    Name VARCHAR(50) NOT NULL ,
    CONSTRAINT PK_Teams PRIMARY KEY ( TeamID )
  ) ;
```

Listing 6-25: Creating the `Teams` table.

Since we wish to forbid access to the base tables, teams will be inserted into the table, one at a time, by calling a stored procedure. Our business rule is simple: team names must be unique. So, we need to decide where to implement this business rule. One choice is to enforce it in the stored procedure, as shown in Listing 6-27.

```
CREATE PROCEDURE dbo.InsertTeam
  @TeamID INT ,
  @Name VARCHAR(50)
AS
  BEGIN ;
        -- This is not a fully-functional stored
        -- procedure. Error handling is skipped to keep
        -- the example short.
        -- Also potential race conditions
        -- are not considered in this simple module
    INSERT   INTO dbo.Teams
           ( TeamID ,
             Name
           )
           SELECT   @TeamID ,
                    @Name
```

```
            WHERE    NOT EXISTS ( SELECT *
                                  FROM   dbo.Teams
                                  WHERE  Name = @Name ) ;
        -- we also need to raise an error if we
        -- already have a team with such a name
    END ;
```

Listing 6-26: The `InsertTeam` stored procedure inserts a team, if the team name does not
already exist in the table.

So, we have a stored procedure that enforces our rule, at least in the absence of high
concurrency. However, what happens when we need another stored procedure that
modifies a single row in the `Teams` table, or one that merges a batch of new rows into
that table? We'll need to re-implement this same logic for every stored procedure that
modifies this table. This is a form of copy-and-paste, and is both time consuming and
error prone.

Besides, unless you can guarantee that no applications can run modifications directly
against the `Teams` table, it's likely that your business rule will be bypassed at some point,
and inconsistent data will be introduced.

It is much easier and safer to just create the business rule once, in one place, as a `UNIQUE`
constraint, as shown in Listing 6-27.

```
ALTER TABLE dbo.Teams
  ADD CONSTRAINT UNQ_Teams_Name UNIQUE(Name) ;
```

Listing 6-27: The `UNQ_Teams_Name` constraint enforces the uniqueness of team names.

We can now let the database engine make sure that this business rule is always enforced,
regardless of the module or command that modifies the table.

Turn to triggers when constraints are not practical

As we have seen, constraints are extremely useful in many simple cases. However, our business rules are often more complex, and it is sometimes not possible or not practical to use constraints. To demonstrate this point, let's add one more table, `TeamMembers`, which references the `Teams` table through the `TeamID` column, as shown in Listing 6-28.

```sql
CREATE TABLE dbo.TeamMembers
  (
    TeamMemberID INT NOT NULL ,
    TeamID INT NOT NULL ,
    Name VARCHAR(50) NOT NULL ,
    IsTeamLead CHAR(1) NOT NULL ,
    CONSTRAINT PK_TeamMembers PRIMARY KEY ( TeamMemberID ) ,
    CONSTRAINT FK_TeamMembers_Teams
      FOREIGN KEY ( TeamID ) REFERENCES dbo.Teams ( TeamID ) ,
    CONSTRAINT CHK_TeamMembers_IsTeamLead
      CHECK ( IsTeamLead IN ( 'Y', 'N' ) )
  ) ;
```

Listing 6-28: Creating the `TeamMembers` table.

Suppose that we need to implement the following business rule: no team can have more than two members. Implementing this business rule in a trigger is quite straightforward, as shown in Listing 6-29, and you only have to do it once. It is possible, but much more complex, to implement this rule via constraints.

```sql
CREATE TRIGGER dbo.TeamMembers_TeamSizeLimitTrigger
    ON dbo.TeamMembers
  FOR INSERT, UPDATE
AS
  IF EXISTS ( SELECT  *
              FROM    ( SELECT  TeamID ,
                                TeamMemberID
                        FROM    inserted
                        UNION
```

195

```
                    SELECT    TeamID ,
                              TeamMemberID
                    FROM      dbo.TeamMembers
                    WHERE     TeamID IN ( SELECT    TeamID
                                          FROM      inserted )
                ) AS t
            GROUP BY TeamID
            HAVING   COUNT(*) > 2 )
    BEGIN ;
      RAISERROR('Team size exceeded limit',16, 10) ;
      ROLLBACK TRAN ;
    END ;
```

Listing 6-29: The `TeamMembers_TeamSizeLimitTrigger` trigger ensures that the teams do not exceed the maximum size.

With our business rule implemented in only one place, we can comprehensively test just one object. In order to test this trigger, we need some test data in our parent table, as shown in Listing 6-30.

```
INSERT  INTO dbo.Teams
        ( TeamID ,
          Name
        )
        SELECT  1 ,
                'Red Bulls'
        UNION ALL
        SELECT  2 ,
                'Blue Tigers'
        UNION ALL
        SELECT  3 ,
                'Pink Panthers' ;
```

Listing 6-30: Adding some test data to the `Teams` table.

The script shown in Listing 6-31, verifies that we can successfully add new team members, as long as the teams' sizes do not exceed the limit imposed by our trigger.

```
-- adding team members to new teams
INSERT   INTO dbo.TeamMembers
        ( TeamMemberID ,
          TeamID ,
          Name ,
          IsTeamLead
        )
        SELECT   1 ,
                 1 ,
                 'Jill Hansen' ,
                 'N'
        UNION ALL
        SELECT   2 ,
                 1 ,
                 'Sydney Hobart' ,
                 'N'
        UNION ALL
        SELECT   3 ,
                 2 ,
                 'Hobart Sydney' ,
                 'N' ;

-- add more team members to existing teams
BEGIN TRANSACTION ;
INSERT   INTO dbo.TeamMembers
        ( TeamMemberID ,
          TeamID ,
          Name ,
          IsTeamLead
        )
        SELECT   4 ,
                 2 ,
                 'Lou Larry' ,
                 'N' ;
ROLLBACK TRANSACTION ;
```

Listing 6-31: Testing the _TeamSizeLimitTrigger trigger with valid INSERTs.

The script shown next, in Listing 6-32, verifies that we can successfully transfer team members between teams, as long as the teams' sizes do not exceed the limit.

```
BEGIN TRANSACTION ;
UPDATE   dbo.TeamMembers
SET      TeamID = TeamID + 1 ;
ROLLBACK ;

BEGIN TRANSACTION ;
UPDATE   dbo.TeamMembers
SET      TeamID = 3 - TeamID ;
ROLLBACK ;
```

Listing 6-32: Testing the _TeamSizeLimitTrigger trigger with valid UPDATEs.

So, we've proved that our trigger allows modifications that do not violate our business rules. Now we need to make sure that it does **not** allow modifications that **do** violate our business rules; there are quite a few cases, and we need to verify them all. First of all, Listing 6-33 verifies that we cannot add new team members if the resulting teams' sizes are too big. All the statements in the script must, and do, fail.

```
-- attempt to add too many team members
-- to a team which already has members
INSERT   INTO dbo.TeamMembers
        ( TeamMemberID ,
          TeamID ,
          Name ,
          IsTeamLead
        )
        SELECT  4 ,
                2 ,
                'Calvin Lee' ,
                'N'
        UNION ALL
        SELECT  5 ,
                2 ,
                'Jim Lee' ,
                'N' ;
GO
    -- attempt to add too many team members to an empty team
INSERT   INTO dbo.TeamMembers
        ( TeamMemberID ,
          TeamID ,
```

```
            Name  ,
            IsTeamLead
        )
    SELECT  4 ,
            3 ,
            'Calvin Lee' ,
            'N'
    UNION ALL
    SELECT  5 ,
            3 ,
            'Jim Lee' ,
            'N'
    UNION ALL
    SELECT  6 ,
            3 ,
            'Jake Lee' ,
            'N' ;
```

Listing 6-33: Testing the `_TeamSizeLimitTrigger` trigger with invalid INSERTs.

We must also make sure that we cannot transfer team members if the resulting teams'
sizes are too big, as shown in Listing 6-34. Again, all following statements fail as expected.

```
-- attempt to transfer members from other teams
-- to a team which is full to capacity
UPDATE  dbo.TeamMembers
SET     TeamID = 1
WHERE   TeamMemberID = 3 ;
GO
    -- attempt to transfer too many team members
    -- to a team that is not full yet
UPDATE  dbo.TeamMembers
SET     TeamID = 2
WHERE   TeamMemberID IN ( 1, 2 ) ;
GO
    -- attempt to transfer too many team members
    -- to an empty team
UPDATE  dbo.TeamMembers
SET     TeamID = 3 ;
```

Listing 6-34: Testing the `_TeamSizeLimitTrigger` trigger with invalid UPDATEs.

199

The amount of testing needed to ensure that a trigger works as expected can be quite substantial. However, this is the easiest alternative; if we were to re-implement this business rule in several stored procedures, then the same amount of testing required for the single trigger would be required for each of these procedures, in order to ensure that every one of them implements our business rule correctly.

Unique filtered indexes (SQL Server 2008 only)

Last, but not least, in some cases filtered indexes also allow us to implement business rules. For example, suppose that we need to make sure that each team has at most one team lead. If you are using SQL Server 2008 and upwards, a filtered index can easily implement this business rule, as shown in Listing 6-35. I encourage you to try out this index and see for yourself that it works.

```
CREATE UNIQUE NONCLUSTERED INDEX TeamLeads
ON dbo.TeamMembers(TeamID)
WHERE IsTeamLead='Y' ;
```

Listing 6-35: The TeamLeads filtered index ensures that each team has at most one team lead.

Summary

The aim of this chapter is to prove to you that a copy-and-paste approach to code reuse will lead to multiple, inconsistent versions of the same logic being scattered throughout your code base, and a maintenance nightmare.

It has also demonstrated how common logic can be refactored into a single reusable code unit, in the form of a constraint, stored procedure, trigger, UDF or index. This careful reuse of code will reduce the possibility of bugs, greatly improve the robustness of our code, and substantially ease the process of team development.

Unfortunately, performance considerations may prevent us from reusing our code to the fullest. Yet, with careful benchmarking, we can usually find a nice compromise and develop code that is easy to maintain but still performs well enough.

Specifically, I hope the chapter has taught you the following lessons in code reuse:

- views are useful for simple reuse of non-parameterized queries

- for reuse of parameterized queries, inline UDFs are often preferable to stored procedures

- be wary of performance issues with scalar and multi-statement table-valued UDFs

- if possible, enforce reusable business logic in a simple constraint, or possibly a filtered index in SQL 2008 and upwards

- for more complex logic, triggers often offer the most convenient means of promoting reuse, but they require extensive testing.

Chapter 7: Maintaining a Code Library

The previous chapter took a practical look at how proper code reuse could reduce the number of bugs in our code, and greatly ease the team development process. It considered specific examples of the types of code modules (stored procedures versus UDFs, and so on) that best promote reuse.

The scale of code reuse can vary, from full enterprise utilities, to useful, reusable functions (see, for example, *Inside T-SQL Querying* by Itzik Ben-Gan, where he creates a function, `fn_nums`, which creates a table of numbers, of varying size, which can be used anywhere), to small snippets of code that can be reused inside other modules to standardize the approach to common problems such as error handling.

There are several difficult aspects to building and maintaining a code library. First, you have to create a place to store the information; you need to write the code in such a way that it can be reused, and you have to validate that it's going to do what you need it to do, every time. This chapter will cover a range of ways to generate, test, and share a library of code modules and snippets amongst the development team, covering use of SSMS templates, text editors, wikis and SQL Prompt. Text editors and wikis bring to the table powerful search capabilities, but at the expense of needing to store the code outside of the normal development environment. SSMS templates and SQL Prompt offer the ability to generate, find, and edit your code directly from a query window, which is probably the best mechanism for ensuring code reuse throughout the enterprise.

Coding for Reuse

In this chapter, I'll present several techniques for promoting and managing the use of reusable code snippets and templates, using tools such as SSMS and SQL Prompt. However, before we examine these techniques, it needs to be emphasized that it's not enough to simply have snippets of code; you need to write these snippets so that they can easily be incorporated into your existing code, in such a way that anyone within the organization can, within reason, incorporate the code into almost any query. In order to make sure a script can be reused, and is reused appropriately, we need to understand what exactly that script does and how it's supposed to be used. This means that it needs to be well written and documented, and we need to be confident in the script, so it also needs to be well tested.

If the code is incomplete and undocumented, you're assuming that everyone who uses it has a complete enough understanding of the appropriate use of the code for them to be able to apply it. Many, maybe even most, of your users will have the requisite knowledge, but far too many are unlikely to understand what they're supposed to do with your code. Keep this class of user in mind as you write and document the snippets that you're going to share. If you just think through how each snippet is likely to be used, you can decide if that snippet has been written in such a way that it can be reused.

Code comments

You need to have a defined process for marking any script that you intend for reuse. This will help you identify the script, and it will help you retrieve it, either from systems where it has been applied, or from the storage system you're using to keep it. It must be clear what your script is doing, when it was updated, what version it is, where it's used, how it's used, and so on.

If you provide insufficient information in your code headers, it will make the code very difficult to reuse. Consider, for example, the CATCH block shown in Listing 7-1, which could be used as a generic, default error handler within the code in your company.

```
/*********************
Name: Catch block
Create Date: 1/1/2010
Notes:
*********************/
BEGIN CATCH
    IF @@TRANCOUNT > 0
        BEGIN
            ROLLBACK TRAN ;
        END
    RETURN ERROR_NUMBER() ;
END CATCH
```

Listing 7-1: A poorly documented error-handling snippet.

The code header leaves quite a bit of doubt about this piece of code. It is a CATCH block, but why is it here, and why is it important? Is there a reason you've stored it in your code snippet management system? It's impossible to know. Listing 7-2 makes things clearer.

```
/*********************
Name: Enterprise Default Catch block
Create Date: 1/1/2010
Version: 2005 or greater
Notes: Does simple rollback, used in most procs.
*********************/
BEGIN CATCH
    IF @@TRANCOUNT > 0
        BEGIN
            ROLLBACK TRAN ;
        END
    RETURN ERROR_NUMBER() ;
END CATCH
```

Listing 7-2: A well documented error-handling snippet.

The header is still terse, and contains what might be considered the minimum of necessary information, but at least it now provides enough information for the developer, on seeing this snippet of code for the first time, to know that it's considered to be the default mechanism for dealing with errors within the entire enterprise, and that it's intended to be used in most stored procedures. Granted, that's not exactly explicit instructions on how to put this to work, but at least the developer will no longer be completely in the dark as to why this thing was created and how it's meant to be used.

The issue of code headers is covered in detail by Phil Factor in Chapter 2, where he proposes a detailed "standard" for the information that should, ideally, be included there, such as a summary of its intended use, example usage, details of revisions made, when and by whom, and so on. However, depending on the script or snippet, it's possible that many such notes could be longer than the code itself. If we use source control, then keeping update history in comments may be considered unnecessary, since the source control system will keep a complete history of who, when, and exactly what was changed.

Parameter naming

A major problem with code reuse is the inappropriate naming of the parameters, temp tables, and other objects used by the code snippet. For example, naming your variables @a, @b, @c is likely to cause problems when you incorporate more than one code snippet into a query, and suddenly you're trying to declare variables multiple times with the same name, or using values between code snippets with incorrect data types or values contained within them. Use very specific values for the names. For example, you may have a code snippet, similar to that shown in Listing 7-3, which you want your enterprise to use for handling deadlocks.

```
/***********************
Name: Enterprise Deadlock Catch block
Create Date: 1/1/2010
Version: 2005 or greater
Notes: Retries a set of code a set number of times in the event of a deadlock,
takes into account that an error can be reentrant without resubmitting the code.
***********************/
DECLARE @Retry AS INT,
    @RetryCount AS INT,
    @MaxRetries AS INT
SET @Retry = 1 ;
SET @RetryCount = 0 ;
SET @MaxRetries = 3 ;
WHILE @Retry = 1
    AND @RetryCount <= @MaxRetries
    BEGIN
        SET @Retry = 0 ;
        BEGIN TRY
            BEGIN TRAN
--insert code here
            COMMIT TRAN
        END TRY
        BEGIN CATCH
            IF ERROR_NUMBER() IN (1205, 3960)
                BEGIN
                    IF XACT_STATE() <> 0
                        ROLLBACK ;
                    SET @Retry = 1 ;
                    SET @RetryCount = @RetryCount + 1 ;
                END
            ELSE
                BEGIN
                    IF XACT_STATE() <> 0
                        ROLLBACK ;
                    SELECT  ERROR_NUMBER() AS ErrorNumber,
                            ERROR_MESSAGE() AS ErrorMessage ;
                    RETURN ERROR_NUMBER() ;
                END
        END CATCH
    END
```

Listing 7-3: A code snippet for handling deadlocks.

You can see that the parameters are named specifically to match the intended purpose; hence, we have **@RetryCount** rather than **@Count**, **@RetriesMax** rather than **@Max**. This adds to the clarity of the snippet, and makes it less likely that this it will cause problems when inserted into existing code. Since variable name length doesn't affect performance in any way, having a clearly defined parameter will only help your code.

Unit tests

For each code snippet or template, we need, either to write a complete function, with every bit of code needed to make it run, or to very carefully document the needs of a piece of code, so that the developer using it knows what's expected. This means you either have to take an approach of Test Driven Development, where you build a test first for any given code snippet, or you can simply maintain a test wrapper appropriate for a given script snippet, as demonstrated in Listing 7-4.

```
CREATE PROCEDURE dbo.TestWrapper
AS
BEGIN TRY
BEGIN TRAN
    RAISERROR ('bigerror',17,1)
COMMIT TRAN
END TRY
/***********************
Name: Enterprise Default Catch block
Create Date: 1/1/2010
Version: 2005 or greater
Notes: Does simple rollback, used in most procs.
***********************/
BEGIN CATCH
    IF @@TRANCOUNT > 0
        BEGIN
            ROLLBACK TRAN ;
        END
    RETURN ERROR_NUMBER() ;
END CATCH
GO
```

```
DECLARE @ErrorNumber INT
EXEC @ErrorNumber = TestWrapper;
SELECT @ErrorNumber
/*Should return 50000*/
GO
DROP PROCEDURE dbo.TestWrapper;
GO
```

Listing 7-4: A test wrapper for our error handling snippet.

You can see how the test uses the code, executes the code, and cleans up after itself. The test wrapper is placed inside of a stored procedure, in this case because it uses a return value which needs to be consumed and validated. These tests can be checked into source control and maintained alongside the code snippets they support.

Storing Script Libraries

You need to come up with a system of storage that allows you to keep, find, retrieve, and reuse the scripts that are important to you. You also have to have a mechanism for sharing the files, which could range from something sophisticated (a source control system), to moderately useful (a shared document location on SharePoint), to primitive (passing around files on thumb drives).

When dealing with full-blown utilities and common processes, such as a shared backup script, you'll need to look at setting up common databases, or unique schemas (e.g. "utils"), where these pieces of code are kept, and can be accessed by any developers who need them (and only by those developers).

In the case of the focus of the discussion in this chapter, script and script snippets which are going to be reused over and over within other scripts and other sets of code, this type of sophisticated storage, access, and security is less critical.

Source control

The one constant in development, like life, is change. You're going to have to change the code on occasion. When you do make changes, you're going to want to have a mechanism in place for managing the change, regardless of how you're storing the script samples. This means keeping track of various versions over time, so that you can retrieve previous versions of the code.

As long as the code we're talking about is T-SQL code, then it is most frequently stored as script text files (CLR code will need to be managed like any other .NET code set). This makes most source management systems ideal for storing your reusable scripts and, as discussed in Chapter 3, any of the products, from Microsoft's Team Foundation Services to Open Source Subversion, can manage text files easily.

For your full application, you should have a development and deployment process that completely synchronizes your databases to the T-SQL code in source control, as outlined in Chapters 3 and 4. Likewise, for code libraries, every effort should be made to ensure that the source that each developer draws from is tightly coupled with what's currently in source control. The versioning capabilities of source management systems allow you to apply named labels to the versions, so that you can keep track of the currently approved version. A good source control system will also allow you to create different branches for your code, and so independently maintain different versions of a given code snippet (e.g. for different versions of SQL Server, or for different applications).

A single file or individual files?

The first decision you'll need to make when it comes to storing your script samples is whether to store everything in a single file or as individual files. Storing everything in a single file can seem an attractive option, since you have a single source of information, one file to check into source control, and one file to share with your development team. There, however, the advantages end.

Use of multiple files makes it much easier to develop versions and branches for each individual code snippet and one can modify, add or delete files individually and safely. Using a single file removes much of this flexibility, and modifying a single file makes it likely that you will accidentally change code you didn't mean to change.

I strongly recommend maintaining a library of individual files. You can check them into source control, and then share the directory with the team. You will also find it much easier to work with, and maintain, these individual files in tools such as SSMS or Red Gate SQL Prompt.

Tools for Creating and Managing Code Libraries

It is possible to simply use Notepad or WordPad within Windows, do a search against the code and snippets to find what you need, and then copy and paste. However, that can be a lot of work and there are, fortunately, better and more efficient tools with which to manage your code library. For example:

- SSMS provides templates which allow us to define our own outlines for creating or modifying database objects

- third-party text-editing tools, such as EditPlus have built in snippet management

- wikis, for example TiddlyWiki or WikidPad, allow us to create a searchable database of scripts, although these tools won't work well with source control

- advanced snippet and code management tools, like Red Gate's SQL Prompt, are also available.

Over the coming sections, we'll discuss the benefits and limitations of each of the listed solutions, but there are other options. You could even go so far as to use publicly available online storage engines, such as SNIPPLR, from HTTP://SNIPPLR.COM/.

SQL Server Management Studio

Most DBAs and database developers do the majority of their work in SSMS, which provides templates as the primary mechanism for generating and maintaining code modules. A template is a script fragment, with placeholders for parameter and variables, to which we can subsequently assign suitable values. These templates are best suited to working with complete scripts containing the full set of necessary code, rather than with snippets. You can use Template Explorer to store code snippets, but then, to apply them, you will need to copy and paste them into whatever script you're editing.

SQL Server comes with a very large number of built-in templates that are used by SSMS itself when creating objects, such as stored procedures. If, within Object Explorer, you right-click on **Stored Procedures**, for example, and select **New Stored Procedure...**, the script window that appears, shown in Listing 7-5, is derived from a template. We can modify these template files in order to have them behave in the manner required for our environment.

```
-- =============================================
-- Template generated from Template Explorer using:
-- Create Procedure (New Menu).SQL
--
-- Use the Specify Values for Template Parameters
-- command (Ctrl-Shift-M) to fill in the parameter
-- values below.
--
-- This block of comments will not be included in
-- the definition of the procedure.
-- =============================================
SET ANSI_NULLS ON
GO
SET QUOTED_IDENTIFIER ON
GO
-- =============================================
-- Author:      <Author,,Name>
-- Create date: <Create Date,,>
-- Description: <Description,,>
```

```
-- -- ===================================================
CREATE PROCEDURE <Procedure_Name, sysname, ProcedureName>
    -- -- Add the parameters for the stored procedure here.
    <@Param1, sysname, @p1> <Datatype_For_Param1, , int> = <Default_Value_For_
Param1, , 0>,
    <@Param2, sysname, @p2> <Datatype_For_Param2, , int> = <Default_Value_For_
Param2, , 0>
AS
BEGIN
    -- -- SET NOCOUNT ON added to prevent extra result sets from
    -- -- interfering with SELECT statements.
    SET NOCOUNT ON;
    -- -- Insert statements for procedure here.
    SELECT <@Param1, sysname, @p1>, <@Param2, sysname, @p2>
END
GO
```

Listing 7-5:   An SSMS template for creating a stored procedure.

One of the most powerful features of templates, as shown by the comments in the header block, is parameter value assignment. With the template open, just hit CTRL+SHIFT+M to open the **Specify Values for Template Parameters** window, as in Figure 7-1.

Parameter	Type	Value
Author		Name
Create Date		
Description		
Procedure_Name	sysname	ProcedureName
@Param1	sysname	@p1
Datatype_For_Param1		int
Default_Value_For_P...		0
@Param2	sysname	@p2
Datatype_For_Param2		int
Default_Value_For_P...		0

Figure 7-1:   Template Parameters selection.

213

We can fill in the appropriate parameter values in the window, and they will automatically be moved into the correct locations within the template. The resulting stored procedure will look something like that shown in Listing 7-6 (I omit the standard template header from here in).

```
SET ANSI_NULLS ON
GO
SET QUOTED_IDENTIFIER ON
GO
-- =====================================================
-- Author:      Grant Fritchey
-- Create date: 11/15/2009
-- Description: Retrieve customer info
-- =====================================================
CREATE PROCEDURE sprCustomerInfo
    -- Add the parameters for the stored procedure here.
    @CustomerId INT = 0 ,
    @Region NVARCHAR(15) = 'N/A'
AS
    BEGIN
    -- SET NOCOUNT ON added to prevent extra result sets from
    -- interfering with SELECT statements.
        SET NOCOUNT ON ;
    -- Insert statements for procedure here.
        SELECT  @CustomerId ,
                @Region
    END
GO
```

Listing 7-6: A `sprCustomerInfo` stored procedure, created from the SSMS template.

Of course, there are limitations to this. What if you don't want two parameters, or what if you want eight? You're not about to edit the parameters in the template and then open the parameter-editing window to fill in the values. It's much easier, in that situation, just to type the inputs as you define the parameters themselves.

In any event, for this example, you can see that a lot of the details have been filled in so that the procedure now has a name, the comment header is filled in with pertinent information, and the two parameters are set up with real names and data types that are correct for the given application. However, notice that the comment headers are of a different format to the "standard" we defined earlier (see Listing 7-2). Let's assume that we want to take the comment header and our default `TRY...CATCH` statement for error trapping, from Listing 7-2, and add it to the template that is used to create stored procedures, so that our own custom header and error handling will appear in every stored procedure that is created using this template.

Fortunately, SSMS provides a means to modify existing templates to meet such requirements. To get started, open the Template Explorer window by clicking on the **View** menu and select the **Template Explorer** menu item. The Template Explorer, by default a docked window on the right side of the screen, shows a series of folders representing all the different types of objects and processes that can be created through T-SQL templates, within SSMS. Scroll down to the **Stored Procedure** folder and expand it, and you'll be presented with the list of template scripts that relate to the creation of different types of stored procedures, and their modification or removal, as shown in Figure 7-2.

Figure 7-2: Stored Procedure folder in Template Explorer.

As this indicates, in order to consistently implement your own custom templates in SSMS you may have to modify quite a large number of scripts. Before you make these changes, it's imperative that you back up the original templates or, better still, put them into source control, so that you can maintain multiple versions of the templates over time, and roll back to the originals with little or no effort. The template files are stored in your documents folder at `\AppData\Roaming\Microsoft\Microsoft SQL Server\100\ Tools\Shell\Templates\Sql.`

Place these files under source control, then you can make changes and additions. Also, once you've got them into source control, and you do make changes, you can share those changes with others on the development and administration team, so that everyone is working from the most recent version of the template. Of course, if you have multiple versions of SQL Server running, or different settings, make sure the code is tested and works in all environments, before sharing it, or keep the code in version-specific branches.

To modify the standard template for creating new stored procedures so that it incorporates our custom header styles and error handling, right-click on the **Create Stored Procedure (New Menu)** template and select **Edit** from the pop-up menu. From there, you can edit the template so that it looks something like that shown in Listing 7-7.

```
CREATE PROCEDURE <Procedure_Name, sysname, ProcedureName>
   -  - Add the parameters for the stored procedure here.
    <@Param1, sysname, @p1> <Datatype_For_Param1, , int> = <Default_Value_For_
Param1, , 0>,
    <@Param2, sysname, @p2> <Datatype_For_Param2, , int> = <Default_Value_For_
Param2, , 0>
AS
/* ********************
Name: <Procedure_Name,,>
Created By: <Created By,,Name>
Created Date: <Created Date,,>
Update By:
Update Date:
Purpose:
Notes:
********************* */
BEGIN TRY
   SET NOCOUNT ON;
   -  - Insert statements for procedure here.
   SELECT <@Param1, sysname, @p1>, <@Param2, sysname, @p2>
   RETURN 0;
END TRY
```

```
BEGIN CATCH
    IF @@TRANCOUNT > 0
    BEGIN
        ROLLBACK TRANSACTION
    END
    RETURN ERROR_NUMBER();
END CATCH
GO
```

Listing 7-7: A customized stored procedure template.

The key thing to remember, when customizing templates, is to follow strictly the format for creating template parameters, namely <parameter, data type, default value>. You're not required to supply either the data type or the default value, but the parameter name must be identical everywhere it is referenced, or you'll simply create a new parameter. Notice, in Listing 7-7, that Procedure_Name is referenced more than once in the template definition.

If you save these changes, the default template will be overwritten to reflect the standards you are attempting to implement within your enterprise. The modified template still retains the functionality of the standard templates; CTRL+SHIFT+M still works and you can fill in the parameter values as described earlier.

Just as you can edit existing templates, you can also create multiple new templates for use within your system, storing them all within the Template Explorer, alongside the system templates. Again, you just need to be sure that you keep a backup of the system templates, and check all the templates into source control so that you can maintain versions and a known change history.

While templates work well as a code generation and sharing mechanism for object creation scripts, you'll also need to create and maintain smaller snippets of code, such as the error handling routine shown earlier and templates are not best suited for this. To maintain a listing of partial code snippets for reuse in multiple scripts, another mechanism is needed. One possibility is to use one of the advanced text editors, such as EditPlus.

Text editors

Since T-SQL code is just text, a primitive way of maintaining a code library would be simply to store all your snippets in a text file. The relevant snippet could be retrieved by a search on its assigned name, and then copied and pasted into your SQL code. This is a very labor-intensive and error-prone approach, so if you do go down this route, it's at least worth investing in a decent text editor that will provide some mechanism for managing the process.

Many modern text editors have built-in mechanisms for maintaining code snippets. For example, EditPlus, one of the better-known shareware text editors, provides the **cliptext** feature which allows us to create and store our own library of code snippets. It works like the clipboard in Office, but has persistence to permanent storage. The library is stored as a file and so can be edited directly and, more importantly, can be checked into source control, in order to maintain different versions of the file, and to share it with other developers and DBAs within the organization.

Testing such a file is more challenging. As was suggested earlier, individual files can be validated using individual, customized tests. A large single file, possibly containing a mix of snippets as well as full templates, will require a fairly sophisticated testing mechanism. It might help to add, to the comment header section for each piece of code, a description of the test for that code, although this still makes automated testing difficult.

To create a new cliptext library, simply navigate to the **cliptext** window, on the left side of the EditPlus screen, right-click on the drop down and select **New**.

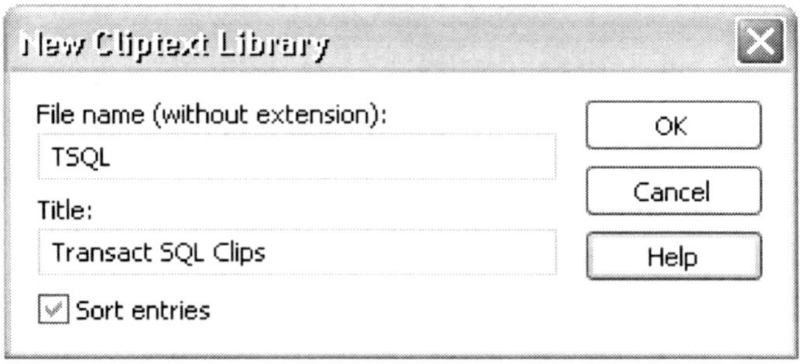

Figure 7-3:   The "New Cliptext Library" window.

This will create a new entry on the cliptext dropdown menu, called "Transact SQL Clips." Click on it and you'll see that the list of selections is empty, but we can now start adding useful snippets of code that are likely to be needed in numerous places within your development project. One such example, shown in Listing 7-8, is the classic table of numbers, or tally table. It's used in all sorts of ways to manipulate data in an efficient manner within T-SQL. Usually it's a better design to simply create a physical tally table, but that's not always possible, so this small, temporary tally table may still come in handy.

```
SELECT TOP 10000
        IDENTITY( INT,1,1 ) AS n
INTO    #Nums
FROM    master.dbo.syscolumns sc1
        CROSS JOIN master.dbo.syscolumns sc2 ;
```

Listing 7-8:   A simple tally table.

To get this code snippet into our **Transact SQL Clips** library, return to the library, right-click inside the empty space and select **Add** from the menu to open the **Add Cliptext Item** window. Then simply add a meaningful title (e.g. "Tally Table") and then type or copy Listing 7-8 into the **Text body** box. Once you've clicked the **OK** button, the snippet will be saved to your cliptext library and available for use the next time you're working on a script in EditPlus. You can drag and drop the entries from the cliptext library into a

T-SQL script or you can double-click on the required snippet. The code is stored in the library "as is," with all formatting, indentation, capitalization, and so on, retained.

Although, in this manner, you can enable a very basic shareable code library, there are many limitations. One big problem with using the cliptext feature, or any similar function in another text-editing tool, is that you're not working within SSMS. So, while you can store reusable code snippets, and you get an editor package that is much more sophisticated than the one that comes with SSMS, you are always working offline, without a connection to a database. You can modify and save files, but you can't perform proper syntax checks (beyond some basic syntax checking supplied through some of these tools). This means that you either have to do all the editing with your text-editing software, and then save the files or copy the code into SSMS, or you have to generate the code snippets within an empty window in the text editor, and then copy and paste the snippet into your code within SSMS. Either way, it's an error-prone, multi-step process.

Furthermore, organization and searching of the scripts is primitive. Only a single list is provided, and the only way to find the required snippet is by its name; there is no key word search or any other type of functionality. The testing of a giant file like this is also difficult to set up, maintain, and automate. Overall, it's a very limited approach and use of a wiki might provide better mechanisms for finding the code you want to use.

Wikis

A wiki is a semi-structured data storage engine, designed to make the storage and retrieval of information as quick and simple as possible. Use of a local wiki, such as the open source WikidPad (HTTP://WIKIDPAD.SOURCEFORGE.NET/), can offer some benefits in terms of organizing and managing your code library.

A wiki will store the files in a searchable tree, allowing you to create the various folders or levels you need to store the code snippets in an organized fashion. With the addition of comment headers to the code, you can define sets of key words to associate with various snippets, which can then be used in searches against the code snippets.

Figure 7-4 shows a basic wiki tree that I created in order to demonstrate some of functionality available for managing code snippets. It consists of basic wiki words that represent either classifications, such as "Statistics and Indexes," or specific definitions for code snippets, such as "Tally Table." For help setting up a basic wiki, please see the previous link, or the equivalent for your wiki of choice.

Figure 7-4: Basic wiki tree structure.

Notice how I've used names that work well as identifying keywords, and that can be quickly searched on within the wiki. Notice, also, that I've created separate "branches" for stored procedure scripts, and statistics and indexes scripts.

Searching in a wiki is far more powerful than with EditPlus, or even SSMS. For example, consider a search on the phrase "error handling," as shown in Figure 7-5.

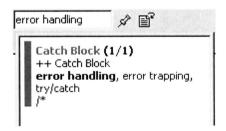

Figure 7-5: Search results in WikidPad.

The search returns one instance of the phrase, found within the **CATCH** block code snippet, which is shown in Listing 7-9.

```
Catch Block
error handling, error trapping, try/catch
/* *******
Name: Enterprise Default Catch block
Create Date: 1/1/2010
Notes: Does simple rollback, use in most procs
******* */
BEGIN CATCH
IF @@TRANCOUNT > 0
BEGIN
ROLLBACK TRAN ;
END
RETURN ERROR_NUMBER() ;
END CATCH
```

Listing 7-9: The **CATCH** block code snippet, as stored in the wiki.

At the top of the listing is the definition, `Catch block`, used by WikidPad to make wiki words. This is followed by a series of word phrases (keywords) that I added to facilitate searching. In this example, I entered the keywords separately from the comment header, but I could just as easily have added them to the comment block.

Having retrieved the required snippet, we can copy and paste it into a script in SSMS, taking care to omit the key words and wiki words. In this instance, because the code is just a snippet, I probably wouldn't even want to copy the comments into the procedure where I'm applying the snippet.

A wiki is a very sophisticated storage engine and you don't need to treat it as if it were only a text field. Figure 7-6 highlights the complex search features, including regex-based searching, which can be put to work within a well-constructed wiki.

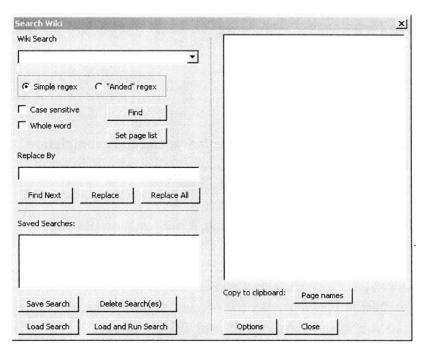

Figure 7-6: Full search capacity of WikidPad.

You can even take advantage of various formatting options, for example, to change the color of the text, or add icons, to make your code snippets easier to browse.

The other feature of a wiki that is very useful, when maintaining a code library, is the built-in change history. This may negate the need to include the wiki in a source control system, although the sophisticated versioning, labeling, and branching that a good source control system provides might not be available in a wiki.

While there is a lot of good functionality provided by a wiki, for managing the code snippets, it still suffers from the weaknesses associated with storing the code outside of SSMS. You still need to copy and paste, in order to put the code to work within your queries. If you do any editing within the wiki, there is no syntax checking. In short, you're working outside of the querying environment. You'll also be hard-pressed to set up testing for a wiki, because the storage format is so different from the usual simple files, so automated testing will also require a lot more work.

SQL Prompt

Red Gate SQL Prompt is an add-on for SSMS which provides advanced code completion functionality along with various code refactoring capabilities, as well as a built-in set of Prompt snippets that can be incorporated into your scripts on the fly.

When SQL Prompt is installed and running on your machine, it puts an icon in your system tray to indicate that it is monitoring activity within T-SQL windows in SSMS and in Visual Studio. It keeps track of the database to which you're currently connected and, in real time, loads each database's objects into its own management area. As you type, it provides keyword completion, and attempts to predict the objects, tables, views, columns, stored procedures, and so on, that you want to use within your T-SQL queries.

Prompt comes with a set of built-in snippets that can be accessed from within an SSMS code window via the appropriate string. For example, if you wish to create a new table in the database, type **ct** in a code window. By default, SQL Prompt will display a list of suggestions, which will include available snippets, along with a second code window, displaying the snippet that will be inserted. This allows you to review the snippet before inserting it into your query. If you type **ct** and then hit the **Tab** key, the `CREATE TABLE` snippet will automatically be added to your code, as shown in Listing 7-10.

```
CREATE TABLE
(
    - - column_name data_type,...
)
```

Listing 7-10: The **ct** (`CREATE TABLE`) snippet.

Other simple examples include typing **w2** to insert the `EXEC sp_who2` snippet, or **mro** to find out the twenty most recently-created objects in the database, as shown in Listing 7-11.

```
SELECT TOP 20 [name], [type], crdate
FROM sysobjects
ORDER BY crdate DESC
```

Listing 7-11: The **mro** (most recent objects) snippet.

These simple examples aren't so much about building code libraries as about faster typing. However, a few of the more sophisticated built-in snippets hint at what's possible. Try, for example, typing **curff** to bring up a snippet that sets up everything you need to create a fast forward cursor, one of the most efficient ways to perform an inefficient operation!

```
DECLARE /* variables */
DECLARE   CURSOR FAST_FORWARD READ_ONLY FOR
/* SELECT statement */
OPEN /* cursor name */
FETCH NEXT FROM /* cursor name */ INTO /* variables */
WHILE @@FETCH_STATUS = 0
BEGIN
/* cursor logic */
FETCH NEXT FROM /* cursor name */ INTO /* variables */
END
CLOSE /* cursor name */
DEALLOCATE /* cursor name */
```

Listing 7-12: The **curff** (CURSOR FAST_FORWARD) snippet.

Despite my grave reservations about the use of cursors, this example does demonstrate how quickly you can lay down the framework for creating and using such an object, including declaration of the variables and the object itself. You may have noticed that, when the snippet was inserted, the cursor was ready and flashing at exactly the point where you needed to enter the object name; more on this shortly.

Creating custom snippets is easy; simply highlight the code you wish to define as a snippet, and then right-click and select **Create Snippet....** In this way, we can define Prompt snippets for the code to create tally tables, and any other piece of code we're likely to need to reuse. For example, let's say that we want to turn into a snippet the query shown in Listing 7-13, which gets the actual definition of all the views, procedures, and functions from the `sys.sql_modules` catalog view.

```
--find the actual code for a particular stored procedure, view, function, etc.
SELECT   OBJECT_NAME(object_ID), definition
FROM     sys.sql_modules
WHERE    OBJECT_NAME(object_ID) = 'MyObjectName'
```

Listing 7-13: Returning object definitions from `sys.sql_modules`.

Sadly, it is impossible to get the build script for tables, along with all its associated objects, columns and indexes, so easily. It isn't stored as such, though it is available via the Object Browser. If you want to get it via code, it has to be generated using SMO.

In the process of creating our snippet, we can highlight another powerful feature of SQL Prompt by replacing `MyObjectName` with the special code word, `$CURSOR$` (uppercase only). Having done this, highlight the code and let's create our snippet, as shown in Figure 7-7.

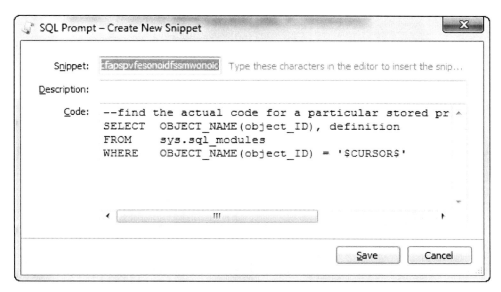

Figure 7-7:   Creating a new snippet in SQL Prompt.

The **Create New Snippet** dialog box is displayed, so that you can enter the snippet name and descriptive text. Notice that a default snippet name is created automatically from the initial letters of the selected text. Give the snippet a more sensible identifying string (such as **fod**, for "find object definition") and a description, and hit Save. Now, if you type **fod** into a code window and hit Tab, the snippet will be automatically inserted, with the cursor placed at the place denoted by $CURSOR$, where you can type in the object name. Note that the $CURSOR$ code word is supported in SSMS templates too, so you can combine the advantages of the template parameters and the cursor placement from SQL Prompt in a single script.

In order to edit an existing snippet, select Snippet Manager from the SQL Prompt menu to bring up the Snippet Manager window, as shown in Figure 7-8.

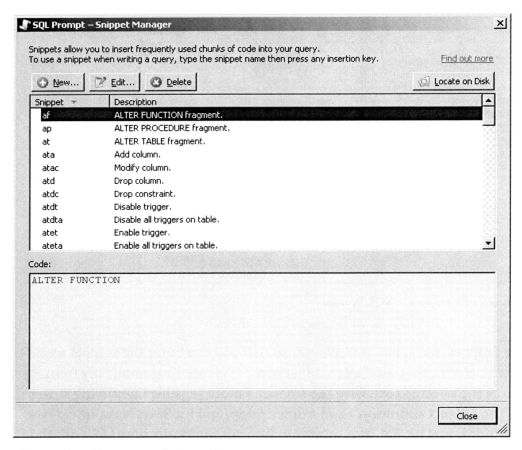

Figure 7-8:   SQL Prompt Snippet Manager.

Clicking the **Edit** button will allow you to change the snippet, the description, and the code. Deleting a snippet deletes the file that stored the snippet. While the description on snippets can't be searched, you can browse the snippets in the Snippet Manager.

The snippets are stored in individual files, located by default at the install directory: `C:\ Documents and Settings\<your user name>\Local Settings\Application Data\Red Gate\SQL Prompt 4\Snippets`. These files can be checked into source control so that they can be versioned and maintained as part of a team environment. Finally, with the snippets individually stored, it's quite easy to create automated tests.

Summary

While you could attempt to manage your code from a text file, and use copy and paste as a means to reuse the code and maintain your library, this can lead to a code base containing lots of subtly different modules that all do more or less the same thing. This then becomes a maintenance nightmare, as you need to make sure that any change to the logic is represented in every single one of those modules.

Code reuse is very difficult to achieve unless you take the time to carefully document your code so that other developers can understand what the code is supposed to do. You will need to treat even small snippets of code just like a fully-fledged application, checking the snippets into source control, and running them through an automated testing routine.

SQL Server Management Studio provides some mechanisms to help you reuse some types of code. It even supplies some mechanisms that allow you to create a code library. Third-party tools, like Red Gate SQL Prompt, can provide even more capabilities to put together very extensive libraries of code that you can apply as needed within your projects.

The point is, a little bit of work up front can save you lots of work later. In addition, it makes your code easier to read and easier to maintain, because you'll be working with familiar material on a regular basis instead of having to divine the intent of the original coders. Creating a library of forms, utilities, and code snippets is not a major formalized process like building a web service. However, many of the same disciplines applied to code reuse can be applied to the building of a code library.

Chapter 8: Exploring your Database Schema

Pretty quickly, if you are doing any serious database development, you will want to know more about a database than SSMS can tell you; there are just more things you might need to know than any one GUI can provide efficiently. There are a number of reasons why you might want to search through your object metadata and data definition language (DDL). For example, if you are doing a review of a development database, there are a number of facts you'll need to establish regarding the database, its tables, keys and indexes, in order to home in on any possible problem areas. Likewise, if you are refactoring or maintaining an existing database that was written by someone else, then you will quickly find that searching through the schema, click by click, using the SSMS Object Explorer, is not really a viable option.

For high-speed searching of your schemas, you need a dedicated tool, or a set of your own search scripts, and most probably both. Fortunately, SQL Server provides any number of ways to get at the metadata you need. The `INFORMATION_SCHEMA` views provide basic metadata about the objects in each database. The far more expansive catalog views offer just about every piece of object metadata that SQL Server currently exposes to the user.

This chapter provides various scripts for interrogating these views to get all sorts of useful information about your database that you would otherwise have to obtain slowly, click by wretched click, from the sluggish SSMS Object browser. Once you've built up your own snippet or template library, you'll find it very easy to access your databases' metadata using SQL Code.

In this chapter, we'll focus on high-level object searches, showing how to use these catalog views and `INFORMATION_SCHEMA` views system to:

- **search the metadata of schema-scoped objects**, to obtain high-level information about the objects in your schema that will help you troubleshoot problems such as: Which tables lack primary keys or indexes? Which objects are owned by whom? And so on.
- **track down object dependencies**. This is vital when, for example, renaming an object.

In the next chapter, we'll step down a level and demonstrate some real magic, showing the code required to enable us to select a database object within a query pane and instantly return the build script for that object, complete with documentation. We'll also see how to search within your DDL and build scripts to find instances of a specific string.

Building a Snippet Library

If you are weaning yourself off dependency on the object browser of SQL Server Management Studio, you'll need a clip library of handy routines instead, which can be shared around the team. It is impossible to keep all the information in your head. I have a range of snippets, recipes, and templates of SQL calls to get the information I want, many of which I present in this chapter. The queries you use for ad hoc work, such as "which index covers this column?" are best put into SSMS templates and dragged/ dropped onto your workspace, or stored as some form of snippet, using SQL Prompt or something like AceText. Typing them out laboriously is not really an option. You can, of course, use a stored procedure if you want to do a general search, or run a utility that queries via ODBC.

How to build and maintain a snippet library, with a tool such as SQL Prompt, is covered in detail in Chapter 7.

Interrogating Information Schema and Catalog Views

Codd's fifth rule (No. 4) of what comprises a relational database states that there must be an active online, inline, relational catalog that is accessible to authorized users by means of their regular query language. This means that users must be able to access the database's structure (catalog) using the same query language that they use to access the database's data, in other words, SQL. And, no, XQuery isn't allowed by Codd's rule.

The `INFORMATION_SCHEMA` views provide a standard means by which to view this metadata for any SQL-based relational databases and, indeed, these views are implemented in SQL Server to comply with the ISO standard. Unfortunately, the standard doesn't cover all the features in a SQL Server database, which means that if you are interested in anything out of the ordinary, such as triggers or extended properties, then you'll be disappointed. The other major drawback, when searching the DDL (covered in Chapter 9), is that the views only return the first 4,000 characters of the definition of an object.

To make up for this and other shortfalls, Sybase and SQL Server always provided the system tables to provide all the information that was required of a database's structure. The system catalog views, and metadata functions, introduced in SQL Server 2005, provide a more efficient and concise way of doing this, even if one loses a bit of the feel for the underlying structure. There are many more views than actual system tables and Microsoft has been assiduous in providing simple ways of getting the metadata that you want.

Before SQL Server 2005, you could see all metadata for all objects in a database, even if you were just assigned the public role. This meant that any user logged on to an instance of SQL Server 2000 or earlier could view metadata for every object in the server, even those objects on which that user had been assigned no rights. In SQL Server 2005 and later, the visibility of metadata is limited to securables that a user either owns, or on which the user has been granted some permission to view. You cannot directly specify whether indexes, check constraints and triggers are visible. If a user has been granted some permission on a table then, by implication, that user can also view the metadata for all the table's subcomponents, such as columns, indexes, check constraints, and triggers. If the user requests information that he has no permission to see, then a NULL is returned.

You can mix the Information Schema views, with the catalog views and their associated metadata functions. To return the entire definition of a routine, for example, you can use the metadata function, Object_Definition(), which is not part of the Information_Schema standard, as shown in Listing 8-1.

```sql
SELECT   full_name ,
         OBJECT_DEFINITION(OBJECT_ID(full_name))
FROM     ( SELECT    Routine_SCHEMA + '.' + routine_name AS Full_Name
           FROM      information_schema.routines
         ) routines
WHERE    full_name LIKE 'MyObjectName'
```

Listing 8-1: Retrieving object definitions from the INFORMATION_SCHEMA views.

This query won't return information about "non-standard" objects such as triggers, but it will also miss views (although you can get this information from information_schema. views). As such, there seems little point in such a query, as the one shown in Listing 8-2, using the catalog views, will give the same information and also provides information about triggers, views, and so on.

```sql
--find the actual code for a particular stored procedure, view, function etc.
SELECT   OBJECT_NAME(object_ID), definition
FROM     sys.sql_modules
WHERE    OBJECT_NAME(object_ID) = 'MyObjectName'
```

Listing 8-2: Retrieving object definitions from the system catalog views.

Searching Structural Metadata in Schema-scoped Objects within a Database

If you are used to glancing at, or clicking away at, the Object Explorer or using SQL Prompt, then you are probably scanning parts of the metadata. As noted, most searching goes on when refactoring or maintaining an existing database. An especially irksome task is renaming a view, table or column. A dependency tracker will find the dependent objects but will, even if working perfectly, miss anything that is in dynamic code, embedded in strings. You may think that code only lurks in stored procedures or functions. Oh, no! What about constraints, computed columns, defaults, rules, triggers or views? What of code in a CLR that accesses a database table? Code appears in a lot of places. Even if you are familiar with the database, it is easy, for example, to forget about a trigger on a table, misspell a column name or overlook an index. For high-speed programming, the "point, click-and-curse" technique isn't really an option.

Using the catalog views along with a metadata function called `OBJECTPROPERTY`, we can find out the intimate details of any schema-scoped objects in the current database. Details of all schema-scoped objects are stored in the `sys.objects` catalog view, from which other views such as `sys.foreign_keys`, `sys.check_constraints`, `sys.tables`, and `sys.views` inherit. These additional views have added information that is specific to the particular type of object. There are database entities that are not classed as objects. Columns, indexes, and parameters to routines, for example, aren't classed by SQL Server as objects. This isn't a problem since they are only meaningful within the context of the database objects they belong to. You'd view them along with the object.

The `OBJECTPROPERTY` function cannot be used for objects that are not schema-scoped, such as DDL triggers and event notifications. You'd need to get the relevant information from the appropriate columns within the view (`sys.server_triggers` and `sys.server_event_notifications` in the examples that follow).

Tables with no primary keys

You'll want to know if there are tables without primary keys, and why. Listing 8-3 provides a way of getting that information from the INFORMATION_SCHEMA.tables view.

```
--Which of my tables don't have primary keys?
SELECT — -we'll do it via information_schema
        TheTables.Table_Catalog + '.' + TheTables.Table_Schema + '.'
        + TheTables.Table_Name AS [tables without primary keys]
FROM    information_schema.tables TheTables
        LEFT OUTER JOIN information_schema.table_constraints TheConstraints
          ON TheTables.table_schema = TheConstraints.table_schema
             AND TheTables.table_name = TheConstraints.table_name
             AND constraint_type = 'PRIMARY KEY'
WHERE   table_Type = 'BASE TABLE'
        AND constraint_name IS NULL
ORDER BY [tables without primary keys]
```

Listing 8-3: Finding tables with no primary key using an INFORMATION_SCHEMA view.

	tables without primary keys
1	ReportServer.dbo.Batch
2	ReportServer.dbo.ExecutionLog
3	ReportServer.dbo.ModelPerspective
4	ReportServer.dbo.ReportSchedule

The code in Listing 8-4, using a catalog view, should give the same result as the previous code, but with less typing. The TableHasPrimaryKey property of the OBJECTPROPERTY function simply returns 1 if a primary key exists, or 0 if not.

```
- — you can save a lot of code by using the catalog views
- — along with the OBJECTPROPERTY() function
SELECT  DB_NAME() + '.' + object_schema_name(t.object_ID) + '.' + t.name
                                       AS [tables without primary keys]
FROM    sys.tables t
WHERE   OBJECTPROPERTY(object_id, 'TableHasPrimaryKey') = 0
        AND OBJECTPROPERTY(object_id, 'IsUserTable') = 1
ORDER BY [tables without primary keys]
```

Listing 8-4:   Finding tables with no primary key using a Catalog view.

Tables with no referential constraints

You can, of course use almost the same query to explore many other characteristics of the tables. You'd certainly want to investigate any tables that seem to have no referential constraints, either as a key or a foreign reference, as shown in Listing 8-5.

```
--Which of my table are waifs? (No referential constraints)
SELECT
  DB_NAME() + '.' + object_schema_name(t.object_ID)
    + '.' + t.name AS [Waif Tables]
FROM    sys.tables t
WHERE   OBJECTPROPERTY(object_id, 'TableHasForeignKey') = 0
        AND OBJECTPROPERTY(object_id, 'TableHasForeignRef') = 0
        AND OBJECTPROPERTY(object_id, 'IsUserTable') = 1
ORDER BY [Waif tables]
```

Listing 8-5:   Finding waif tables.

237

	Waif Tables
1	ReportServer.dbo.Batch
2	ReportServer.dbo.ChunkData
3	ReportServer.dbo.ConfigurationInfo
4	ReportServer.dbo.Event
5	ReportServer.dbo.ExecutionLog
6	ReportServer.dbo.History
7	ReportServer.dbo.Keys
8	ReportServer.dbo.RunningJobs
9	ReportServer.dbo.ServerParametersInstance
10	ReportServer.dbo.SnapshotData
11	ReportServer.dbo.UpgradeInfo

Tables with no indexes

You'd also be interested in those tables without clustered indexes, and want to find out the reason why.

```
SELECT  DB_NAME() + '.' + Object_Schema_name(t.object_ID) + '.' + t.name
                                AS [Tables without Clustered index]
FROM    sys.tables t
WHERE   OBJECTPROPERTY(object_id, 'TableHasClustIndex') = 0
        AND OBJECTPROPERTY(object_id, 'IsUserTable') = 1
ORDER BY [Tables without Clustered index]
```

Listing 8-6: Tables without clustered indexes.

And you'd certainly scratch your head a bit if there were tables of any great size without any index at all.

238

```
SELECT   DB_NAME() + '.' + Object_Schema_name(t.object_ID) + '.' + t.name
                                  AS [Tables without any index]
FROM     sys.tables t
WHERE    OBJECTPROPERTY(object_id, 'TableHasIndex') = 0
         AND OBJECTPROPERTY(object_id, 'IsUserTable') = 1
ORDER BY [Tables without any index]
```

Listing 8-7:   Tables with no indexes.

	Tables without any index
1	PhoneProblem.dbo.CallLog
2	PhoneProblem.dbo.PhoneTariff
3	PhoneProblem.dbo.PhoneTariffCharges

A one-stop view of your table structures

We can pull of this together in a single query against the **sys.tables** catalog view to find out which objects (indexes, constraints, and so on) do, or don't, exist on a given database. This handy query, shown in Listing 8-8, provides a very useful at-a-glance summary of the characteristics of your tables' structure.

```
SELECT   DB_NAME() + '.' + Object_Schema_name(t.object_ID) + '.' + t.name
                                  AS [Qualified Name] ,
         CASE WHEN
--Table has an active full-text index.
                   OBJECTPROPERTY(object_id, 'TableHasActiveFulltextIndex') = 0
              THEN 'no'
              ELSE 'yes'
         END AS [FT index] ,
         CASE WHEN
--Table has a CHECK constraint.
                   OBJECTPROPERTY(object_id, 'TableHasCheckCnst') = 0 THEN 'no'
              ELSE 'yes'
         END AS [Check Cnt] ,
         CASE WHEN
```

239

```
--Table has a clustered index.
                    OBJECTPROPERTY(object_id, 'TableHasClustIndex') = 0
            THEN 'no'
            ELSE 'yes'
        END AS [Clustered ix] ,
        CASE WHEN
--Table has a DEFAULT constraint.
                    OBJECTPROPERTY(object_id, 'TableHasDefaultCnst') = 0
            THEN 'no'
            ELSE 'yes'
        END AS [Default Cnt] ,
        CASE WHEN
--Table has a DELETE trigger.
                    OBJECTPROPERTY(object_id, 'TableHasDeleteTrigger') = 0
            THEN 'no'
            ELSE 'yes'
        END AS [Delete Tgr] ,
        CASE WHEN
--Table has a FOREIGN KEY constraint.
                    OBJECTPROPERTY(object_id, 'TableHasForeignKey') = 0
            THEN 'no'
            ELSE 'yes'
        END AS [FK Cnt] ,
        CASE WHEN
--referenced by a FOREIGN KEY constraint.
                    OBJECTPROPERTY(object_id, 'TableHasForeignRef') = 0
            THEN 'no'
            ELSE 'yes'
        END AS [FK Ref] ,
--Table has an identity column.
        CASE WHEN OBJECTPROPERTY(object_id, 'TableHasIdentity') = 0 THEN 'no'
            ELSE 'yes'
        END AS [Identity Col] ,
--Table has an index of any type.
        CASE WHEN OBJECTPROPERTY(object_id, 'TableHasIndex') = 0 THEN 'no'
            ELSE 'yes'
        END AS [Any index] ,
        CASE WHEN
--Object has an INSERT trigger.
                    OBJECTPROPERTY(object_id, 'TableHasInsertTrigger') = 0
            THEN 'no'
            ELSE 'yes'
        END AS [Insert Tgr] ,
        CASE WHEN
```

```
--Table has a nonclustered index.
                OBJECTPROPERTY(object_id, 'TableHasNonclustIndex') = 0
            THEN 'no'
            ELSE 'yes'
        END AS [nonCl Index] ,
        CASE WHEN
--Table has a primary key
                OBJECTPROPERTY(object_id, 'TableHasPrimaryKey') = 0
            THEN 'no'
            ELSE 'yes'
        END AS [Primary Key] ,
        CASE WHEN
--ROWGUIDCOL for uniqueidentifier col
                OBJECTPROPERTY(object_id, 'TableHasRowGuidCol') = 0
            THEN 'no'
            ELSE 'yes'
        END AS [ROWGUIDCOL] ,
        CASE WHEN
--Table has text, ntext, or image column
                OBJECTPROPERTY(object_id, 'TableHasTextImage') = 0 THEN 'no'
            ELSE 'yes'
        END AS [Has Blob] ,
        CASE WHEN
--Table has a timestamp column.
                OBJECTPROPERTY(object_id, 'TableHasTimestamp') = 0 THEN 'no'
            ELSE 'yes'
        END AS [Timestamp] ,
        CASE WHEN
--Table has a UNIQUE constraint.
                OBJECTPROPERTY(object_id, 'TableHasUniqueCnst') = 0
            THEN 'no'
            ELSE 'yes'
        END AS [Unique Cnt] ,
        CASE WHEN
--Table has an Update trigger.
                OBJECTPROPERTY(object_id, 'TableHasUpdateTrigger') = 0
            THEN 'no'
            ELSE 'yes'
        END AS [Update Tgr]
FROM    sys.tables t
WHERE   OBJECTPROPERTY(object_id, 'IsUserTable') = 1
ORDER BY [Qualified Name]
```

Listing 8-8: Which objects exist in a database?

Qualified Name	FT i...	Che...	Clus...	Def...	Dele...	FK ...	FK Ref
AdventureWorks.dbo.AWBuildVersion	no	no	yes	yes	no	no	no
AdventureWorks.dbo.DatabaseLog	no	no	no	no	no	no	no
AdventureWorks.dbo.ErrorLog	no	no	yes	yes	no	no	no
AdventureWorks.dbo.JobCandidates	no	no	yes	no	no	no	no
AdventureWorks.dbo.sysdiagrams	no	no	yes	no	no	no	no
AdventureWorks.HumanResources.Department	no	no	yes	yes	no	no	yes
AdventureWorks.HumanResources.Employee	no	yes	yes	yes	yes	yes	ye
AdventureWorks.HumanResources.EmployeeAddress	no	no	yes	yes	no	ye	
AdventureWorks.HumanResources.EmployeeDepartme...	no	yes	yes	yes	no	yes	
AdventureWorks.HumanResources.EmployeePayHistory	no	yes	yes	yes	no	yes	
AdventureWorks.HumanResources.JobCandidate	no	no	yes	yes	no		
AdventureWorks.HumanResources.Shift	no	no	yes	yes	no		
AdventureWorks.Person.Address	no	no	yes	yes			
AdventureWorks.Person.AddressType	no	no	yes	yes			
AdventureWorks.Person.Contact	no	yes	yes				
AdventureWorks.Person.ContactType	no	no	yes				
AdventureWorks.Person.CountryRegion	no	no					
AdventureWorks.Person.StateProvince							
AdventureWorks.Production.BillOfMaterials							

How many of each object...

Since the **OBJECTPROPERTY** function generally returns either a 1 or a 0, it can be used pretty simply in order to find out, not just whether there are constraints, defaults, rules or triggers on individual tables, but also how many of them there are.

```
--Which of my tables have constraints, defaults, rules or triggers on them?
--If so, how many?
SELECT  DB_NAME() + '.' + Object_Schema_name(s.[object_ID]) + '.' + p.name
                        AS [Qualified_Name] ,
        COUNT(*) ,
        SUM(OBJECTPROPERTY(s.object_ID, 'IsPrimaryKey')) AS [Pk] ,
        SUM(OBJECTPROPERTY(s.object_ID, 'IsCheckCnst')) AS [ChkCns] ,
```

```
        SUM(OBJECTPROPERTY(s.object_ID, 'IsDefaultCnst')) AS [DefCns] ,
        SUM(OBJECTPROPERTY(s.object_ID, 'IsForeignKey')) AS [Fk] ,
        SUM(OBJECTPROPERTY(s.object_ID, 'IsConstraint')) AS [Cnstrnt] ,
        SUM(OBJECTPROPERTY(s.object_ID, 'IsDefault')) AS [Default] ,
        SUM(OBJECTPROPERTY(s.object_ID, 'IsTrigger')) AS [Trigger]
FROM    sys.objects S — -to get the objects
        INNER JOIN sys.objects p — -to get the parent object
— -and then the name of the table
        ON s.parent_Object_ID = p.[object_ID]
WHERE   OBJECTPROPERTY(p.object_ID, 'IsTable') <> 0
GROUP BY DB_NAME() + '.' + Object_Schema_name(s.[object_ID]) + '.' + p.name
```

Listing 8-9: How many of each object?

	Qualified_Name	total	Pk	Ch...	De...	Fk	Cnst...	Def...	Trigger
1	AdventureWorks.Sales.SalesOrderHeader	26	1	6	9	9	25	0	1
2	AdventureWorks.Production.Product	20	1	10	4	4	19	0	1
3	AdventureWorks.HumanResources.Employee	17	1	6	6	2	15	0	2
4	AdventureWorks.Purchasing.PurchaseOrderHeader	17	1	5	7	3	16	0	1
5	AdventureWorks.Sales.SalesPerson	15	1	5	6	2	14	0	1
6	AdventureWorks.Sales.SalesTerritory	12	1	4	6	0	11	0	1
7	AdventureWorks.Purchasing.ProductVendor	12	1	6	1	3	11	0	1
8	AdventureWorks.Production.BillOfMaterials	12	1	4	3	3	11	0	1
9	AdventureWorks.Purchasing.PurchaseOrderDetail	10	1	4	1	2	8	0	2
10	AdventureWorks.Sales.SpecialOffer	10	1	4	4	0	9	0	1
11	AdventureWorks.Sales.SalesOrderDetail	10	1	3	3	2	9	0	1
12	AdventureWorks.Production.WorkOrderRouting	10	1			2	9	0	1

Too many indexes...

By a slightly different route, we can also find out which of our tables have the most indexes on them. Are any of them duplications? For example, you might use the query in Listing 8-10 to see where indexes have gathered in undue numbers.

```
--Which of my tables have the most indexes?
SELECT TOP 10
        COUNT(*) AS [Indexes] ,
        DB_NAME() + '.' + Object_Schema_name(t.object_ID) + '.' + t.name
                                  AS [table]
FROM    sys.indexes i
        INNER JOIN sys.objects t ON i.object_ID = t.object_ID
WHERE   USER_NAME(OBJECTPROPERTY(i.object_id, 'OwnerId')) NOT LIKE 'sys%'
GROUP BY DB_NAME() + '.' + Object_Schema_name(t.object_ID) + '.' + t.name
ORDER BY COUNT(*) DESC
```

Listing 8-10: Which tables have the most indexes?

	Indexes	table
1	5	AdventureWorks.HumanResources.Employee
2	5	AdventureWorks.Production.ProductModel
3	5	AdventureWorks.Sales.Individual
4	5	AdventureWorks.Sales.SalesOrderHeader
5	4	AdventureWorks.Person.Address
6	4	AdventureWorks.Person.Contact
7	4	AdventureWorks.Person.StateProvince
8	4	AdventureWorks.Production.Product
9	4	AdventureWorks.Sales.Customer
10	4	AdventureWorks.Sales.Store

Seeking out troublesome triggers

I find triggers particularly troublesome as it is not always obvious that they are there. I'm not the only developer who has spent an hour trying to work out why the result of an update is nothing like what one was expecting, only to be struck by the thought that some crazed code-jockey has inexplicably placed an UPDATE trigger on one of my tables. Yes, there it is. The code in Listing 8-11 should winkle out these lurking problems, and much more besides.

```
--Which of my tables have triggers on them, and how many?
SELECT — -firstly, we'll search the names of the basic objects
        DB_NAME() + '.' + Object_Schema_name(s.[object_ID]) + p.name
                                        AS [Qualified_Name] ,
        COUNT(*) AS [how many]
FROM    sys.objects S — -to get the objects
        INNER JOIN sys.objects p — -to get the parent object
        ON s.parent_Object_ID = p.[object_ID]
WHERE   OBJECTPROPERTY(s.object_ID, 'IsTrigger') <> 0
        AND OBJECTPROPERTY(p.object_ID, 'IsTable') <> 0
GROUP BY DB_NAME() + '.' + Object_Schema_name(s.[object_ID]) + p.name
```

Listing 8-11: Finding tables with triggers.

From this, you can drill down to see the sort of triggers your tables have, as shown below.

```
SELECT   DB_NAME() + '.' + Object_Schema_name(t.[object_ID]) + '.' + t.name
                                        AS [Qualified_Name] ,
        CASE WHEN OBJECTPROPERTY(t.object_ID, 'HasAfterTrigger') <> 0
            THEN 'yes'
            ELSE 'no'
        END AS [After] ,
        CASE WHEN OBJECTPROPERTY(t.object_ID, 'HasDeleteTrigger') <> 0
            THEN 'yes'
            ELSE 'no'
        END AS [Delete] ,
        CASE WHEN OBJECTPROPERTY(t.object_ID, 'HasInsertTrigger') <> 0
            THEN 'yes'
            ELSE 'no'
        END AS [Insert] ,
        CASE WHEN OBJECTPROPERTY(t.object_ID, 'HasInsteadOfTrigger') <> 0
            THEN 'yes'
            ELSE 'no'
        END AS [Instead Of] ,
        CASE WHEN OBJECTPROPERTY(t.object_ID, 'HasUpdateTrigger ') <> 0
            THEN 'yes'
            ELSE 'no'
        END AS [Update]
FROM    sys.tables t
```

Listing 8-12: What types of trigger exist on each table?

245

	Qualified_Name	After	Delete	Insert	Instead Of	Update
1	AdventureWorks.Production.ProductProductPhoto	yes	no	no	no	yes
2	AdventureWorks.Sales.StoreContact	yes	no	no	no	yes
3	AdventureWorks.Person.Address	yes	no	no	no	yes
4	AdventureWorks.Production.ProductReview	yes	no	no	no	yes
5	AdventureWorks.Production.TransactionHistory	yes	no	no	no	yes
6	AdventureWorks.Person.AddressType	yes	no	no	no	yes
7	AdventureWorks.Production.ProductSubcategory	yes	no	no	no	yes
8	AdventureWorks.dbo.AWBuildVersion	yes	no	no	no	yes
9	AdventureWorks.Production.TransactionHistoryArch...	yes	no	no	no	yes
10	AdventureWorks.Purchasing.ProductVendor	yes	no	no	no	yes
11	AdventureWorks.Production.BillOfMaterials	yes	no	no	no	yes
12	AdventureWorks.Production.UnitMeasure	yes	no	no	no	yes
13	AdventureWorks.Purchasing.Vendor	yes	yes	no	yes	yes
14	AdventureWorks.Purchasing.PurchaseOrderDetail	yes	no	yes	no	yes
15	AdventureWorks.Person.Contact	yes	no	no	no	yes
16	AdventureWorks.Purchasing.VendorAddress	yes	no	no	no	yes
17	AdventureWorks.Purchasing.VendorContact	yes	no	no	no	yes
18	AdventureWorks.Purchasing.PurchaseOrderHeader	yes	no	no	no	yes

What objects have been recently modified?

If you are working with others on a database, then one of the more useful code snippets to share amongst your team is the one shown in Listing 8-13, which tells you the date at which your database objects were last modified. This is the full code, but you'll generally modify it slightly, as you'll just want to know the twenty or so latest modifications, or maybe list all the objects modified in the past week. Sadly, it will not tell you what has been deleted!

```
SELECT    [Qualified_Name] ,
          Object_Type ,
          CONVERT(CHAR(17), Created, 113) ,
          CONVERT(CHAR(17), Last_Modified, 113)
FROM      ( SELECT - -firstly, we'll search the names of the basic objects
                    DB_NAME() + '.' + Object_Schema_name(s.[object_ID]) + '.'
                    + COALESCE(p.name + '.', '') + s.name AS [Qualified_Name] ,
                    REPLACE(SUBSTRING(v.name, 5, 31), 'cns', 'constraint')
                    + ' name' AS Object_Type ,
                    s.create_date AS 'Created' ,
                    s.modify_date AS 'Last_Modified'
          FROM      sys.objects S - -to get the objects
                    LEFT OUTER JOIN master.dbo.spt_values v
  - -to get the type of object
                    ON s.type = SUBSTRING(v.name, 1, 2) COLLATE database_default
                       AND v.type = 'O9T'
                    LEFT OUTER JOIN sys.objects p - -to get any parent object
                    ON s.parent_Object_ID = p.[object_ID]
          WHERE     Object_Schema_name(s.object_ID) NOT LIKE 'sys%'
          UNION ALL - -now search the XML schema collection names
          SELECT    DB_NAME() + '.' + name ,
                    'XML Schema Collection name' ,
                    create_date AS 'created' ,
                    modify_date AS 'Last Modified'
          FROM      sys.xml_schema_collections
          UNION ALL
          SELECT    DB_NAME() + '.' + name ,
                    LOWER(type_desc) COLLATE database_default ,
                    create_date AS 'created' ,
                    modify_date AS 'Last Modified'
          FROM      sys.triggers
          WHERE     parent_class = 0--only DDL triggers
          UNION ALL - -names of CLR assemblies
          SELECT    DB_NAME() + '.' + name ,
                    'CLR Assembly' ,
                    create_date AS 'created' ,
                    modify_date AS 'Last Modified'
          FROM      sys.assemblies
          UNION ALL - -almost done. We do the agent jobs too here
          SELECT DISTINCT
                    'Agent' + '.' + DB_NAME() + '.' + [name]
                                     COLLATE database_default ,
                    'Agent Job' ,
                    date_created ,
```

247

```
                        date_modified
        FROM            MSDB.dbo.sysJobs Job
                        INNER JOIN MSDB.dbo.sysJobSteps Step
                                        ON Job.Job_Id = Step.Job_Id
        WHERE           Database_name LIKE DB_NAME() COLLATE database_default
      ) objects
ORDER BY Last_Modified DESC
```

Listing 8-13: Which objects have been recently modified?

Querying the documentation in extended properties

Catalog queries are a powerful way of querying the documentation in order to find out more about the business rules governing the database structure. There are several useful queries that you can use if you have been sensible enough to structure your documentation, such as listing out your procedures and functions, along with a brief synopsis of how they are used, and why. Here, we'll just restrict ourselves to a useful list of all the tables that have no documentation in the extended properties. There really aren't any other places to put your table documentation, so you can be fairly sure that these tables have no documentation at all.

```
--Which tables do not have any documentation in extended properties?
SELECT  DB_NAME() + '.' + Object_Schema_name(s.[object_ID]) + '.' + s.name
                                        AS [Undocumented Table]
FROM    sys.objects s
        LEFT OUTER JOIN sys.extended_properties ep
            ON s.object_ID = ep.major_ID
            AND minor_ID = 0
WHERE   type_desc = 'USER_TABLE'
        AND ep.value IS NULL
```

Listing 8-14: Which tables have no documentation?

Object permissions and owners

There are a whole variety of things you will need information on, in addition to details of the database objects; lists of permissions on each object, and the type of permissions they represent, for example. Listing 8-15 provides a query that lists the database-level permissions for the users (or particular user, if the final condition that is currently commented out is used.)

```
SELECT   CASE WHEN class_desc = 'DATABASE' THEN DB_NAME()
              WHEN class_desc = 'SCHEMA' THEN SCHEMA_NAME(major_id)
              WHEN class_desc = 'OBJECT_OR_COLUMN' THEN OBJECT_NAME(major_id)
              WHEN class_desc = 'DATABASE_PRINCIPAL' THEN USER_NAME(major_id)
              WHEN class_desc = 'TYPE' THEN TYPE_NAME(major_id)
              ELSE 'Huh??'
         END ,
         USER_NAME(grantee_principal_id) AS grantee ,
         USER_NAME(grantor_principal_id) AS grantor ,
         type ,
         Permission_Name ,
         State_Desc
FROM     sys.database_permissions
WHERE    Class_Desc IN ( 'DATABASE', 'SCHEMA', 'OBJECT_OR_COLUMN',
                         'DATABASE_PRINCIPAL', 'TYPE' )
- - and grantee_principal_id = DATABASE_PRINCIPAL_ID('public');
```

Listing 8-15: Finding database-level permissions for each user.

A different task is to explore the ownership of the various objects in your database, a task that Listing 8-16 makes a lot simpler.

```
--find the user names of all the objects
SELECT  [Entity Type] ,
        [Owner name] ,
        [Object Name]
FROM    ( SELECT    REPLACE(SUBSTRING(v.name, 5, 31), 'cns', 'constraint')
                                                    AS [entity type] ,
                    USER_NAME(OBJECTPROPERTY(object_id, 'OwnerId'))
                                                    AS [owner name] ,
                    DB_NAME() + '.' + Object_Schema_name(o.object_ID) + '.'
                    + o.name AS [Object Name]
          FROM      sys.objects o
                    LEFT OUTER JOIN master.dbo.spt_values v — -object type
                    ON o.type = SUBSTRING(v.name, 1, 2)
                                        COLLATE database_default
                        AND v.type = 'O9T'
          UNION
          SELECT    'Type' ,
                    USER_NAME(TYPEPROPERTY(SCHEMA_NAME(schema_id) + '.' + name,
                                    'OwnerId')) ,
                    DB_NAME() + '.' + SCHEMA_NAME(schema_ID) + '.' + name
          FROM      sys.types
          UNION
          SELECT    'XML Schema Collection' ,
                    COALESCE(USER_NAME(xsc.principal_id),
                        USER_NAME(s.principal_id)) ,
                    DB_NAME() + '.' + SCHEMA_NAME(xsc.schema_ID) + '.'
                    + xsc.name
          FROM      sys.xml_schema_collections AS xsc
                    JOIN sys.schemas AS s ON s.schema_id = xsc.schema_id
        ) f
WHERE   [owner Name] NOT LIKE 'sys'
```

Listing 8-16: Who owns which objects?

Searching All Your Databases

You can use these various routines on all databases, or on a list of databases. You can use undocumented code, of course, but a better approach would be to use yet another system catalog called **sys.Databases**. You can then execute the code against all databases, collecting the result into a single table. Listing 8-17 provides an example of how to return tables without primary keys, across all databases.

```sql
DECLARE @ii INT , — -loop counter
    @iiMax INT , — -loop counter upper limit
    @CurrentDatabase VARCHAR(255) , — -variable holding name of current database
    @command NVARCHAR(2000)
--the dynamic command
DECLARE @whatWeSearch TABLE — -the table of all the databases we search
    (
        Database_ID INT IDENTITY(1, 1) ,
        DatabaseName VARCHAR(255)
    )
DECLARE @Result TABLE — -the result
    (
        [Tables Without Primary Keys] VARCHAR(255)
    )
INSERT   INTO @whatWeSearch
        ( DatabaseName
        )
        SELECT   name
        FROM     sys.Databases
        WHERE    name NOT IN ( 'Master', 'TempDB', 'Model', 'MSDB',
                               'Distribution', 'mssqlresource' )
--get all the databases we want to search
SELECT   @ii = MIN(Database_ID) ,
         @iiMax = MAX(Database_ID)
FROM     @whatWeSearch
--and do them all one after another
WHILE @ii <= @iiMax
    BEGIN
        SELECT   @CurrentDatabase = QUOTENAME(DatabaseName)
        FROM     @whatWeSearch
        WHERE    Database_ID = @ii
```

```
          SET @Command = N'Use ' + @CurrentDatabase + ';
          Select DB_NAME()+''.''+Object_Schema_name(t.object_ID)+''.''
                              +t.name  as [tables without primary keys]
          FROM sys.tables t
          WHERE OBJECTPROPERTY(object_id,''TableHasPrimaryKey'') = 0
          ORDER BY [tables without primary keys]'
          INSERT  INTO @Result
                  ( [Tables Without Primary Keys] )
                  EXEC sp_executesql @Command
          SELECT  @ii = @ii + 1 — -and on to the next database
     END
SELECT  [Tables Without Primary Keys]
FROM    @Result
```

Listing 8-17: Search all databases for tables lacking a primary key.

Investigating Foreign Key Relationships

When you are exploring a database, it is interesting to check out the FOREIGN KEY constraints. These will only tell you the relationships between tables if they have been properly defined (i.e. not implicitly defined). However, if they have been, then it becomes absurdly easy to construct queries that describe the foreign key relationships, either graphically, or via system views.

I've used several ways of "walking" the foreign key relationships, in the past, but my preferred method, which I'll demonstrate here, expresses the relationship in terms of the actual SQL clause that defines it. For example, if we request to see the foreign key relationship between two tables, SalesOrderDetail and SpecialOfferProduct, then l like to see it expressed as shown in Listing 8-18.

```
ON Sales.SalesOrderDetail.SpecialOfferID =
                            Sales.SpecialOfferProduct.SpecialOfferID
   AND Sales.SalesOrderDetail.ProductID = Sales.SpecialOfferProduct.ProductID
```

Listing 8-18: SQL clause defining the FK relationship between two tables.

Even better, is to return a complete query, as shown in Listing 8-19.

```
SELECT TOP 20
       *
FROM    Sales.SalesOrderDetail
        INNER JOIN Sales.SpecialOfferProduct
                ON Sales.SalesOrderDetail.SpecialOfferID =
                            Sales.SpecialOfferProduct.SpecialOfferID
               AND Sales.SalesOrderDetail.ProductID =
                            Sales.SpecialOfferProduct.ProductID
-- - FK_SalesOrderDetail_SpecialOfferProduct_SpecialOfferIDProductID
```

Listing 8-19: Full query defining the FK relationship between two tables.

This way, you can then quickly execute it to see the data, or paste it into SSMS to get a graphical representation (highlight the query, right-click and select "Design Query in Editor").

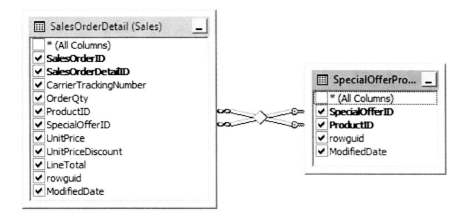

You'll notice that in this example from AdventureWorks, the `SalesOrderDetail` contains a compound foreign key, containing more than one column. There could, in theory, be more. You could sniff them out in your database using the code shown in Listing 8-20.

253

```
SELECT   fk.name
FROM     sys.foreign_Key_columns fkc
         INNER JOIN sys.foreign_keys fk ON fkc.constraint_object_id = fk.object_id
GROUP BY fk.name
HAVING   COUNT(*) = 1
```

Listing 8-20: Finding composite foreign keys.

This complicates the SQL that you'd use to generate these relationships, as you can see from Listing 8-21, which shows the SQL to get all the relationships for a particular table in the database, in this case, the **HumanResources.Employee** table.

```
SELECT   SUBSTRING(( SELECT   ' AND ' + Object_Schema_name(fk.Parent_object_ID)
                            + '.' + OBJECT_NAME(fk.Parent_object_ID) + '.'
                            + cr.name + ' = '
                            + Object_Schema_name(fkc.referenced_object_id)
                            + '.' + OBJECT_NAME(fkc.referenced_object_id)
                            + '.' + c.NAME
                   FROM     sys.foreign_Key_columns fkc
                            INNER JOIN sys.columns c
                                ON fkc.referenced_column_id = c.column_id
                                    AND fkc.referenced_object_id = c.object_id
                            INNER JOIN sys.columns cr
                                ON fkc.parent_column_id = cr.column_id
                                    AND fkc.parent_object_id = cr.object_id
                   WHERE    fkc.constraint_object_id = fk.OBJECT_ID
                   FOR
                     XML PATH('')
                   ), 6, 2000) + ' — — ' + fk.name
FROM     sys.foreign_keys fk
WHERE    fk.referenced_object_ID = OBJECT_ID('HumanResources.Employee')
         OR fk.parent_object_id = OBJECT_ID('HumanResources.Employee')
```

Listing 8-21: A query to find all the FK relationships for a given table.

We would, of course, enshrine this in a procedure or function. Listing 8-22 shows an example procedure that produces the full SQL queries that define the FK relationships for a table, allowing you to then look at a sample of the result that would be created. Try it and see; it is quite handy.

```
CREATE PROCEDURE FKRelationshipsFor
    @objectName SYSNAME = NULL
/*summary:    >
This procedure gives SQL Scripts to show sample (20 row)
results of the joins that can be made from
relationships defined in  all the foreign key constraints
associated with the table specified (all if no parameter give)
Author: Phil Factor
Revision:
 — 1.1 added select statement to the ON clause
 — date: 20 sept 2010
Revision
 — 1.1 added facility to list everything
 — date: 21 sept 2010
example:
 — code: FKRelationshipsFor 'HumanResources.Employee'
example:
 — code: FKRelationshipsFor 'Sales.SpecialOfferProduct'
example:
 — code: FKRelationshipsFor 'Production.ProductInventory'
example:
 — FKRelationshipsFor — -do them all
Returns:    >
single column Varchar(MAX) result called 'Script'.
**/
AS
    IF @objectName IS NOT NULL
        IF OBJECT_ID(@objectName) IS NULL
            BEGIN
                RAISERROR(
    'Hmm. Couldn''t find ''%s''. Have you qualified it with the schema name?',
    16,1,@ObjectName)
                RETURN 1
            END
    SELECT 'SELECT TOP 20 *
FROM ' + Object_Schema_name(fk.referenced_object_id) + '.'
            + OBJECT_NAME(fk.referenced_object_id) + '
  INNER JOIN ' + Object_Schema_name(fk.parent_object_id) + '.'
            + OBJECT_NAME(fk.parent_object_id) + '
```

```
   ON '
              + SUBSTRING(( SELECT    ' AND '
                                     + Object_Schema_name(fk.Parent_object_ID)
                                     + '.' + OBJECT_NAME(fk.Parent_object_ID)
                                     + '.' + cr.name + ' = '
                                     + OBJECT_NAME(fkc.referenced_object_id)
                                     + '.' + c.NAME
                           FROM      sys.foreign_Key_columns fkc
                                     INNER JOIN sys.columns c
                                      ON fkc.referenced_column_id = c.column_id
                                      AND fkc.referenced_object_id = c.OBJECT_ID
                                     INNER JOIN sys.columns cr
                                      ON fkc.parent_column_id = cr.column_id
                                      AND fkc.parent_object_id = cr.OBJECT_ID
                           WHERE     fkc.constraint_object_id = fk.OBJECT_ID
                          FOR
                          XML PATH('')
                          ), 5, 2000) + CHAR(13) + CHAR(10) + ' -- -- ' + fk.name
                                                                        AS script
   FROM       sys.foreign_keys fk
   WHERE      fk.referenced_object_ID = COALESCE(OBJECT_ID(@objectName),
                                         fk.referenced_object_ID)
              OR fk.parent_object_id = COALESCE(OBJECT_ID(@objectName),
                                         fk.parent_object_ID)
GO
```

Listing 8-22: A stored procedure the full SQL queries that define the FK relationships for a table.

A useful extension to this would be to develop code that would give you the entire SQL to do the joins, when supplied with a list of tables, up to six, say – an exercise left for the reader.

Interrogating Object Dependencies

If you are faced with the difficult task of refactoring code whilst keeping everything running reliably, one of the most useful things you can determine is the chain of dependencies of database objects. You'll need this information if you are considering renaming anything in the database, changing a column in a table, moving a module, or replacing a data type.

Unfortunately, the information you get back from the metadata about dependencies isn't particularly reliable. One problem is that some entities used in an application can contain caller-dependent references or one-part name references (e.g. they don't specify the schema). This can cause all sorts of problems because the binding of the referenced entity depends on the schema of the caller and so the reference cannot be determined until the code is run. Additionally, if code is stored in a string and executed, then the entities that the code is referencing cannot be recorded in the metadata.

One thing you can do, if you are checking on the dependencies of a routine (non-schema-bound stored procedure, user-defined function, view, DML trigger, database-level DDL trigger, or server-level DDL trigger) is to update its metadata. This is because the metadata for these objects, such as data types of parameters, can become outdated because of changes to their underlying objects. This is done by using `sys.sp_refresh-sqlmodule`, e.g.

```
sys.sp_refreshsqlmodule 'dbo.ufnGetContactInformation'
```

Even so, bear in mind that the information you get back from metadata queries is to be taken with a pinch of salt. If you're looking for an alternative, more reliable approach, you might consider a tool such as Red Gate's SQL Dependency Tracker.

Finding the closest relations

It is reasonably easy to get a list of what objects refer to a particular object, and what objects are referred to by an object. Variations of the query shown in Listing 8-23 will do it for you, using the SQL Server 2005 catalog view, **sys.sql_dependencies**.

```
--List all the dependencies in the database.
--Normally you'll have a WHERE clause to pick just the object you want.
SELECT  Object_Schema_name(object_id) + '.' + COALESCE(OBJECT_NAME(object_id),
                                             'unknown')
        + COALESCE('.' + COL_NAME(object_id, column_id), '') AS [referencer] ,
        Object_Schema_name(referenced_major_id) + '.'
        + OBJECT_NAME(referenced_major_id)
              + COALESCE('.'
                         + COL_NAME(referenced_major_id,
                                    referenced_minor_id),
                    '') AS [Referenced]
FROM    sys.sql_dependencies
WHERE   class IN ( 0, 1 ) — -AND referenced_major_id = OBJECT_ID('HumanResources.
Employee')
ORDER BY COALESCE(OBJECT_NAME(object_id), 'x') ,
        COALESCE(COL_NAME(object_id, column_id), 'a')
```

Listing 8-23: Finding directly referring, and referred to, objects.

	referencer	Referenced
1	Production.CK_BillOfMaterials_BOMLevel	Production.BillOfMaterials.ProductAssemblyID
2	Production.CK_BillOfMaterials_BOMLevel	Production.BillOfMaterials.BOMLevel
3	Production.CK_BillOfMaterials_BOMLevel	Production.BillOfMaterials.PerAssemblyQty
4	Production.CK_BillOfMaterials_EndDate	Production.BillOfMaterials.StartDate
5	Production.CK_BillOfMaterials_EndDate	Production.BillOfMaterials.EndDate
6	Production.CK_BillOfMaterials_PerAssemblyQty	Production.BillOfMaterials.PerAssemblyQty
7	Production.CK_BillOfMaterials_ProductAssemblyID	Production.BillOfMaterials.ComponentID
8	Production.CK_BillOfMaterials_ProductAssemblyID	Production.BillOfMaterials.ProductAssemblyID
9	Person.CK_Contact_EmailPromotion	Person.Contact.EmailPromotion
10	Sales.CK_Customer_CustomerType	Sales.Customer.CustomerType
11	Production.CK_Document_Status	Production.Document.Status
12	HumanResources.CK_Employee_BirthDate	HumanResources.Employee.BirthDate
13	HumanResources.CK_Employee_Gender	HumanResources.Employee.Gender
14	HumanResources.CK_Employee_HireDate	HumanResources.Employee.HireDate
15	HumanResources.CK_Employee_MaritalStatus	HumanResources.Employee.MaritalStatus
16	HumanResources.CK_Employee_SickLeaveHours	HumanResources.Employee.SickLeaveHours
17	HumanResources.CK_Employee_VacationHours	HumanResources.Employee.VacationHours
18	HumanResources.CK_EmployeeDepartmentHistory_EndD...	HumanResources.EmployeeDepartmentHistory.StartDate
19	HumanResources.CK_EmployeeDepartmentHistory_EndD...	HumanResources.EmployeeDepartmentHistory.EndDate

Finding the dependency chain

If you are altering the behavior of the object, then you will need, not only the dependent objects of the object you are re-engineering, but also the objects that are dependent on these dependent objects, and so on – and watch out for mutual dependency! In other words, you need the dependency chains, which is exactly what is provided by the DependencyChainOf function shown in Listing 8-24.

```
CREATE FUNCTION DependencyChainOf ( @Object_Name SYSNAME )
/**
  summary:   >
             The DependencyChainOf function takes as a
             parameter either a table, view, function or
             procedure name or a column name. It works
             best with the full object name of
             schema.object(.column). Returns a table that
             gives the dependency chain with both forward
             and backward links so that you can see what
             objects are likely to be affected by the
             changes you make, and what objects your
             object is referencing.
  Revisions:
  - version: 1
             Modification: Created Table-valued
                                         function
             Author: Phil Factor
             Date:   01/03/2010
  - version: 2
             Modification: added catch for mutual
                                         dependency
             Author: Phil Factor
             Date:   02/03/2010
  example:
  - code:
             Select distinct *
             from DependencyChainOf('VEmployee')
             order by The_level,TheName
  - code:
             EXEC sys.sp_refreshsqlmodule 'MyProc1'
             Select distinct *
             from DependencyChainOf('MyTable')
             order by The_level,TheName
  **/
RETURNS @Referenced TABLE
    (
      TheName VARCHAR(200) ,
      The_Object_ID BIGINT ,
      Column_ID INT ,
      Class INT ,
      The_Level INT
    )
AS
```

```
    BEGIN
--identify the object or  column
--get the referencing entity
        INSERT  INTO @referenced
                ( The_Object_ID ,
                  Column_ID ,
                  Class ,
                  The_Level
                )
                SELECT TOP 1
                        object_ID ,
                        Column_ID ,
                        class ,
                        1
                FROM    ( SELECT Object_Schema_name(object_id) + '.'
                                    + COALESCE(OBJECT_NAME(object_id),
                                        'unknown') + COALESCE('.'
                                            + COL_NAME(object_id,
                                                column_id), '')
                                                AS [name] ,
                                    d.object_ID ,
                                    d.column_ID ,
                                    class
                            FROM    sys.sql_dependencies d
                        ) names
                WHERE CHARINDEX(REVERSE(@Object_Name), REVERSE(names.name)) = 1
                        OR OBJECT_NAME([Object_ID]) = @Object_Name
        IF NOT EXISTS ( SELECT  1
                        FROM    @referenced )
            INSERT  INTO @referenced
                ( The_Object_ID ,
                  Column_ID ,
                  Class ,
                  The_Level
                )
                SELECT TOP 1
                        object_ID ,
                        Column_ID ,
                        class ,
                        1
                FROM    ( SELECT     Object_Schema_name(referenced_major_id)
                                        + '.'
                                        + OBJECT_NAME(referenced_major_id)
                                        + COALESCE('.'
```

```
                                            + COL_NAME(referenced_major_id,
                                                    referenced_minor_id),
                                            '') AS [name] ,
                            d.Referenced_Major_ID AS [object_ID] ,
                            d.Referenced_Minor_ID AS [column_ID] ,
                            class
                FROM       sys.sql_dependencies d
            ) names
        WHERE    CHARINDEX(REVERSE(@Object_Name),
                        REVERSE(names.name)) = 1
                OR OBJECT_NAME([Object_ID]) = @Object_Name
DECLARE @Currentlevel INT ,
    @RowCount INT
SELECT  @Currentlevel = 1 ,
        @Rowcount = 1
WHILE @Rowcount > 0
    AND @currentLevel < 50--guard against mutual dependency
    BEGIN
        INSERT  INTO @referenced
                ( The_Object_ID ,
                  Column_ID ,
                  Class ,
                  The_Level
                )
                SELECT  Referenced_Major_ID ,
                        Referenced_Minor_ID ,
                        d.class ,
                        The_Level + 1
                FROM    @referenced r
                        INNER JOIN sys.sql_dependencies d
                            ON The_Object_ID = object_ID
- -AND r.column_ID=d.Column_ID
                                AND r.class = d.Class
                                AND @Currentlevel = The_Level
        SELECT  @rowcount = @@Rowcount ,
                @CurrentLevel = @CurrentLevel + 1
    END
SELECT  @Currentlevel = 1 ,
        @Rowcount = 1
WHILE @Rowcount > 0
    AND @currentLevel > — 50--guard against mutual dependency
    BEGIN
        INSERT  INTO @referenced
                ( The_Object_ID ,
```

```
                                Column_ID ,
                                Class ,
                                The_Level
                            )
                    SELECT  Object_ID ,
                            d.column_ID ,
                            d.class ,
                            The_Level — 1
                    FROM    @referenced r
                            INNER JOIN sys.sql_dependencies d
                                ON The_Object_ID = Referenced_Major_ID
  — -AND r.column_ID=d.Referenced_Major_ID
                                    AND r.class = d.Class
                                    AND @Currentlevel = The_Level
                SELECT   @rowcount = @@Rowcount ,
                         @CurrentLevel = @CurrentLevel — 1
            END
      UPDATE    @Referenced
      SET       TheName = DB_NAME() + '.' + Object_Schema_name(The_object_ID)
                + '.' + OBJECT_NAME(The_object_ID) + COALESCE('.'
                                    + COL_NAME(The_object_ID,
                                    column_id), '')

      RETURN
  END
```

Listing 8-24: Finding the dependency chain.

	TheName	The_Object_ID	Column_ID	Class	The_Level
1	DependencyChainSample.dbo.MyProc3	485576768	0	0	0
2	DependencyChainSample.dbo.MyProc2	469576711	0	0	1
3	DependencyChainSample.dbo.MyProc1	453576654	0	0	2
4	DependencyChainSample.dbo.MyView.c1	437576597	1	0	3
5	DependencyChainSample.dbo.MyTable.c1	421576540	1	0	4
6	DependencyChainSample.dbo.MyTable.c2	421576540	2	0	4

263

It's worth noting that, in SQL Server 2008, you would use the `sys.sql_expression_dependencies` table, which has a much improved way of working out dependencies. There is a very full discussion, with example code, in the article, *Reporting SQL Dependencies* (HTTP://MSDN.MICROSOFT.COM/EN-US/LIBRARY/BB677168.ASPX).

Summary

With the various scripts, suggestions and illustrations in this article, I hope I've given you a taste for using the catalog (or Information Schema) views for getting all sorts of useful information about the objects in your databases and the dependencies that exist.

Some of this information is available from the SSMS Object browser but it is slow going. Once you've built up your own snippet or template library, you'll find it quicker and easier to take the Spartan approach, and search your databases' catalog using SQL.

Chapter 9: Searching DDL and Build Scripts

Often, a database developer needs to go beyond high-level object searches, to find occurrences of a specific string, such as a parameter name, within the DDL of the databases you manage. It's at these times that the absence of an effective search utility in SSMS really hits home. Of course, there is a "Find" menu item (CTRL+ F) but it won't work in the Object Explorer pane of SSMS to find things in your database schema. You also have an object search feature in SSMS 2008 within the Object Explorer "Details" window, but that only searches the names of objects, not their definitions. It also doesn't search all objects, not even columns. Obviously, you can find strings within the current query window, but this is only a small fraction of what you actually need when you're developing a database. You want to search for all your database objects, their names, their definitions and their comments.

In this chapter, I'll show how to **search within the object definitions** in your build scripts to find occurrences of a specific string, using:

- SQL Search – a free search tool provided by Red Gate
- custom scripts – based on the catalog and `INFORMATION_SCHEMA` views.

With these scripts to hand, and a few more, I'll move on to how to make use of SSMS shortcut keys to enable you select the name of an object, particularly a table, and to instantly see, at a keystroke, the build script in the results pane, complete with the documentation and, in the case of a table, the referential constraints. I'll also show how to get a list of all the places in the database where the object's name appears.

A dream? Read on...

Searching Within the DDL

The SSMS Object Explorer must have a great deal of information about the objects in it but, unfortunately, it does not really make much of it accessible. Very limited searching by name is available through the Object Explorer Details window (F7 opens it up), but what's really needed is the ability to search through the full code (definition) for a given objects.

Why isn't it in SSMS?

I don't know for sure, but I suspect that the reason there is no way of searching through the code, as well as the name, in SSMS is that it isn't straightforward within the architecture that Microsoft has chosen to use, without breaking a few rules.

One problem is that there could be quite a few database objects around, such as those in the list below.

- Tables (system tables and user tables)

- Views

- Indexes

- Stored procedures

- Constraints (CHECK, DEFAULT, UNIQUE, foreign keys primary keys, rules)

- T-SQL functions (scalar, table-valued, inline)

- CLR functions (scalar, table-valued), CLR stored procedures, CLR DML triggers

- Extended stored procedures

- XML Schema collections

- Other objects, such as plan guides, replication filters, service queues.

Quite a few of these objects will have code in them. The code, or definition, of objects will be found in user-defined rules, defaults, unencrypted Transact-SQL stored procedures, user-defined Transact-SQL functions, triggers, computed columns, CHECK constraints, views, or system objects such as a system stored procedure. Even if you can search through all the code, you'd also probably need to look at the extended properties too.

The most potentially powerful means of searching your database objects is by use of Server Management Objects (SMO). The problem with using SMO is that it provides an object-oriented programmatic model, in place of the real way that SQL Server stores information about its objects such as tables, procedures and columns, and the hierarchical structure of objects. It is clever, it is useful, but it is dead slow to navigate when you're looking at a large database, and trying to extract the contents of routines.

So how do you do it?

Over the coming sections, we'll go through the various alternative approaches to searching for stuff in your database definition.

Get the free tool: SQL Search

If you don't want to get immersed in SQL code to do this, SQL Search is free, and you don't even have to give anyone your email address to get it.

This is perfect for the majority of requirements. At the moment, SQL Search (WWW.RED-GATE.COM/PRODUCTS/SQL_SEARCH/INDEX.HTM) will search through the code for most of the main database objects (tables, views, stored procedures, constraints, triggers, and so on), but it currently misses out indexes, and also won't search the contents of extended properties.

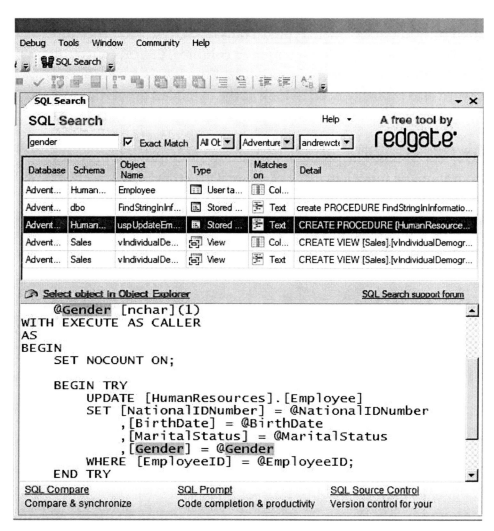

Figure 9-1: Red Gate SQL Search.

This means that it does not, at the moment, entirely replace the requirement for a T-SQL-based solution. However, you can see that it does more than the Object Explorer Details search of SSMS, since it will find the search term in the text, or definition, of the stored procedure, as well as finding it in the name.

Searching the entire build script

Let's start with the very simplest, but one of the most reliable methods of searching. You get out your build script. No build script? You generate it. If you like clicking at things, then use SSMS; otherwise use an automated procedure with PowerShell and SMO (remember that you have to regenerate the build script every time someone else makes an alteration). I still use a slightly retro stored procedure with DMO (see www. SIMPLE-TALK.COM/SQL/DATABASE-ADMINISTRATION/MORE-DATABASE-ADMINISTRATION-AND-DEVELOPMENT-AUTOMATION-USING-DMO/); it works very well for me. Then, you read it into your favorite text editor and use the search facilities in it. This sounds clunky, but if your editor uses RegEx search, then a lot can be done, including the automatic generation of lists. Personally, I am pretty happy with this approach, but it isn't always convenient.

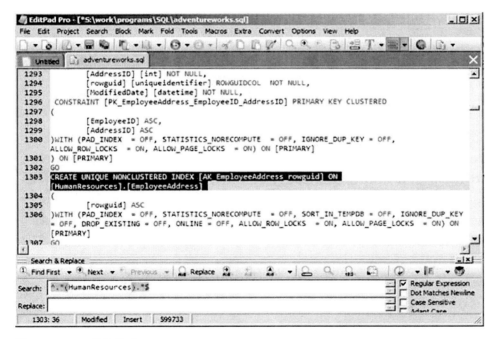

Figure 9-2: EditPad.

The use of a query pane with the build script in it is almost as good, but you don't have the regular expressions, or the performance of a programmer's text editor. It also doesn't help with some of the more advanced operations that you might need. I like making lists, with the help of a RegEx string, of the lines, or context, where each match happened. I can then scan them quickly to find a particular occurrence (see the *T-SQL Regular Expression Workbench* – WWW.SIMPLE-TALK.COM/SQL/T-SQL-PROGRAMMING/TSQL-REGULAR-EXPRESSION-WORKBENCH/ – for an introduction to RegEx). With a Grep tool, and SQLCMD, you can get lists of lines containing your search string.

The "Help" system procedures: a toe in the water

There are a number of "traditional" approaches to looking at your structural metadata, but they aren't going to help much. If you just want a list of the most important objects, then just use…

```
- — list all objects in sys.sysobjects table
Execute sp_help
```

…but you will miss out on columns and indexes, and quite a few of the less important objects, as well. There are other similar stored procedures, some of which are listed below, which are fine for getting specific information, but not much use for answering questions like "Where, in the database, is a date conversion used with a German (104) date format?" The famous **sp_helptext** is fine for getting the text of a particular object but no more than that. There is also the following:

- **sp_helpconstraint** – all constraint types, their user-defined or system-supplied name, the columns on which they have been defined, and the expression that defines the constraint

- **sp_helpdb** – reports information about a specified database

- **sp_helpextendedproc** – currently defined extended stored procedures

- **sp_helpfile** – the physical names and attributes of files associated with the current database

- **sp_helpfilegroup** – lists file groups

- **sp_helpgroup** – lists roles

- **sp_helpindex** – lists indexes, and the columns on which the index is built

- **sp_helptext** – displays the definition of a routine

- **sp_helptrigger** – lists the triggers and their types.

Going standard: using Information_Schema

You can use the `Information_Schema` views for searching your DDL, if you don't want too much. However, as noted in the previous chapter, they only store the first 4,000 characters of the definition of an object. If you write long stored procedures, you can move on to a later part of this chapter, or stick cozily to the idea of using a traditional programmer's text editor, as I've already described. Also, you'll only get information on objects considered part of the Standard, so you won't be able to search the DDL of triggers, or search inside extended properties.

Of course, you can "get around" the 4,000 character limit using the `OBJECT_DEFINITION` function like this:

```
SELECT OBJECT_DEFINITION(OBJECT_ID(SPECIFIC_SCHEMA + '.' + SPECIFIC_NAME)), * FROM
INFORMATION_SCHEMA.ROUTINES
```

However, since this function is a wrapper around the SQL Server system views, you've rather defeated the purpose of using `Information_Schema` in the first place, which is designed to be a portable standard.

Listing 9-1 shows a procedure that does what it can to search your database, using `Information_Schema`.

```
IF EXISTS ( SELECT  *
            FROM    information_Schema.routines
            WHERE   specific_name = 'FindStringInInformationSchema' )
    DROP PROCEDURE FindStringInInformationSchema
go
CREATE PROCEDURE FindStringInInformationSchema
/**
 summary:    >
This finds the string that you specify within the name of many database objects
including indexes and parameters of routines. It searches within the text
(definition) for every routine. It displays the full path of the database object
and the object type. This cannot find the text (Definition) or names of triggers,
and knows nothing of extended properties.
example:
 — code:    FindStringInInformationSchema '' — -list every object, along with
                                              creation date etc
 — code:    FindStringInInformationSchema 'getdate'--find where the string
                                              'getdate' appears!
 — code:    FindStringInInformationSchema 'gender'--find where the string
                                              'gender' appears!
returns:    >
result
**/ @SearchString VARCHAR(2000)
AS
    IF CHARINDEX('%', @SearchString) = 0
        SELECT  @SearchString = '%' + @SearchString + '%'
    SELECT--report on the routines first, name and definition
            Specific_Catalog + '.' + Specific_Schema + '.' + Specific_Name
                                              AS Qualified_Name ,
            LOWER(Routine_Type) + ' '
            + CASE WHEN specific_name LIKE @SearchString THEN 'name'
                ELSE 'definition'
              END AS Object_Type
    FROM    information_Schema.routines
    WHERE   specific_name LIKE @SearchString
            OR routine_Definition LIKE @SearchString
```

```
UNION ALL
SELECT--and search view definitions
        Table_Catalog + '.' + Table_Schema + '.' + Table_Name ,
        'view definition'
FROM    information_Schema.views
WHERE   View_Definition LIKE @SearchString
UNION ALL
SELECT  Table_Catalog + '.' + Table_Schema + '.' + Table_Name ,
        LOWER(table_type) + ' Name'
FROM    information_Schema.tables
WHERE   Table_name LIKE @SearchString
UNION ALL
SELECT  Table_Catalog + '.' + Table_Schema + '.' + Table_Name + '.'
        + constraint_name ,
        LOWER(Constraint_type) + ' constraint Name'
FROM    information_Schema.table_constraints
WHERE   constraint_name LIKE @SearchString
UNION ALL
SELECT  catalog_name + '.' + Schema_name ,
        'Schema'
FROM    information_Schema.schemata
WHERE   schema_name LIKE @SearchString
        AND schema_name NOT LIKE 'db_%'
        AND schema_name NOT LIKE 'information_Schema%'
UNION ALL
SELECT  Table_Catalog + '.' + Table_Schema + '.' + Table_Name + '.'
        + column_name ,
        'TVF Column name'
FROM    information_Schema.ROUTINE_COLUMNS
WHERE   column_name LIKE @SearchString
UNION ALL
SELECT DISTINCT
        Constraint_Catalog + '.' + constraint_Schema + '.'
        + constraint_Name ,
        'Foregn Key constraint'
FROM    information_Schema.Referential_constraints
WHERE   constraint_name LIKE @SearchString
UNION ALL
SELECT DISTINCT
        Unique_Constraint_Catalog + '.' + Unique_constraint_Schema + '.'
        + Unique_constraint_Name ,
        'Unique constraint'
FROM    information_Schema.Referential_constraints
WHERE   Unique_constraint_name LIKE @SearchString
```

273

```
UNION ALL
SELECT   Specific_Catalog + '.' + Specific_Schema + '.' + Specific_Name
         + '(' + Parameter_name + ')' ,
         'routine parameter'
FROM     information_schema.parameters
WHERE    parameter_name <> ''
         AND parameter_name LIKE @SearchString
UNION ALL
SELECT   Table_Catalog + '.' + Table_Schema + '.' + Table_Name + '.'
         + Column_Name ,
         'column Name'
FROM     INFORMATION_SCHEMA.COLUMNS
WHERE    column_name LIKE @SearchString
UNION ALL
SELECT   Table_Catalog + '.' + Table_Schema + '.' + Table_Name + '.'
         + Column_Name + '.default' ,
         'default constraint text'
FROM     INFORMATION_SCHEMA.COLUMNS
WHERE    column_default LIKE @SearchString
```

Listing 9-1: Searching your database using INFORMATION_SCHEMA views.

Learning patience: using SMO

You can get a huge range of database and server objects with SMO, as long as you don't mind waiting, and if you like coding in a .NET language. The problems come when you try to tackle a large database. You are soon in trouble if you have a lot of tables and columns, because you have to walk the hierarchy of SMO objects, rather than do a set-oriented operation. SMO provides a logical and consistent interface into a database, but it does not represent the reality of the way that this information is actually stored in the database.

SMO comes into its own as a way of quickly finding out how to access a "difficult" database object. If you use SMO, and run Profiler at the same time to see what SQL is being executed as a result of running an SMO job, you can quickly achieve SQL MegaStar status in your development team.

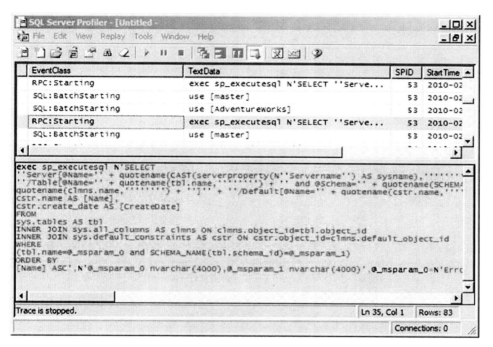

Figure 9-3: Using SMO and Profiler.

Using the object catalog views

I love the object catalog views. In the previous chapter, I showed some simple examples of how to search them to find tables with no primary keys, or indexes, and so on; even Edgar Codd might have grudgingly approved.

However, when searching for specific strings within an object definition, using the catalog views, I wouldn't suggest using them "raw," as they are not as "unwrapped" or denormalized as the `Information_Schema` views are. Really, the only way to survive is to have all the information tucked into a stored procedure that you'd call up to find the things you wanted. Here is the routine I use to search through as much as possible of the structure of databases. I've written it like a Lego tower, with a series of UNION ALLs so as to allow you to break it up and create your own Lego tower. I've included in Listing 9-2 enough of the code to give you the idea. The full code is available from the code download page for this book (see the Introduction).

```
IF EXISTS ( SELECT   *
            FROM    information_Schema.routines
            WHERE   specific_name = 'FindString' )
    DROP PROCEDURE FindString
go
CREATE PROCEDURE FindString
/**
 summary:   >
This finds the string that you specify within the name of every database object
including indices, agent jobs, extended properties and parameters of routines.
It  searches within the text (definition) for every routine, and within the value
of every extended property. It displays the full path of the database object, the
object type, the dates of creation and modification (sometimes that of the parent
if this information isn't available) as well as the name of the parent of the
object.
example:
 - code: findstring '' - -list every object, along with creation date etc
example:
 - code: findString 'GetDate'--find where the string 'getdate' appears!
example:
 - code: findstring 'b[aeiou]t'--find but, bot,bit,bet and bat!
returns:   >
    Qualified_Name  Varchar
This is the fully-qualified name of the object so that you know where it lurks.
Sometimes, the path is a bit artificial, but it should be obvious how the
convention works.
    Object_Type  Varchar
A description of the type of object the string was found in. 'Definition' refers to
the code within the routine.
    created DateTime
The date that either the object or its parent was created.
    Last_Modified DateTime
The date that either the object or its parent was last modified
    Parent Varchar
The name of the parent of the object if known
**/ @SearchString VARCHAR(2000)
AS - --------------------------------------------------------------------
    IF CHARINDEX('%', @SearchString) = 0 - -if user hasn't specifed search
 - -string in the SQL wildcard format.
```

```sql
        SELECT  @SearchString = '%' + @SearchString + '%' -- -add it
SELECT -- -firstly, we'll search the names of the basic objects
        DB_NAME() + '.' + Object_Schema_name(s.[object_ID]) + '.'
        + COALESCE(p.name + '.', '') + s.name AS [Qualified_Name] ,
        REPLACE(SUBSTRING(v.name, 5, 31), 'cns', 'constraint') + ' name'
                                                        AS Object_Type ,
        s.create_date AS 'Created' ,
        s.modify_date AS 'Last_Modified' ,
        COALESCE(p.name, '-') AS 'parent'
FROM    sys.objects S -- -to get the objects
        LEFT OUTER JOIN master.dbo.spt_values v -- -to get the type of object
        ON s.type = SUBSTRING(v.name, 1, 2) COLLATE database_default
            AND v.type = 'O9T'
        LEFT OUTER JOIN sys.objects p -- -to get any parent object
        ON s.parent_Object_ID = p.[object_ID]
WHERE   s.name LIKE @SearchString--string you want to search for
        AND Object_Schema_name(s.object_ID) NOT LIKE 'sys%'
UNION ALL
SELECT--and search all the names of the  columns too
        DB_NAME() + '.' + Object_Schema_name(s.object_ID) + '.' + '.'
        + s.name + '.' + c.name AS [name] ,
        'Column name' AS [object_type] ,
        s.create_date AS 'created' ,
        s.modify_date AS 'Last Modified' ,
        COALESCE(s.name, '-') AS 'parent'
FROM    sys.columns c
        INNER JOIN sys.objects S -- -get table data
        ON c.object_ID = s.object_ID
WHERE   c.name LIKE @SearchString--string you want to search for
        AND Object_Schema_name(s.object_ID) NOT LIKE 'sys%'
UNION ALL
SELECT--and search all the definitions of the computed columns too
        DB_NAME() + '.' + Object_Schema_name(s.object_ID) + '.' + s.name
        + ',' + c.name AS [name] ,
        'computed Column definition' AS [object_type] ,
        s.create_date AS 'created' ,
        s.modify_date AS 'Last Modified' ,
        COALESCE(s.name, '-') AS 'parent'
FROM    sys.computed_columns c
        INNER JOIN sys.objects S ON c.object_ID = s.object_ID
WHERE   c.definition LIKE @SearchString--string you want to search for
        AND Object_Schema_name(s.object_ID) NOT LIKE 'sys$'
UNION ALL -- -now search the XML schema collection names
SELECT  DB_NAME() + '.' + name ,
```

277

```
                    'XML Schema Collection name' ,
            create_date AS 'created' ,
            modify_date AS 'Last Modified' ,
            '-' AS 'parent'
    FROM    sys.xml_schema_collections
    WHERE   name LIKE @SearchString
    UNION ALL — -and now search the names of the DDL triggers (they aren't in sys.
objects)
    SELECT  DB_NAME() + '.' + name ,
            LOWER(type_desc) COLLATE database_default ,
            create_date AS 'created' ,
            modify_date AS 'Last Modified' ,
            '-' AS 'parent'
    FROM    sys.triggers
    WHERE   name LIKE @SearchString--string you want to search for
            AND parent_class = 0--only DDL triggers
    UNION ALL — -and search the names of all the indexes
    SELECT  DB_NAME() + '.' + Object_Schema_name(p.object_ID) + '.' + p.name
            + '.' + i.name ,
            LOWER(i.type_desc) + ' index name' COLLATE database_default ,
            create_date AS 'created' ,
            modify_date AS 'Last Modified' ,
            p.name AS 'parent'
    FROM    sys.indexes i
            INNER JOIN sys.objects p ON i.object_ID = p.object_ID
    WHERE   i.name LIKE @SearchString--string you want to search for
            AND Object_Schema_name(i.object_ID) NOT LIKE 'sys%'
            AND is_primary_key = 0
            AND i.type_desc <> 'HEAP'
    UNION ALL--and we want to know the parameters to the routines
    SELECT  DB_NAME() + '.' + Object_Schema_name(s.[object_ID]) + +s.name
            + '(' + pa.name + ')' AS [name] ,
            SUBSTRING(v.name, 5, 31) + ' parameter name' AS [object_type] ,
            s.create_date AS 'created' ,
            s.modify_date AS 'Last Modified' ,
            COALESCE(s.name, '-') AS 'parent'
    FROM    sys.parameters pa
            INNER JOIN sys.objects S — -to get the objects
            ON pa.object_ID = S.object_ID
            LEFT OUTER JOIN master.dbo.spt_values v
                ON s.type = SUBSTRING(v.name, 1, 2) COLLATE database_default
                    AND v.type = 'O9T'
    WHERE   pa.name <> ''
            AND pa.name LIKE @SearchString--string you want to search for
```

278

```
            AND Object_Schema_name(s.object_ID) NOT LIKE 'sys%'
UNION ALL--and the text (definition) of the default constraints
SELECT  DB_NAME() + '.' + Object_Schema_name(d.parent_object_id) + '.'
        + OBJECT_NAME(d.parent_object_id) + '.' + c.name + '.' + d.name ,
        'default constraint definition' ,
        NULL AS 'created' ,
        NULL AS 'Last Modified' ,
        OBJECT_NAME(d.parent_object_id) AS 'parent'
FROM    sys.default_constraints d
        INNER JOIN sys.columns c ON d.parent_column_id = c.column_id
                                AND d.parent_object_ID = c.object_ID
WHERE   definition LIKE @SearchString
UNION ALL — -the text of other table objects
<...snip...>
```

Listing 9-2:   The `FindString` stored procedure.

Qualified_Name	Object_Type	Created	Last_Modified	parent
AdventureWorks.Sales..vIndividualDemographics.DateFirstPu...	Column name	2005-10-14...	2005-10-14 ...	vIndi...
AdventureWorks.Person..vAdditionalContactInfo.FirstName	Column name	2005-10-14...	2005-10-14 ...	vAd...
AdventureWorks.HumanResources..vEmployee.FirstName	Column name	2005-10-14...	2009-11-23 ...	vEm...
AdventureWorks.HumanResources..vEmployeeDepartment.Fi...	Column name	2005-10-14...	2005-10-14 ...	vEm...
AdventureWorks.HumanResources..vEmployeeDepartmentHi...	Column name	2005-10-14...	2005-10-14 ...	vEm...
AdventureWorks.Sales..vIndividualCustomer.FirstName	Column name	2005-10-14...	2005-10-14 ...	vIndi...
AdventureWorks.Person..Contact.FirstName	Column name	2005-10-14...	2005-10-14 ...	Cont...
AdventureWorks.Sales..vSalesPerson.FirstName	Column name	2005-10-14...	2005-10-14 ...	vSal...
AdventureWorks.Sales..vStoreWithDemographics.FirstName	Column name	2005-10-14...	2005-10-14 ...	vSto...
AdventureWorks.Purchasing..vVendor.FirstName	Column name	2005-10-14...	2005-10-14 ...	vVe...
AdventureWorks.dbo..ufnGetContactInformation.FirstName	Column name	2005-10-14...	2005-10-14 ...	ufnG...
AdventureWorks.HumanResources..vJobCandidate.Name.First	Column name	2005-10-14...	2005-10-14 ...	vJob...
AdventureWorks.Person.vAdditionalContactInfo	view definition	2005-10-14...	2005-10-14 ...	-
AdventureWorks.HumanResources.vEmployee	view definition	2005-10-14...	2009-11-23 ...	-
AdventureWorks.HumanResources.vEmployeeDepartment	view definition	2005-10-14...	2005-10-14 ...	-

You'll notice that we access an old Sybase table, using `master.dbo.spt_values where the v.type = 'O9T'`. This table lists a whole range of enumerations, and `O9T` refers to the system object types.

279

At some point, someone decided to use the special value of 0 to denote the description of the type, which you can see from...

```
SELECT name,* FROM master.dbo.spt_values WHERE number=0 ORDER BY type
```

...but the scheme soon fell foul of the fact that some enumerations, such as binary 'Yes'/'No', required a zero!

Using System Tables (pre-SQL 2005)

If you are stuck on SQL Server 2000 or older, this shouldn't stop you dead in your tracks, because there are still ways to get at this metadata. Instead of using the catalog views, you have to use the system tables. The mapping between the system tables and the system catalog views are all listed for you on Books Online. The big problem is that the code is complicated by the fact that each routine is stored in as many NVARCHAR(4000) chunks as are required to hold the entire definition. A solution that I use for searching through the definitions of routines in SQL Server 2000 database is given at: WWW.SIMPLE-TALK. COM/COMMUNITY/BLOGS/PHILFACTOR/ARCHIVE/2006/06/03/854.ASPX.

Using SSMS to Explore Table Metadata

Using some of the previously-presented scripts, and a little ingenuity, we can use SSMS to do a detailed exploration of the metadata of our routines and tables. To provide a feel for the sort of magic that is possible, let's start with a brief demo. I have a blank query window. I wonder what tables I have in my database and what they're for. I hit my query shortcut, CTRL+6. The output shown in Figure 9-4 appears in the results pane.

Figure 9-4: A list of tables, columns, and table description, for a given database.

I have a list of tables for the database we are investigating (**AdventureWorks**, in this case). Hmm. I'll pop them into the query pane in order to explore them. So, what is this table, **ProductReview**? I hit CTRL+3 and instantly out pops the build script for that table, as shown in Figure 9-5.

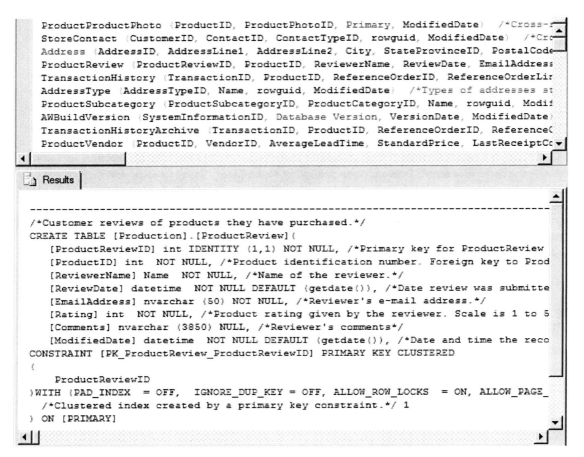

```
ProductProductPhoto (ProductID, ProductPhotoID, Primary, ModifiedDate)  /*Cross-r
StoreContact (CustomerID, ContactID, ContactTypeID, rowguid, ModifiedDate)  /*Cro
Address (AddressID, AddressLine1, AddressLine2, City, StateProvinceID, PostalCode
ProductReview (ProductReviewID, ProductID, ReviewerName, ReviewDate, EmailAddress
TransactionHistory (TransactionID, ProductID, ReferenceOrderID, ReferenceOrderLir
AddressType (AddressTypeID, Name, rowguid, ModifiedDate)  /*Types of addresses st
ProductSubcategory (ProductSubcategoryID, ProductCategoryID, Name, rowguid, Modif
AWBuildVersion (SystemInformationID, Database Version, VersionDate, ModifiedDate)
TransactionHistoryArchive (TransactionID, ProductID, ReferenceOrderID, Reference(
ProductVendor (ProductID, VendorID, AverageLeadTime, StandardPrice, LastReceiptCc
```

Results

```
---------------------------------------------------------------------------
/*Customer reviews of products they have purchased.*/
CREATE TABLE [Production].[ProductReview](
    [ProductReviewID] int IDENTITY (1,1) NOT NULL, /*Primary key for ProductReview
    [ProductID] int  NOT NULL, /*Product identification number. Foreign key to Prod
    [ReviewerName] Name  NOT NULL, /*Name of the reviewer.*/
    [ReviewDate] datetime  NOT NULL DEFAULT (getdate()), /*Date review was submitte
    [EmailAddress] nvarchar (50) NOT NULL, /*Reviewer's e-mail address.*/
    [Rating] int  NOT NULL, /*Product rating given by the reviewer. Scale is 1 to 5
    [Comments] nvarchar (3850) NULL, /*Reviewer's comments*/
    [ModifiedDate] datetime  NOT NULL DEFAULT (getdate()), /*Date and time the reco
CONSTRAINT [PK_ProductReview_ProductReviewID] PRIMARY KEY CLUSTERED
(
    ProductReviewID
)WITH (PAD_INDEX  = OFF,  IGNORE_DUP_KEY = OFF, ALLOW_ROW_LOCKS  = ON, ALLOW_PAGE_
  /*Clustered index created by a primary key constraint.*/ 1
) ON [PRIMARY]
```

Figure 9-5: A complete build script for the ProductReview Table.

I have turned this query window into a powerful table-inspector, and I could do the same thing for procedures, functions or triggers.

How about telling me where the string ProductReview occurs? I select it, hit CTRL+4, and I see the output shown in Figure 9-6, showing all the objects where this string occurs.

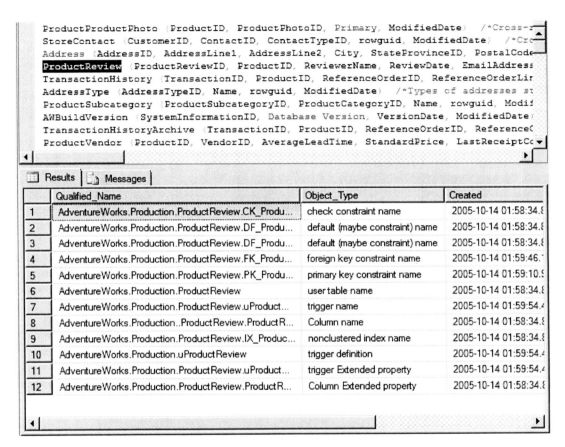

Figure 9-6: All objects that contain a given string.

How do I do this? It's a combination of SSMS shortcut keys, and some useful metadata queries and stored procedures.

SSMS shortcut keys

There exists in SSMS a very useful facility for executing particular stored procedures or simple SQL expressions of your choice. There are a number of special keyboard shortcuts that are reserved for the user. These are called the query shortcuts and are accessed with ALT+F1, CTRL+F1, CTRL+1, CTRL+2, and so on, up to CTRL+0, as shown in Figure 9-7.

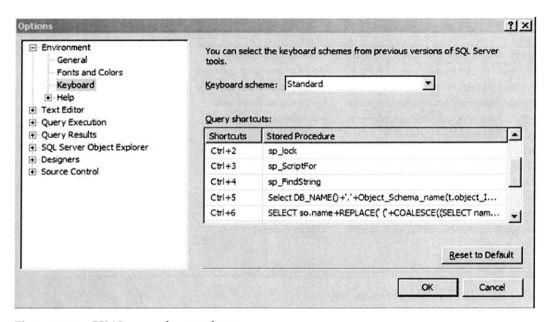

Figure 9-7:   SSMS query shortcut keys.

Normally, you use these keys to invoke the system stored procedures, such as `sp_Help`, `sp_HelpText` and `sp_Who`. The other nine slots are left enticingly blank for your own routines or queries. You can get in there and add your own, but these will only work in Query Windows that you open subsequently!

Of course, for information such as that build script, you'll probably need to set the results window to "text," and increase the number of characters displayed in each column to a sensible level, such as 8,000 chars.

If you highlight text in the code pane of the query window in SSMS or QA, and then invoke code that is slotted into one of these keyboard shortcuts, whatever you highlight is appended "as-is" to what is executed. This means that if you want to pass a string to a procedure it will need to be a valid delimited string, escaped if necessary. If it is a valid object name, it is coerced successfully into a string. This means that you can pass the name of an object, but a qualified object name would have to be delimited properly.

Most of the code that I have in query shortcuts is for getting lists of tables, procedures, parameters and so on. I haven't hit a limit for the length of the expression, but it has to be all in one line. To force a query onto a single line, you can simply do a find-and-replace in SSMS (CTRL+F), and replace "\n" with nothing (or a single space).

Useful shortcut queries

Every grey-muzzled database programmer will have a "thumb-drive" of favorite utility queries and routines to ease the development process. If you are clever with these, the requirement to continually poke and click all over SSMS to get anything done soon diminishes to a tolerable level, and so your subsequent development work can get much faster.

For any query that requires parameters, you'll have to use a stored procedure, as we'll discuss in more detail shortly, but there are a number of queries that can go on one line and that provide useful information. Each time, simply shrink it down to a single line, and paste it into one of the shortcut keys. Let's start with a simple query, shown in Listing 9-3, which lists all tables, functions, stored procedures, and triggers for a given database.

```
/*list all the tables*/
SELECT   name AS [Tables]
FROM     sys.objects
WHERE    OBJECTPROPERTY(object_id, 'isUserTable') <> 0
/*list all the Scalar functions*/
SELECT   name AS [Scalar functions]
```

```
FROM      sys.objects
WHERE     OBJECTPROPERTY(object_id, 'IsScalarFunction') <> 0
/*list all the Table Functions*/
SELECT    name AS [Table Functions]
FROM      sys.objects
WHERE     OBJECTPROPERTY(object_id, 'IsTableFunction') <> 0
/*list all the Procedures*/
SELECT    name AS [Procedures]
FROM      sys.objects
WHERE     OBJECTPROPERTY(object_id, 'IsProcedure') <> 0
/*list all the Triggers*/
SELECT    name AS [Triggers]
FROM      sys.objects
WHERE     OBJECTPROPERTY(object_id, 'IsTrigger') <> 0
```

Listing 9-3: Listing objects in a given database.

There are a host of other queries you can work out from here. Of course, you can elaborate them. Listing 9-4 shows some code that will return all your functions along with their parameters, and any extended properties.

```
SELECT    so.name + REPLACE('('
                       + COALESCE(( SELECT    name + ', '
                                    FROM      sys.parameters sp
                                    WHERE     sp.object_ID = so.object_ID
                                              AND parameter_ID > 0
                                    ORDER BY parameter_ID
                                    FOR
                                    XML PATH('')
                                 ), '') + ')', ', ', ')', ')')
          + COALESCE('  /*' + CONVERT(VARCHAR(300), value) + '*/', '')
                                              [Scalar functions]
FROM      sys.objects so
          LEFT OUTER JOIN sys.extended_properties ep
                       /*get any extended properties*/
                                 ON ep.name LIKE 'MS_Description'
                       AND major_ID = so.object_ID
WHERE     OBJECTPROPERTY(object_id, 'IsScalarFunction') <> 0
```

Listing 9-4: A query to return all functions and their parameters.

How about listing out all tables along with a list of columns that can then be used for **SELECT** and **UPDATE** statements? Easy: the query is remarkably similar to the one for the functions, and is the table-lister I used earlier for the CTRL+6 shortcut key.

```sql
SELECT   so.name + REPLACE(' ('
                          + COALESCE(( SELECT    name + ', '
                                       FROM      sys.columns sp
                                       WHERE     sp.object_ID = so.object_ID
                                                 AND column_ID > 0
                                       ORDER BY column_ID
                                     FOR
                                       XML PATH('')
                                     ), '') + ')', ', )', ')')
         + COALESCE('  /*' + CONVERT(VARCHAR(300), value) + '*/', '') [Tables]
FROM     sys.objects so
         LEFT OUTER JOIN sys.extended_properties ep
                                          /* get any extended properties*/
         ON ep.name LIKE 'MS_Description'
            AND major_ID = so.object_ID
            AND minor_ID = 0
WHERE    OBJECTPROPERTY(object_id, 'IsUserTable') <> 0
```

Listing 9-5:   A query to return all tables and their columns.

You can just keep the table list handy somewhere when doing some development work (I use AceText but you can use Notepad if you have nothing better).

With a moment's thought, you'll notice that you can elaborate on this, as shown in Listing 9-6, to give yourself the complete **SELECT** statement for tables, including all the comments, for all your database tables. This is suddenly powerful magic.

```sql
SELECT   '/* ' + qualifiedName + ' */' + CHAR(13) + CHAR(10)
       + REPLACE(REPLACE
           (STUFF(SelectScript, /*delete final comma line-terminator*/
                  LEN(SelectScript) - CHARINDEX('|,|',
                                            REVERSE(SelectScript)
                                            + '|') - 1, 3,
                  ''), '\n', CHAR(13) + CHAR(10)), '|,|', ',') /*put in new-
                                            lines and convert token to comma*/
FROM     ( SELECT    so.name AS Name ,
                     OBJECT_SCHEMA_NAME(so.object_ID) + '.' + so.name
                                               AS qualifiedName ,
                     'SELECT '
                     + REPLACE(COALESCE(
                           ( SELECT '\n       ' + QUOTENAME(sp.name)
                                    + '|,|' + COALESCE(' /*'
                                          + CONVERT(VARCHAR(MAX), value)
                                          + '*/', '')
                             FROM   sys.columns sp
                               LEFT OUTER JOIN sys.extended_properties ep
                                    ON sp.object_id = ep.major_ID
                                       AND sp.column_ID = minor_ID
                                       AND class = 1
                               WHERE  sp.object_ID = so.object_ID
                                    AND column_ID > 0
                               ORDER BY column_ID
                             FOR
                               XML PATH('')
                           ), '1'), ',||', '') + '\nFROM  '
                     + QUOTENAME(OBJECT_SCHEMA_NAME(so.object_ID)) + '.'
                     + QUOTENAME(so.name) + COALESCE('  /*'
                                          + CONVERT(VARCHAR(300), value)
                                          + '*/', '') [SelectScript]
           FROM      sys.objects so
                     LEFT OUTER JOIN sys.extended_properties ep /* get any
                                               extended properties */
                           ON ep.name LIKE 'MS_Description'
                               AND major_ID = so.object_ID
                               AND minor_ID = 0
           WHERE     OBJECTPROPERTY(object_id, 'IsUserTable') <> 0
         ) f
ORDER BY name
```

Listing 9-6: Generate the SELECT statements from all tables in a given database.

This routine will create a **SELECT** statement for every table in your database, including both table and column comments in extended properties. Listing 9-7 shows some sample output for a single table.

```
/* Person.Address */
SELECT
      [AddressID], /*Primary key for Address records.*/
      [AddressLine1], /*First street address line.*/
      [AddressLine2], /*Second street address line.*/
      [City], /*Name of the city.*/
      [StateProvinceID], /*Unique identification number for the state or province.
Foreign key to StateProvince table.*/
      [PostalCode], /*Postal code for the street address.*/
      [rowguid], /*ROWGUIDCOL number uniquely identifying the record. Used to
support a merge replication sample.*/
      [ModifiedDate] /*Date and time the record was last updated.*/
FROM  [Person].[Address]  /*Street address information for customers, employees,
and vendors.*/
```

Listing 9-7: **SELECT** statement generated for the **Person.Address** table in **AdventureWorks**.

You may wonder why I put the name of the table in comments at the start: this is to make it easier to locate the **SELECT** statements if your results pane is set to "grid" view, as shown in Figure 9-8.

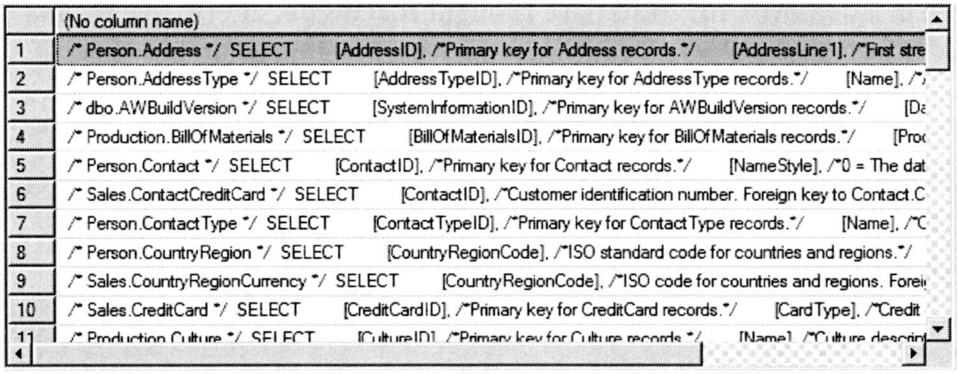

Figure 9-8: The opening comments make it easier to locate the **SELECT** statement for a table.

289

The equivalent script for executing table-valued functions is even more complex, but it, and the script for executing procedures, can be useful if you take care to document your code using extended properties (I use SQL Doc to make this easier to do). Your code starts looking a lot more readable and understandable.

Useful shortcut stored procedures

You'll notice a catch when you want to get to the next level of complexity. We want to be able to highlight a string in a query window and have it supplied as a parameter to a query we have loaded into one of our shortcut keys. In fact, in this case, we can't use a query since the parameter ends up being appended. This is a killer. We have to use a stored procedure instead.

Here we hit a particular problem, in that these keyboard query shortcuts are designed purely for use by system stored procedures, and they don't easily lend themselves to use with normal stored procedures, unless you propagate them to every database on which you are working.

As a general practice, I put my kit of development tools in the **Model** database, in a dev schema, so it automatically gets propagated to all my development databases as I create them. However, this is useless for a keyboard shortcut tool, and it can end up being accidentally included in a deployment. You'd have thought that a safer alternative would be to create a special "Dev" database for all your metadata-pummeling tools, but this would mean that your tools could only be invoked for that database! The only alternative to placing your dev routines in each database is to put them in the **Master** database. We are faced with needing to make a special plea to the DBA to be allowed to do this, adding the **sp_** prefix, and registering the stored procedure as a system stored procedure, but you would end up having to redo it on every service pack and upgrade.

As such, putting routines into the `Master` database isn't generally a good idea, but I'm afraid that this particular extension of SSMS requires it if you wish to have more than the standard development stored procedures such as `sp_help` and `sp_helptext`.

One very useful stored procedure to have in your query shortcuts is `FindString`, presented in the previous chapter, which searches for any occurrence of a given string in a database (see Figure 9-6). As discussed, you'll to change its name by giving it an `sp_` prefix, and put it in the `Master` database, making sure you register it, too.

Generating Build Scripts

If you haven't got SQL Prompt, table build scripts can be gotten from SSMS just by opening up the browser, clicking on the database, clicking on "Tables," and then right-clicking on the required table. Then you need to select "script tables as" and finally choose a suitable target. When you finally get the table build script, you'll see that it isn't really designed for humans to look at. The comments (`MS_Description`) for each column aren't shown with the table, and the description of the table is lost halfway down the page. It isn't usually clear which columns are foreign keys or what they are referring to (they don't use the clearer "REFERENCES" syntax for single-column foreign key constraints).

In short, it isn't programmer-friendly. Doing things this way is fine for the database of your CD collection, but not much else. For serious exploration of metadata, you need something much better. Ideally, of course, you'll have everything to hand using SQL Doc, or some other third-party documenter, but the method I'm describing isn't bad, and can be honed to your exact requirements.

So, let's say we want to highlight the name of a routine or table, in a query window, and hit a keyboard shortcut to get a build script. With stored procedures, views, triggers and functions, SQL Server stores the source and so the build script is easy to fetch out, as shown in Listing 9-8.

```
--find the actual code for a particular stored procedure, view, function, etc.
SELECT   OBJECT_NAME(object_ID) ,
         definition
FROM     sys.SQL_Modules
WHERE    OBJECT_NAME(object_ID) = 'vEmployeeDepartment'
--find the actual code for a particular stored procedure, view, function, etc.
SELECT   name ,
         object_definition(object_ID)
FROM     sys.objects
WHERE    object_ID = OBJECT_ID('HumanResources.vEmployeeDepartment')
```

Listing 9-8: Generating the build script for stored procedures, views, triggers, and functions.

If fetching table scripts were that easy, you wouldn't need the rather scary script coming up next. However, tables aren't held in script form in SQL Server because it would be difficult to synchronize the script with any changes you made to its child objects, such as columns or constraints. Instead, each time you request a table build script in SSMS, it uses SMO to reconstitute the script. It is an elaborate process. Unlike in MySQL, there is no SQL Server command to produce a table build script. Either we have to use SMO, or hand-craft a stored procedure to do it.

Table build scripts are hard to get right, and they're a moving target with every revision of SQL Server. However, here is my take on the problem, which aims to provide the script for any object. Remember, before you use this, that the **sp_ScriptFor** stored procedure, shown in Listing 9-9, is intended to allow you to get information about your objects such as tables, functions, procedures, and so on. The table section, in particular, will not give you a complete build script, as I don't bother with indexes and **CHECK** constraints, or all those messy extended property build expressions. Oh no, this is for looking at.

```
USE MASTER
SET ANSI_NULLS ON
GO
SET QUOTED_IDENTIFIER ON
GO
IF EXISTS (SELECT 1 FROM sys.objects WHERE name LIKE 'sp_ScriptFor')
      DROP PROCEDURE sp_ScriptFor
go
CREATE PROCEDURE [dbo].[sp_ScriptFor]
@Identifier NVARCHAR(776)
/**
summary:   >
This procedure returns an object build script as a single row, single column
result. Unlike the built-in OBJECT_DEFINITION, it also does tables.
It copies the SMO style where possible but it uses the more intuitive
way of representing referential constraints and includes the documentation
as comments that was, for unknown reasons, left out by Microsoft.
You call it with the name of the table, either as a string, a valid table name,
or as a schema-qualified table name in a string.
Author: Phil Factor
Revision: 1.1 dealt properly with heaps
date: 20 Apr 2010
example:
 - code: sp_ScriptFor 'production.TransactionHistory'
example:
 - code: sp_ScriptFor 'HumanResources.vEmployee'
example:
 - code: execute phone..sp_ScriptFor 'holidays'
example:
 - code: execute AdventureWorks..sp_ScriptFor TransactionHistory
example:
 - code: sp_ScriptFor 'HumanResources.uspUpdateEmployeeHireInfo'
returns:    >
single row, single column result Build_Script.
**/
--sp_helptext sp_help 'jobcandidate'
AS
DECLARE @Script VARCHAR(MAX)
DECLARE         @dbname         SYSNAME
DECLARE @PrimaryKeyBuild VARCHAR(MAX)
IF CHARINDEX ('.',@identifier)=0
      SELECT @Identifier=QUOTENAME(Object_Schema_name(s.object_id))
                  +'.'+QUOTENAME(s.name)
      FROM sys.objects s WHERE s.name LIKE @identifier
```

293

```
SELECT @dbname = PARSENAME(@identifier,3)
        IF @dbname IS NULL
                SELECT @dbname = DB_NAME()
        ELSE IF @dbname <> DB_NAME()
                BEGIN
                        RAISERROR(15250,-1,-1)
                        RETURN(1)
                END
SELECT @Script=object_definition(OBJECT_ID(@Identifier))
IF @script IS NULL
        IF (SELECT TYPE FROM sys.objects
            WHERE object_id=OBJECT_ID(@Identifier))
        IN ('U','S')--if it is a table
                BEGIN
                SELECT @Script='/*'+CONVERT(VARCHAR(2000),value)+'*/
        FROM  sys.extended_properties ep
                        WHERE ep.major_ID = OBJECT_ID(@identifier)
                        AND  minor_ID=0 AND class=1
SELECT @Script=COALESCE(@Script,'')+'CREATE TABLE '+@Identifier+'(
    ' +
(SELECT     QUOTENAME(c.name)+ ' '+ t.name+' '
        + CASE WHEN is_computed=1 THEN ' AS '+ --do DDL for a computed column
                        (SELECT definition FROM sys.computed_columns cc
                          WHERE cc.object_id=c.object_id
                                AND cc.column_ID=c.column_ID)
                + CASE WHEN
                        (SELECT is_persisted FROM sys.computed_columns cc
                                        WHERE cc.object_id=c.object_id
                                        AND cc.column_ID=c.column_ID)
                        =1 THEN 'PERSISTED' ELSE '' END
-- -we may have to put in the length
                WHEN t.name IN ('char', 'varchar','nchar','nvarchar') THEN '('+
                CASE WHEN c.max_length=-1 THEN 'MAX'
                        ELSE CONVERT(VARCHAR(4),
                                    CASE WHEN t.name IN ('nchar','nvarchar')
                                    THEN  c.max_length/2 ELSE c.max_length END )
                        END +')'
                WHEN t.name IN ('decimal','numeric')
                        THEN '('+ CONVERT(VARCHAR(4),c.precision)+','
                            + CONVERT(VARCHAR(4),c.Scale)+')'
                        ELSE '' END
                + CASE WHEN is_identity=1
                        THEN 'IDENTITY ('
                        + CONVERT(VARCHAR(8),IDENT_SEED(Object_Schema_Name
```

```
                                              (c.object_id)
          +'.'+OBJECT_NAME(c.object_id)))+','
          + CONVERT(VARCHAR(8),IDENT_INCR(Object_Schema_Name
                                             (c.object_id)
          +'.'+OBJECT_NAME(c.object_id)))+')' ELSE '' END
    + CASE WHEN c.is_rowguidcol=1 THEN ' ROWGUIDCOL' ELSE '' END
    + CASE WHEN XML_collection_ID<>0 THEN -- -deal with object
-- -schema names
                        '('+ CASE WHEN is_XML_Document=1
                                  THEN 'DOCUMENT '
                                  ELSE 'CONTENT ' END
        + COALESCE(
            (SELECT QUOTENAME(ss.name)+'.' +QUOTENAME(sc.name)
             FROM sys.xml_schema_collections sc
             INNER JOIN  Sys.Schemas ss
                ON sc.schema_ID=ss.schema_ID
             WHERE sc.xml_collection_ID=c.XML_collection_ID)
            ,'NULL')
          +')' ELSE '' END
    + CASE WHEN  is_identity=1
        THEN CASE WHEN OBJECTPROPERTY(object_id, 'IsUserTable') = 1
                AND COLUMNPROPERTY(object_id, c.name,
                                        'IsIDNotForRepl') = 0
            AND OBJECTPROPERTY(object_id, 'IsMSShipped') = 0
        THEN '' ELSE ' NOT FOR REPLICATION ' END ELSE '' END
    + CASE WHEN c.is_nullable=0 THEN ' NOT NULL' ELSE ' NULL' END
    + CASE WHEN c.default_object_id <>0
        THEN ' DEFAULT '+object_Definition(c.default_object_id)
        ELSE '' END
    + CASE WHEN c.collation_name IS NULL THEN ''
        WHEN  c.collation_name<>
                (SELECT collation_name FROM sys.databases
                    WHERE name=DB_NAME()) COLLATE Latin1_General_CI_AS
        THEN COALESCE(' COLLATE '+c.collation_name,'')
        ELSE '' END+'|,|'
    + CASE WHEN ep.value IS NOT NULL
        THEN ' /*'+CAST(value AS VARCHAR(100))+ '*/'
        ELSE '' END
    + CHAR(10)+'    '
FROM sys.columns c INNER JOIN sys.types t
        ON c.user_Type_ID=t.user_Type_ID
LEFT OUTER JOIN sys.extended_properties ep
        ON c.object_id = ep.major_ID
            AND c.column_ID = minor_ID AND class=1
```

295

```
                LEFT OUTER JOIN
                (SELECT 'REFERENCES '
            +COALESCE(SCHEMA_NAME(fkc.referenced_object_id)+'.','')
            +OBJECT_NAME(fkc.referenced_object_id)+'('+c.name+') '--+
            + CASE WHEN delete_referential_action_desc <> 'NO_ACTION'
                    THEN 'ON DELETE '
                    + REPLACE(delete_referential_action_desc,'_',' ')
                  COLLATE database_default
                  ELSE '' END
            + CASE WHEN update_referential_action_desc <> 'NO_ACTION'
                    THEN 'ON UPDATE '
                    + REPLACE(update_referential_action_desc,'_',' ')
                  COLLATE database_default
                  ELSE '' END
                        AS reference, parent_column_id
                    FROM sys.foreign_key_columns fkc
                    INNER JOIN sys.foreign_keys fk ON
                                        constraint_object_id=fk.object_ID
                    INNER JOIN sys.columns c
                    ON c.object_ID = fkc.referenced_object_id
                        AND c.column_ID = referenced_column_id
                     WHERE fk.parent_object_ID = OBJECT_ID(@identifier)
                    AND constraint_object_ID NOT IN -- -include only
    -- -single-column keys
                    (SELECT 1 FROM sys.foreign_key_columns multicolumn
                             WHERE multicolumn.parent_object_id
                                            =fk.parent_object_ID
                             GROUP BY constraint_object_id
                             HAVING COUNT(*)>1)) column_references
            ON  column_references.parent_column_ID=c.column_ID
        WHERE object_id = OBJECT_ID(@identifier)
        ORDER BY c.column_ID
              FOR XML PATH(''))--join up all the rows!
              SELECT @Script=LEFT(@Script,LEN(@Script)-1)
    -- -take out the trailing line feed
              SELECT TOP 1 @PrimaryKeyBuild= '
CONSTRAINT ['+i.name+'] PRIMARY KEY '
                    +CASE WHEN type_desc='CLUSTERED' THEN 'CLUSTERED'
                        ELSE '' END+'
   (
          '  + COALESCE(SUBSTRING((SELECT ','+COL_NAME(ic.object_id,ic.column_id)
              FROM  sys.index_columns AS ic
              WHERE ic.index_ID=i.index_ID AND ic.object_id=i.object_id
              ORDER BY key_ordinal
```

```
                   FOR XML PATH('')),2,2000),'?')+'
     )WITH (PAD_INDEX  = '
         +CASE WHEN is_Padded<>0 THEN 'ON' ELSE 'OFF' END
         +',  IGNORE_DUP_KEY = '
             +CASE WHEN ignore_dup_key<>0 THEN 'ON' ELSE 'OFF' END
         +', ALLOW_ROW_LOCKS  = '
             +CASE WHEN allow_row_locks<>0 THEN 'ON' ELSE 'OFF' END
         +', ALLOW_PAGE_LOCKS  = '
             +CASE WHEN allow_page_locks<>0 THEN 'ON' ELSE 'OFF' END
         +') ON [PRIMARY]'+
             + CASE WHEN ep.value IS NOT NULL THEN '
    /*'+CAST(value AS VARCHAR(100))+'*/' ELSE '' END
                FROM sys.indexes i
                LEFT OUTER JOIN sys.extended_properties ep
                     ON i.object_id = ep.major_ID
                        AND i.index_ID = minor_ID AND class=7
                WHERE OBJECT_NAME(object_id)=PARSENAME(@identifier,1)
                   AND is_primary_key =1
   - -and add the primary key build script and the ON PRIMARY, deleting the
   - - last comma-line-terminator if necessary. conver the |,| to commas
                IF @PrimaryKeyBuild IS NULL
                     SELECT @Script=STUFF(@Script,--delete final comma
   - -line-terminator
                               LEN(@Script)-CHARINDEX('|,|',
                               REVERSE(@Script)+'|')-1,3
                               ,'')
                SELECT @Script=REPLACE(@Script,'|,|',',')
                     +COALESCE(@PrimaryKeyBuild,'')+'
   ) ON [PRIMARY]'
   END
   SELECT COALESCE(@Script,'- — could not find '''+@identifier+''' in '
          +DB_NAME(),'null identifier.')
       AS Build_Script
   GO
   IF NOT EXISTS
     (SELECT 1 FROM sys.objects WHERE NAME = 'sp_ScriptFor' AND IS_MS_SHIPPED=1)
       EXEC sp_ms_marksystemobject 'sp_ScriptFor'
   GO
```

Listing 9-9: The sp_ScriptFor stored procedure.

So, all you need to do now is to collect up the other scripts you find useful, and configure up your SSMS query shortcuts to give you extra speed for your database development work, especially if you are refactoring someone else's database. The reason I like doing this sort of thing is because I like to hone my development environment to my own particular tastes. Your tastes will be different, but I hope you agree with the principle that it is good to take some time to make sure you can develop things quickly and without frustrating delays. There is nothing more frustrating than wrestling with an IDE designed by people who don't seem to understand how database developers do their work.

Summary

I use all the methods I've described for perusing the structures in databases. If I want quick information in the course of writing a database routine, I use SQL Search. When I'm doing some intensive refactoring, I'll use the full Build script, but always in a Programmers Text Editor rather than SSMS (I once hit "Execute" instead of "Open file," and deleted a database). I use `Information_Schema` views wherever possible, as they are reasonably future proof and open standard. I use object catalog views when I can't get what I want from `Information_Schema` views, and I use system tables when I have to use older versions of SQL Server.

Index

Index

....

SQL Server
and .NET tools
from Red Gate Software

SQL Compare Pro® $595

Compare and synchronize SQL Server database schemas

↗ Automate database comparisons, and synchronize your databases

↗ Simple, easy to use, 100% accurate

↗ Save hours of tedious work, and eliminate manual scripting errors

↗ Work with live databases, snapshots, script files, or backups

> **"SQL Compare and SQL Data Compare are
> the best purchases we've made in the .NET/
> SQL environment. They've saved us hours
> of development time, and the fast, easy-to-
> use database comparison gives us maximum
> confidence that our migration scripts are correct.
> We rely on these products for every deployment."**
>
> **Paul Tebbutt** Technical Lead, Universal Music Group

SQL Data Compare Pro™ $595

Compare and synchronize SQL Server database contents

↗ Compare your database contents

↗ Automatically synchronize your data

↗ Row-level data restore

↗ Compare to scripts, backups, or live databases

> **"We use SQL Data Compare daily
> and it has become an indispensable
> part of delivering our service to our
> customers. It has also streamlined
> our daily update process and cut back
> literally a good solid hour per day."**
>
> **George Pantela** GPAnalysis.com

Visit **www.red-gate.com** for a 14-day, free trial

SQL Server backup compression tools
High performance compression and encryption as standard

If you're looking for an end-to-end backup compression tool with powerful job management, network resilience, and advanced restore options, try SQL Backup Pro.

If you want to manage your compressed backups with native SQL Server maintenance plans and the option to back up to .zip for flexible restores, try SQL HyperBac.

SQL Backup™ Pro $795
Compress, encrypt, and strengthen SQL Server backups

- ↗ Compress SQL Server database backups by up to 95% for faster, smaller backups
- ↗ Protect your data with up to 256-bit AES encryption
- ↗ Strengthen your backups with network resilience to enable a fault-tolerant transfer of backups across flaky networks
- ↗ Control your backup activities through an intuitive interface, with powerful job management and an interactive timeline

> "With version 6 introducing a fourth level of compression and network resilience, SQL Backup will be a REAL boost to any DBA."
> **Jonathan Allen** Senior Database Administrator

SQL HyperBac™ $795
Silent compression for faster, smaller SQL Server backups

- ↗ Silently compress SQL Server backups by up to 95%
- ↗ Works seamlessly with T-SQL commands and requires no changes to existing backup techniques
- ↗ Protect your data with 256-bit AES encryption
- ↗ Back up to .zip for restores to any server, free from proprietary formats

> "The beauty of SQL HyperBac is that you do not need to alter what you are doing. Just install the software, configure the service, and you are essentially done; no messy re-writes of backup jobs. The backup time is also significantly reduced, along with the actual size of the backup file."
> **Doug Johns** MCDBA

HYPERBAC® POWERED

Visit **www.red-gate.com** for a 14-day, free trial

SQL Virtual Restore™ $495

Rapidly mount live, fully functional databases direct from backups

- ↗ Turn backups into live databases for quick and easy access to data, without requiring a physical restore
- ↗ Live databases mounted by SQL Virtual Restore require significantly less storage space than a regular physical restore
- ↗ Recreate a fully functional database - databases mounted with SQL Virtual Restore support both read/write operations
- ↗ Perform smart object level recovery - SQL Virtual Restore is ACID compliant and gives you access to full, transactionally consistent data, with all objects visible and available
- ↗ Verify your backups - run DBCC CHECKDB against databases mounted by SQL Virtual Restore, without requiring the space and time for a full restore

HYPERBAC® POWERED

> "SQL Virtual Restore offers several important benefits to DBAs that a standard restore can't provide: substantial space savings, and substantial restore time savings."
> **Brad McGehee** Director of DBA Education, Red Gate Software

SQL Storage Compress™ $1,595

Silent data compression to optimize SQL Server storage

- ↗ Reduce the storage footprint of live SQL Server databases by up to 90% to save on space and hardware costs
- ↗ Works seamlessly with compressed files – databases compressed with SQL Storage Compress are live and fully functional
- ↗ Integrates seamlessly with SQL Server and does not require any configuration changes
- ↗ Protect the data in your live databases with 256-bit AES encryption

HYPERBAC® POWERED

Visit **www.red-gate.com** for a 14-day, free trial

SQL Monitor™

Proactive SQL Server performance monitoring and alerting

↗ Intuitive overviews at global, machine, SQL Server and database levels for up-to-the minute performance data

↗ SQL Monitor's web UI means you can check your server health and performance on the go with many mobile devices, including tablets

↗ Intelligent SQL Server alerts via email and an alert inbox in the UI, so you know about problems first

↗ Comprehensive historical data, so you can go back in time to identify the source of a problem fast

↗ Generate reports via the UI and with SQL Server Reporting Services

↗ Investigate long-running queries, SQL deadlocks, blocked processes, and more, to resolve problems sooner

↗ Fast, simple installation and administration

> "Being web-based, SQL Monitor is readily available to you, wherever you may be on your network. You can check on your servers from almost any location, via most mobile devices that support a web-browser."
>
> **Jonathan Allen** Senior DBA, Careers South West Ltd

Due for release Q4 2010

SQL Toolbelt™ $1,995

The essential SQL Server tools for
database professionals

You can buy our acclaimed SQL Server tools individually or bundled. Our most popular deal is
the SQL Toolbelt: fourteen of our SQL Server tools in a single installer, with **a combined value of
$5,930 but an actual price of $1,995**, a saving of 66%.

Fully compatible with SQL Server 2000, 2005, and 2008.

SQL Toolbelt contains:

↗ **SQL Compare Pro**   ↗ **SQL Doc**

↗ **SQL Data Compare Pro**   ↗ **SQL Dependency Tracker**

↗ **SQL Source Control**   ↗ **SQL Packager**

↗ **SQL Backup Pro**   ↗ **SQL Multi Script Unlimited**

↗ **SQL Response**   ↗ **SQL Refactor**

↗ **SQL Prompt Pro**   ↗ **SQL Comparison SDK**

↗ **SQL Data Generator**   ↗ **SQL Object Level Recovery Native**

> **"The SQL Toolbelt provides tools
> that database developers, as well
> as DBAs, should not live without."**
> **William Van Orden** Senior Database Developer,
> Lockheed Martin

Visit **www.red-gate.com** for a 14-day, free trial

.NET Reflector ®   Free

Explore, browse, and analyze .NET assemblies

↗ View, navigate, and search through the class hierarchies of .NET assemblies, even if you don't have
   the source code for them

↗ Decompile and analyze .NET assemblies in C#, Visual Basic and IL

↗ Understand the relationships between classes and methods

↗ Check that your code has been correctly obfuscated before release

.NET Reflector Pro® $195

Step into decompiled assemblies whilst debugging in Visual Studio

↗ Integrates the power of .NET Reflector into Visual Studio

↗ Decompile third-party assemblies from within VS

↗ Step through decompiled assemblies and use all the debugging techniques
   you would use on your own code

SmartAssembly™   from $795

.NET obfuscator and automated error reporting

↗ First-rate .NET obfuscator: obfuscate your .NET code and protect your application

↗ Automated error reporting: get a complete state of your program when it crashes (including the values
   of all local variables)

↗ Improve the quality of your software by fixing the most recurrent issues

Visit **www.red-gate.com** for a 14-day, free trial

Performance Tuning with SQL Server Dynamic Management Views

Louis Davidson and Tim Ford

This is the book that will de-mystify the process of using Dynamic Management Views to collect the information you need to troubleshoot SQL Server problems. It will highlight the core techniques and "patterns" that you need to master, and will provide a core set of scripts that you can use and adapt for your own requirements.

ISBN: 978-1-906434-47-2
Published: October 2010

Defensive Database Programming

Alex Kuznetsov

Inside this book, you will find dozens of practical, defensive programming techniques that will improve the quality of your T-SQL code and increase its resilience and robustness.

ISBN: 978-1-906434-49-6
Published: June 2010

Brad's Sure Guide to
SQL Server Maintenance Plans
Brad McGehee

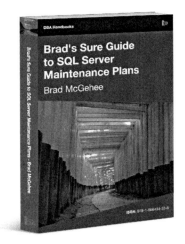

Brad's Sure Guide to Maintenance Plans shows you how to use the Maintenance Plan Wizard and Designer to configure and schedule eleven core database maintenance tasks, ranging from integrity checks, to database backups, to index reorganizations and rebuilds.

ISBN: 78-1-906434-34-2
Published: December 2009

SQL Server Tacklebox
Rodney Landrum

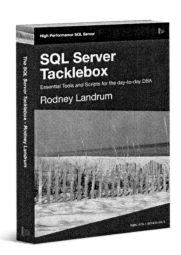

As a DBA, how well prepared are you to tackle "monsters" such as backup failure due to lack of disk space, or locking and blocking that is preventing critical business processes from running, or data corruption due to a power failure in the disk subsystem? If you have any hesitation in your answers to these questions, then Rodney Landrum's SQL Server Tacklebox is a must-read.

ISBN: 978-1-906434-25-0
Published: August 2009

Lightning Source UK Ltd.
Milton Keynes UK
UKOW020630120612

194270UK00001B/4/P